Contents map

The world of work	8 When I am eighteen			
	Are you ready?	plans	future forms	
	8.1 Jobs	jobs	articles; general use of *you* and passive; (*would + like / love / hate to*; *really*)	D
	8.2 The world of work	part-time / summer jobs	phrasal verbs; infinitives of purpose	D
	8.3 Applying for jobs	application forms, CVs	modal verbs; (adverbs of sequence: *firstly*, *next*, *thirdly*, *finally*)	D
	8.4 Starting a business	business	reported speech; reported speech: commands	D
	8.5 Thinking about the future	future work plans	future plans: *think + will, want to, would like to, might, be going to*, present simple + fixed time	D
	Our world: Young business people			D
	Review			
	Words and phrases - Unit 8			
	Revision 4 (Unit 7 and Unit 8)			
The international world	9 Meeting new people			
	Are you ready?	formal and informal greetings	passive; (exclamations with *how* and *what*)	
	9.1 We are all different	school exchanges	modal passives	E
	9.2 Let's celebrate!	celebrations	suffixes	E
	9.3 What we eat	typical food	two verbs in a sentence	A/E
	9.4 Globalization	across the world	adverbs of degree	E
	9.5 We are world citizens	world citizens	second conditional	E
	Our world: Cultural melting pots			C/E
	Review			
	Words and phrases - Unit 9			
	10 Communication and technology			
	Are you ready?	documents and texts	(Adverbs of degree)	
	10.1 Technology and me	experiences of technology	tag questions; * (nouns as verbs; *anyway*)	C
	10.2 Life then and now	technology in the past	past tense; *about to* + infinitive	C
	10.3 Technology in the home	home technology	phrasal verbs 4 : *turn* + preposition (*be like* for general descriptions)	C
	10.4 Technology in the future	future technology	predictions with *think*; (discourse markers: *also, instead, and ..., so*)	C
	10.5 New worlds	technology and business	past perfect	C
	Our world: World languages			C/E
	Review			
	Words and phrases - Unit 10			
	Revision 5 (Unit 9 and Unit 10)			

*Tag questions are not in the Cambridge IGCSE English (as an Additional Language) syllabus so this grammar point is extension material.

How to use this course

Welcome to *Collins Cambridge IGCSE™ English (as an Additional Language)*, a course carefully designed and written to help you to develop as an independent and effective learner and to provide you with the knowledge and skills you need to prepare for success in your Cambridge IGCSE English (as an Additional Language) studies.

IGCSE English (as an Additional Language) consists of a Student's Book and a Workbook, as well as accompanying audio and teacher support materials.

STUDENT'S BOOK

The Student's Book covers the full content of the syllabus. It is divided into 10 units. These 10 units cover the vocabulary, grammar and topic areas from the syllabus and also give comprehensive practice in the four skills: listening, reading, speaking and writing. It is designed in this way:

At the start of the book

1   A detailed **Contents map** on pages 4–6 gives you a summary of the course and helps you to find topics or language areas easily when you are revising.

2   Next, there are six Starter units welcoming you to the course. These show you what you know and what you need to learn. They also help your teacher know how to help you. There are also activities to help you to learn some simple words and phrases that you can use in the classroom.

In each unit

1   The **Are you ready?** lesson of each unit gets you ready for the topic of the unit. It introduces some words and phrases related to the topic of the unit.

2   **Lessons .1–.5** then follow the same pattern.

•   A list of **learning aims** at the start of each lesson tells you what skills and activities are in the lesson.

> ### Learning aims
> •   Listen to a conversation describing a family photo
> •   Describe my family
> •   Discuss family trees

•   **Starter questions** at the start of each lesson encourage you and your classmates to start talking about the topic.

   Discuss. *Is your family big or small?*
   Who is in your family?

This helps you to remember some of the language you already know and shows you what the lesson is about. If you need help answering these questions, you can listen to your teacher answer them first.

•   There are **activities** to practise all four language skills (listening, reading, speaking and writing). The activities are designed to be interesting and fun, and are usually about things that you experience in your daily life. The activities help you to learn and understand the key language and skills. Try all the activities and do your best. It's OK to make mistakes – that's how we learn. Language is presented and practised so you move from being able to understand language while reading and listening to being able to speak and write by the end. You are given opportunities throughout the course to build on your knowledge and to apply what you learn in different situations. As well as working on your own, you have the chance to work in pairs and as part of a group. The activities are also designed to develop reading and thinking skills, to help you become a better and more independent learner.

- Key vocabulary is highlighted in **Vocabulary** boxes. The vocabulary is often presented in a phrase to help you to learn how to use the words. Use these boxes to review vocabulary. There is also a list of all the key words and phrases at the end of each unit.

Vocabulary

I study ...
art
biology
chemistry
computer science (IT)
drama
geography
history
languages
maths
music
physical education (PE)
physics
religious education (RE)
science

- Key grammar points are explained in **Grammar** boxes. Each box also contains a note to the more detailed Grammar reference at the back of the Student's Book.

Grammar

Present continuous
Use the present continuous to talk about what you are doing now.

Use *am/are/is* + verb + *-ing*.

*What **are** you **doing**?*
*I'm **having** a shower.*
***Are** you **watching** TV?*
*No, **I'm not**. / Yes, I **am**.*

More? → Grammar

- **Language support** boxes help you to develop fluency in your speaking and writing.

| Use *then* to say that one thing happens after another. | I go home and do my homework. ***Then*** I have dinner. |

- **Study tips** boxes offer advice on how to improve your English and also how to how to learn better so you start good study habits as soon as possible.

Study tip

When you read or hear a word or phrase you don't know, look it up in a dictionary or ask someone what it means. Then write a new sentence using the word or phrase. Try and use the new word or phrase in your next conversation in English.

3 The **Our world** lesson focuses on a topic outside the classroom so that you can learn about life outside of your studies. This lesson has a longer reading text so that you can develop your reading even further. There are comprehension activities and tasks to encourage discussion in pairs or in groups or as a class. For example, **Find out** boxes encourage you to do research related to the topic, **Discuss** boxes give you interesting questions to talk to your classmates about and **The same … but different** boxes introduce ideas about different cultures and how they are similar to or different from your own.

Discuss

What do you think the sentence in bold in the text means? Do you agree with it?

I think it means that …
What do you think?
I agree with this sentence because …
I don't agree with this sentence because …

Find out

1 *Look on a world map. Where is Ontario?*

2 *Is there an International Duke of Edinburgh Award in your country?*

The same …

In most of Canada, there are two official languages: English and French. In Vancouver in the east of Canada, most people speak English, but in Quebec in the west, most people speak French. About 20% of Canadians can speak both languages. *What languages do people speak in your country?*

but different

4 The **Review** lesson at the end of the unit offers you the chance to check how much of the unit you understand. It starts with activities that review the language from the unit. The **How are you doing?** table at the end helps you to think about how you are doing and what you need to practise more. The lesson ends with some advice on how to keep developing your English skills.

5 There is a list of **Words and phrases** at the end of each unit. This contains all the key language from the unit, plus additional vocabulary on the same topic. There are lines next to each word or phrase to add notes or pictures to help you remember the words or phrases. You can also listen to the words and phrases on the audio recording so that you can practise your pronunciation.

Audio

If you see this icon, it means that there is an audio file for you to listen to.

Underneath the audio icon is the number of the audio file. All the audio files for the Student's Book are available online at www.collins.co.uk/internationalresources.

Other parts of the Student's Book

1 The five **Revision units** give you the opportunity to review language through short listening, reading, writing and speaking tests. These units come after Units 2, 4, 6, 8 and 10. They focus mainly on the language of the two previous units. For example, Revision 2 comes after Unit 4 and covers the language of Units 3 and 4. However, the Revision units also build on things you have learned earlier in the course.

2 The **Grammar** reference at the end of the book gives more information on all the Grammar topics in the syllabus, with examples.

3 There are some **exam-style questions** at the end of the Student's Book so you know what to expect on the day and how to prepare yourself.

WORKBOOK

The Workbook provides further practice of reading, writing, grammar and vocabulary. Each of the main lessons of the Student's Book units (**Lessons .1–.5**) has a corresponding lesson in the Workbook. You can do these activities independently and they are therefore also suitable for homework.

Welcome to the world of English

Starter 1

1 Listen and repeat. 0.1

a b c d e f g h i j k l m n o p q r s t u v w x y z

A B C D E F G H I J K L M N O P Q R S T U V W X Y Z

2 Listen and write the girl and the boy's names. 0.2

Hi. My name's _____.

Hi. I'm _____.

Vocabulary

What's your name?
My name's (Sally).
I'm (Sally).
How do you spell that?
What's = What is
name's = name is
I'm = I am

Grammar

Capital letters
You use capital letters at the beginning of a sentence or question.
What's your name?
My name's ...
You also use captital letters for languages:
English
Spanish

More? → Grammar

3 Ask and answer.

What's your name?   How do you spell that?

4 Listen and match speakers 1–5 to photos a–g. 0.3

a
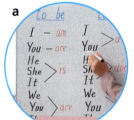
English

b

maths

c

biology

d

chemistry

e
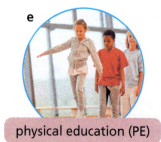
physical education (PE)

f
history

g
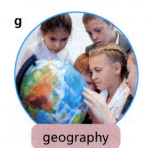
geography

5 Copy and complete the sentences with the words from the box. Then listen and check. 🔊0.4

are   is

- What **1** _____ your favourite subject, Eva?
- My favourite subject **2** _____ chemistry.

- What **3** _____ your favourite subjects, Raheem?
- My favourite subjects **4** _____ biology and history.

6 Ask and answer.

What's your favourite subject?

7 Choose the correct form of the verb *to be* to complete the sentences.

1 **Am / Are / Is** your favourite subject geography?

2 My parents **am / are / is** at home.

3 I **am / are / is** at school.

4 Sara **am / are / is** happy today.

5 **Am / Are / Is** Raf and Sophia 18 years old?

6 What **am / are / is** your name?

7 **Am / Are / Is** your phone in your bag?

8 I **am / are / is** sixteen years old.

8 Rewrite these sentences using the negative forms of the verb *to be*.

1 English and maths are my favourite subjects.

2 The cat is hungry.

3 The books are in my bag.

4 Bella is nine years old.

5 I'm a boy.

6 You are a teacher.

7 We are tired.

8 It's Tuesday.

Grammar

The verb *to be*
The verb *to be* is an irregular verb. You say:
I'm = I am
You're = You are
He's = He is
She's = She is
It's = It is
We're = We are
They're = They are
Am, *are* and *is* are followed by:
Nouns:
*Mr Brown **is** a teacher. It **isn't** my book.*
***Are** you a student?*
Adjectives:
*She**'s** tall. I**'m** sad. It**'s** blue.*
***Are** the pens green?*
A place or time:
*Amira**'s** at school. It**'s** one o'clock.*
*The pens **are** on the desk.*
An age:
*Charlie **is** fifteen.*
*May **is** fourteen years old.*
*Ted **isn't** sixteen.*
You make the negative of the verb *to be* by adding not.
*I'm **not** Sally.*
*We're **not** friends.*
You can say:
*You're **not** James.*
*He's **not** Tom.*
or
*You **aren't** James.*
*He **isn't** Tom.*
Remember:
aren't = are not
isn't = is not

More? ➔ Grammar

Starter 2

1 Listen and order the colours as you hear them.

2 Copy and write the missing numbers.

1 one _____ three _____ five

2 eleven _____ thirteen fourteen _____

3 ten twenty _____ forty fifty _____

4 twenty-one thirty-two forty-three _____

5 first second _____ fourth _____ sixth

3 Match the numbers and words.

a	25	eighty-eight
b	15	one hundred
c	64	seventy-five
d	100	fifteen
e	91	nineteen
f	19	seventy-two
g	88	sixty-four
h	18	twenty-five
i	72	ninety-one
j	75	eighteen

4 Write the ordinal numbers in words.

a 17th   b 11th   c 3rd

d 20th   e 1st   f 22nd

Vocabulary

What colour is it?
It's …
black
blue
brown
green
grey
orange
pink
purple
red
yellow

5 **Answer the questions.**

1 How many days are there in a week?

2 How many months are there in a year?

6 **Copy and complete the days of the week. Then put them in order.**

1 M o n day   [1]

2 F _ _ day

3 Th _ _ _ day

4 Sat _ _ day

5 T _ _ _ _ day

6 S _ _ day

7 W _ _ _ _ _ day

7 **Complete the calendar with the months from the box.**

> April   August   January   July   May   November   October

A

S	M	T	W	T	F	S
					1	2
3	4	5	6	7	8	9
10	11	12	13	14	15	16
17	18	19	20	21	22	23
24	25	26	27	28	29	30
31						

February

S	M	T	W	T	F	S
	1	2	3	4	5	6
7	8	9	10	11	12	13
14	15	16	17	18	19	20
21	22	23	24	25	26	27
28						

March

S	M	T	W	T	F	S
	1	2	3	4	5	6
7	8	9	10	11	12	13
14	15	16	17	18	19	20
21	22	23	24	25	26	27
28	29	30	31			

B

S	M	T	W	T	F	S
				1	2	3
4	5	6	7	8	9	10
11	12	13	14	15	16	17
18	19	20	21	22	23	24
25	26	27	28	29	30	

C

S	M	T	W	T	F	S
						1
2	3	4	5	6	7	8
9	10	11	12	13	14	15
16	17	18	19	20	21	22
23	24	25	26	27	28	29
30	31					

June

S	M	T	W	T	F	S
		1	2	3	4	5
6	7	8	9	10	11	12
13	14	15	16	17	18	19
30	21	22	23	24	25	26
27	28	29	30			

D

S	M	T	W	T	F	S
				1	2	3
4	5	6	7	8	9	10
11	12	13	14	15	16	17
18	19	20	21	22	23	24
25	26	27	28	29	30	31

E

S	M	T	W	T	F	S
1	2	3	4	5	6	7
8	9	10	11	12	13	14
15	16	17	18	19	20	21
22	23	24	25	26	27	28
29	30	31				

September

S	M	T	W	T	F	S
			1	2	3	4
5	6	7	8	9	10	11
12	13	14	15	16	17	18
19	20	21	22	23	24	25
26	27	28	29	30		

F

S	M	T	W	T	F	S
					1	2
3	4	5	6	7	8	9
10	11	12	13	14	15	16
17	18	19	20	21	22	23
24	25	26	27	28	29	30
31						

G

S	M	T	W	T	F	S
	1	2	3	4	5	6
7	8	9	10	11	12	13
14	15	16	17	18	19	20
21	22	23	24	25	26	27
28	29	30				

December

S	M	T	W	T	F	S
			1	2	3	4
5	6	7	8	9	10	11
12	13	14	15	16	17	18
19	20	21	22	23	24	25
26	27	28	29	30	31	

8 **Write the dates.**

1 1 / 4 *the first of April*

2 20 / 12

3 5 / 6

4 19 / 2

5 11 / 10

6 8 / 11

7 3 / 7

8 22 / 3

9 14 / 8

10 25 / 5

9 **Listen and match the speakers to their ages and birthdays.**

Ana	12	the first of May
Emiko	15	the fifth of June
Tom	16	the twenty-third of November

> **Vocabulary**
>
> How old are you?
> I'm fifteen.
> When is your birthday?
> It's on the 1st of May.

Starter 3

1 **Complete the sentences. Use *a*, *an*, *the* or -.**

1 Write ___*a n*___ answers in your notebook.

2 I have _____ English lessons on Monday, Tuesday, Wednesday and Friday.

3 In my pencil case there is _____ pencil, _____ pen, ___*a*___ pencil sharpener, _____ eraser, _____ ruler and _____ highlighter pen.

4 Look up words you don't know in _____ dictionary.

5 Open _____ book and look at _____ page 24.

6 There's _____ interactive whiteboard in every classroom.

7 Be quiet! _____ teacher is talking.

8 Your books are on _____ desk.

9 I like _____ new poster on the classroom wall.

2 **Write the word for each picture. (Look for them in activity 1.)**

1
pencil case

2

3

4

5

6

7

8

9

10

11

12
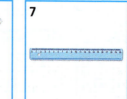

13

14

15

Grammar

Articles
You use the indefinite articles *a* or *an* to talk about things that are not known to the person speaking or writing and to the person listening or reading.
*I have **a** pen.*
You use *an* in front of nouns that start with a vowel.
*Is this **an** apple?*
You use *the* definite article the to talk about things that are known.
***The** books are in my bag.*
With plurals you don't need an article.
I love cats.

More? ➔ Grammar

Vocabulary

American English and British English
Some words are different in American English to British English. For example, in American English you say *eraser* and in British English you say *rubber*.

3 **Where is the pen? Match the sentences with the pictures.**

> The pen is **in** the pencil case.   The pen is **on** the notebook.
> The pen is **under** the desk.

1    **2**    **3**

4 **Work with a partner. Talk about what's in your bag, on your desk and in your classroom. Use the words from activity 2 and prepositions of place.**

The teacher is in the classroom.   My pencil case is on the desk.   My ruler is in the pencil case.

5 **Look at the photos. Listen and repeat.** 🔊 0.7

boy

girl

boys

girls

child

adults

woman

man

children

women

men

6 **Look at the photos. Choose the correct word.**

They are adults / children.   They are adults / children.

7 **Work with a partner. Answer the questions.**

- How many girls are there in your class?
- How many boys are there in your class?
- How many adults are there in your class?

Starter 4

1 Choose the best options to complete the conversations. Then listen and check. 🎧 0.8

- **1 Good morning / Goodbye**, I'm Mr Harper.
- **2 Thanks / Hello**, Mr Harper. I'm Nick.

- Here's a pen.
- **3 Thanks / Please.**
- **4 You're welcome / Goodbye.**

- Can I have a book, **5 hello / please?**
- Yes. Here you are.
- **6 Good evening / Thank you.**

2 Work with a partner. Practise the conversations in activity 1.

3 Listen and complete these useful phrases. 🎧 0.9

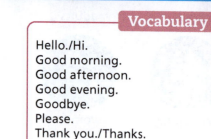

> Can don't help How me mean sorry spell

1 Excuse _____ Miss/Sir.
2 What does this word _____?
3 How do you _____ it?
4 _____ you repeat that, please?
5 Can you _____ me, please?
6 I'm _____, but I don't understand.
7 _____ do you say this in English?
8 I _____ know.

Vocabulary

Hello./Hi.
Good morning.
Good afternoon.
Good evening.
Goodbye.
Please.
Thank you./Thanks.

4 Listen and complete the text. 🎧 0.10

Name: David (**1**) _____
Address: (**2**) _____ Kew Road.
Telephone number: (**3**) _____
Age: (**4**) _____
Birthday: (**5**) _____
Favourite subjects: (**6**) _____, biology and maths.

5 **Choose the best options to complete the sentences. Listen again and check.** (10.10)

- Good morning. **1 My / I** name is Miss Wells. **2 My am/ I'm** the English teacher here at Oldman College. What's **3 you / your** name?
- What are **4 your / you** favourite subjects, David?
- Um … I think **5 my / I** favourite subjects are …

6 **Complete the answers with personal pronouns.**

1 Where is England? _____ is in Europe.

2 How is your brother? _____ is fine, thanks.

3 What do Mr and Mrs Smith like to eat? _____ like pizza.

4 What lesson is your class doing? _____ are doing maths.

7 **Complete these sentences with possessive adjectives.**

1 Do you like _____ new shoes?

2 Lisa and _____ brother are both sixteen.

3 Hello. What is _____ name?

4 England is famous for _____ queen.

8 **Read the answers and write the questions. Use the noun in brackets + 's.**

1 Her name is Miss Taylor. **(teacher)** What's your teacher's name?

2 Her favourite colour is blue. **(Julie)**

3 His birthday is the fifth of July. **(Dad)**

4 His favourite subjects are music and art. **(Adam)**

9 **Work with a partner. Ask and answer.**

- *What's your name?*
- *How do you spell your surname?*
- *What's your address?*
- *What's your telephone number?*
- *How old are you?*
- *When's your birthday?*
- *What are your favourite subjects?*

10 **Now talk about your partner from activity 9.**

This is ….

His/ Her name is …

He / She is … years old.

Grammar

Personal pronouns
You use subject pronouns with a verb to say who is doing something.
I
you
he
she
it
we
they
I am sixteen.

More? ➜ Grammar

Grammar

Possessive adjectives
You use possessive adjectives when you say that something belongs to someone.
my
your
his
hers
its
our
their
My birthday is in October.
You can also use noun + 's.
This is Lucy's house.

More? ➜ Grammar

Starter 5

1 **Match words a–c to shapes 1–3.**

a triangle   b circle   c square

1 2 3

Grammar

Nouns are words for people, places, feelings and things.
This is a circle.
Adjectives describe nouns.
A circle is round.

nouns	adjectives
circle	round
square	square
triangle	triangular

More? ➜ Grammar

2 **Copy and complete the sentences with the words from the box.**

round   square   triangular

1 The clock is _____.

2 The sign is _____.

3  The window is _____.

Study tip

When you learn a new word, record if it is a noun, an adjective or a verb etc. Write it in a sentence to help you remember how to use it.

3 **Choose the best word to complete each sentence.**

1 The girl is **tall / short**.
   The boy is **tall / short**.

2 The computer is **big / small**.
   The phone is **big / small**.

4 **Play *Find it!* Work in small groups. Find these things in your classroom:**

1 a tall person

2 a square thing

3 a round thing

4 a short person

5 a small and triangular thing

6 a big and round thing

5 **Read the text. Match the activities with the clocks below.**

Hi Years 8, 9 & 10,

Sports day schedule for Friday 18th May.

- meet at the sports centre – quarter to nine
- running races – quarter past nine
- swimming races – half past ten
- lunch – quarter past one
- table tennis – two o'clock
- skateboarding – quarter to three
- football match – teachers against students – half past three
- end of the day – five o'clock

See you there!
PE department

1

table tennis

2

3

4

5

6

7

8

Vocabulary

am and *pm*
When you talk about time, you use *am* to talk about the morning (before 12 o'clock midday) and *pm* to talk about the afternoon/evening (after 12 o'clock midday). You say *am* and *pm* as letters: a-m. / p-m.

When you use *am* or *pm*, you don't say *o'clock*.

6 **Complete the questions with the words from the box.**

How   How many   What   When   Where   Which   Who   Why

1 _____ is your birthday?

2 _____ time is it?

3 _____ people are in this classroom?

4 _____ is your favourite singer?

5 _____ tall are you?

6 _____ do you live?

7 _____ is your favourite sport?

8 _____ do you want to learn English?

Grammar

Questions
We use question words (*How, How many, What, When, Where, Who, Which, Why* …) to ask questions.
At the end of questions there is a question mark: **?**

More? ➜ Grammar

7 **Write your answers to the questions in activity 6.**

Starter 6

1 Work with a partner, play *Guess the word* using the words below.

eat   cook   drink   go

like   read   run   study

think   walk   write

2 Read and complete the text with the correct form of the verbs in brackets.

My name **1** _____ **(be)** Pippa. I **2** _____ **(be)** 14 years old. I **3** _____ **(go)** to the Beaufort Academy and I **4** _____ **(be)** in year 9. I **5** _____ **(live)** with my parents and my sister, Elsa.

We **6** _____ **(have)** a cat called Ginger. My brother Matt **7** _____ **(be)** 23 years old and he **8** _____ **(live)** in London.

He **9** _____ **(work)** in a primary school. Sometimes I **10** _____ **(go)** to London and visit him.

My favourite subjects **11** _____ **(be)** maths and PE. I **12** _____ **(like)** swimming and running. I **13** _____ **(not like)** football. On Sundays, my friends and I **14** _____ **(meet)** in the city centre and **15** _____ **(go)** shopping or go to the cinema.

3 Work with your partner. Say what is the same or different for you and Pippa.

My name *isn't* Pippa.   I am 14 years old *too*.

| We use *too* to say that something is the same. | *I am 14 years old **too**.* |

Useful verbs
be
eat
cook
do
drink
go
have
know
like
live
make
meet
read
run
study
think
visit
walk
work
write

Grammar

Present simple
You use the present simple to talk about things that are always true, and about general facts about our lives.
*I **like** history. I **live** in the UK.*

The form of the verb changes with *he / she / it*.
*She **likes** history. He **lives** in the UK.*

You use *do / does* + verb to make questions in the present simple.
***Do** you **like** history?*
***Does** Otto **like** maths?*

You use *don't / doesn't* to make negatives in the present simple.
*No, I **don't** (like history).*
*No, he **doesn't** (like maths).*

More? ➜ Grammar

4 Complete the sentences with *do, does, don't* or *doesn't*.

1 _____ you like the colour orange?

2 _____ Ali have a favourite subject?

3 _____ your teachers eat lunch at school?

4 I _____ have a TV.

5 Selma _____ study on Saturdays.

6 We eat at 8 pm. We _____ eat at 9 pm.

5 Order the words to make correct sentences.

1 food / my / is / fish and chips / favourite / .

2 in / band / I'm / singer / a / a / .

3 school / isn't / my / big / very / .

4 has / our / garage/ a / house / .

5 like / chocolate / I / don't / .

6 office / she / in / works / an / .

7 beach / the / grandparents / my / near / live / .

8 for / one hour / study / every day / I / .

9 tennis / Adam / well / plays / very / .

10 at / eat / dinner / 7.30 pm / we / .

6 Write a text about you. Use Pippa's text in activity 2 as a model.

Talk about your school, your family, your home, your hobbies, what you do at the weekend.

1 This is me

- Describe myself and others
- Write simple sentences describing myself
- Listen to people describing other people

1 Match the words in the box with the parts of the photo.

> eye   face   glasses   hair   mouth   nose

2 Listen to people describing other people. Number the photos 1–6. 🎧 1.1

3 Take turns to describe the photos in activity 2 for your partner to guess who.

- *This boy/girl has …*
- *This boy/girl doesn't have …*
- *His/Her … is/are …*
- *His/Her … isn't/aren't …*

4 Discuss. In activity 2 who do you think is:

> pretty   old   thin   young

> I think the girl in photo a is young and pretty.

5 Can you remember? What are the opposites of *pretty* and *thin*? Are these words you should use often? Discuss.

6 Describe yourself to your partner.

- *I have …*
- *I don't have …*
- *My … is / are …*
- *My … isn't / aren't …*
- *I wear …*
- *I don't wear …*

7 Your friend's mum is meeting you at the bus station. She doesn't know what you look like. Write a description for her.

1.1 This is my family

1 Discuss. *Is your family big or small?*
Who is in your family?

2 Complete the labels for Bella's family tree with the words in the box.

> aunt   brother   cousin   grandfather   mother   sister

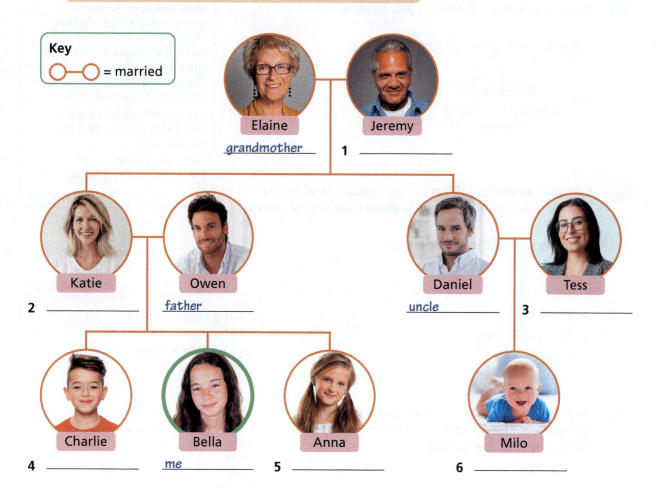

Key

○—○ = married

Elaine — grandmother

Jeremy — **1** _____

Katie — **2** _____

Owen — father

Daniel — uncle

Tess — **3** _____

Charlie — **4** _____

Bella — me

Anna — **5** _____

Milo — **6** _____

3 Answer the questions about Bella's family tree.

1 How many children do have Elaine and Jeremy have?
2 How many grandchildren do Elaine and Jeremy have?
3 Who is Tess's husband?
4 Who are Milo's parents?
5 Who is Owen's son?
6 Who are Daniel's nieces?
7 Who is Katie's nephew?

4 Listen to Maud and Jemima talking about Maud's family. Who is John? 🎧 1.2

5 Listen again. How many relatives are there in the photo? Compare your answer with a partner's. 🎧 1.2

6 Match the questions and answers.

1 What's your family like?

2 How many people are there in your family?

3 Who's this?

4 Do you have any cousins?

5 Do you have any brothers?

6 Is your sister older than you?

a Yes, I do. I have two.

b There are twelve.

c Yes, she is.

d He's my grandfather, his name's John. I call him Grandpa.

e It's big.

f No, I don't but I have a sister.

7 Draw and label your own family tree.

8 Work with a partner. Use your family trees to ask and answer questions about your families.

Who's this?

What's your family like?

How many … do you have?

Do you have any …?

Who's the oldest?

My family is …

These are my …

I don't have…

I have …

This is my …

Vocabulary

What's your family like?
This man / woman is my … / This man / woman is his / her …
I have a / an … / He / She has a / an …
I don't have a / an … / He / She doesn't have a / an …

father mother
dad / mum
brother / sister
son / daughter
grandson / granddaughter
grandfather / grandmother
husband / wife
niece / nephew
aunt / uncle
cousin
relative
parent

I'm / He's / She's …
married
single
elderly
older
the youngest

Grammar

Present simple
You use present simple tense to talk about general facts.

*My family **is** big. My uncles **aren't** married. I **have** three sisters. I **don't have** a brother. He **has** an older sister. She **doesn't have** a brother.*

More? ➜ Grammar

Grammar

Comparatives and superlatives
You use comparatives and superlatives to compare people and things.

*They're **older than** me.
I'm **the youngest**.*

More? ➜ Grammar

1.2 These are my friends

1 **Discuss.** *What is a good friend?*

Learning aims

- Describe my friends and friendships
- Listen to people talk about their friendships
- Read and write about a best friend
- Use adverbs of frequency to talk about how often my friends do something

2 With your partner, play *Guess the word* using the words below. Use your dictionary to find the meanings.

| angry | boring | curious | funny |

| happy | intelligent | interesting | kind |

| nice | quiet | sensible | serious |

3 Listen to Henry talking about his friends. Who is Henry's best friend? 🎧 1.3

4 Listen again. Copy and complete the table. 🎧 1.3

Friend	He / She is ...
Alex	funny
Noah	and
Emilio	
Fred	

Study tip

Record new words with definitions. For example: rude – when people are rude they are not polite; for example they never say please or thank you.

5 Complete the phrases with the words from the box. Listen again to check your answers. 🎧 1.3

| never   makes   very   happy   best   me |

1 He _____ me laugh a lot.
2 Noah's _____ intelligent.
3 Emilio's always _____.
4 He makes _____ smile a lot.
5 Fred's my _____ friend.
6 He's _____ boring.

Grammar

make for feelings
To talk about how people feel when someone does something, you use *make* + pronoun + adjective or verb.

He makes me laugh / cry / smile / happy / sad / angry.

More? → Grammar

6 Complete the sentences about your best friend.

1 My best friend is called …

2 He / She's very …

3 He / She makes me …

4 She's / He's always / usually / often / rarely / never …

Grammar

Adverbs of frequency
You can use adverbs of frequency to talk about how often people do something:

always, never, often, rarely, usually

*She **rarely** cries.*
*She's **never** angry.*
*He's **always** quiet.*

More? → Grammar

7 Read Fred's paragraph about Henry. Decide if the sentences are true (T) or false (F).

Henry and I are in the same science and history classes. We've been friends for two years. He's interesting, funny and very kind, and we talk a lot. We don't like going to the park. We really like going for long walks together and we like finding new places. We like the same music, and he makes me laugh a lot. I make him laugh a lot too. That's why he's my best friend.

1 Henry and Fred go to the same school.   T/F

2 They often go to the park together.   T/F

3 Henry makes Fred sad.   T/F

4 Fred thinks Henry is very serious.   T/F

8 Ask and answer with your partner.

• *Who are your friends?*

• *How long have you been friends for?*

To ask and answer questions about the length of your friendships:	*How long have you been friends for?* *We've been friends for two years.*

9 Write about your best friend(s) in your notebook. Answer these questions.

• Who is your best friend?

• What is he / she like?

• Why is he / she your best friend?

• How long have you been friends for?

• What do you like doing together?

1.3 These are my pets

1 **Discuss.** *Do you have pets?*
What pets do you have?

Learning aims
- Understand descriptions of pets
- Describe my pets using pronouns and adjectives
- Ask and answer questions about pets

2 **Match the photos 1–10 with the names of the animals a–j.**

a	bird	**f**	mouse
b	cat	**g**	rabbit
c	dog	**h**	rat
d	fish	**i**	snake
e	horse	**j**	spider

Some nouns have irregular plurals. For example:	one fish > two fish one mouse > two mice

Study tip

Some people like to record new words with a drawing. For example:
a mouse

3 **Take turns to ask and answer questions about the pets in activity 2.**

What colour is the mouse?　It's white.

How many legs does the horse have?　It has four.

Does the cat have ears?　Yes, it has.

4 Listen to some students talking about their pets. 🎧 1.4

Match the person to their pet. There is ONE pet you do not need.

Alma
Grace
Leon
Tom
Adam

bird
rat
fish
horse
snake
cat

5 Listen again. Answer the questions. 🎧 1.4

1 Does Alma have a lot of pets?
2 Which person in Alma's family doesn't like pets?
3 What colour is Grace's pet?
4 Who has an old pet?
5 Why don't some people like Adam's pet?
6 Which two pets live in a bedroom?

6 Complete the phrases with the words from the box. Listen again to check your answers. 🎧 1.4

| amazing I'd lucky quite time very |

1 _____ like to have lots of animals.
2 My mum doesn't like them _____ much.
3 I'm very _____ because I have a big brown horse called Humphrey.
4 Snakes are _____.
5 Bob's _____ old now.
6 Freda cleans herself all the _____.

7 Ask and answer the questions with your partner.

• *What pets do you have?*
• *What is its name? / What are their names?*
• *What colour is it? / What colour are they?*
• *How old is it? / How old are they?*
• *Where do they live?*
• *What pet would you like to have?*

| To talk about something you don't have, but you want, you use *would like*. | What pet *would you like* to have?
I*'d like* to have a rabbit.
(I'd = I would) |

Grammar

Pronouns
Pronouns are words that you use to talk about someone or something when you do not need to use a noun.
They're blue and white.
I keep them in my bedroom.

More? ➜ Grammar

Vocabulary

My fish lives ... / My snake lives ... / My pet rat lives ...
in a glass bowl in my bedroom
in a glass box
in her cage on my desk in my bedroom

Grammar

Order of adjectives
You put adjectives before the noun in English. Adjectives of size come first, then colour. For example:
a big brown horse

More? ➜ Grammar

1.4 This is my home

Learning aims
- Read descriptions of homes
- Talk about my home
- Use conjunctions to describe my home
- Write about my home

1 **Discuss.** *Do you live in a house or a flat?*
What's your favourite room in your home?

2 **Listen and find the word. Copy the words into your notebook. Then listen again and number the parts of the home as you hear them.** 🎧 1.5

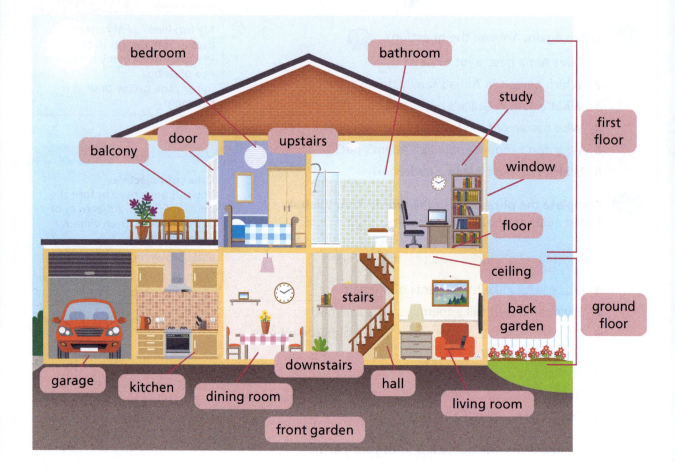

bedroom
bathroom
study
first floor
balcony
door
upstairs
window
floor
ceiling
back garden
ground floor
stairs
downstairs
hall
garage
kitchen
dining room
living room
front garden

3 **Work with a partner. Say what you have and don't have in your home.**

Compound nouns	*living room bedroom upstairs*
A compound noun is a noun made of two words. There are some in the Vocabulary box. In compound nouns you usually stress the first syllable.	*A **green**house – a place where you grow plants* (compound noun) *A green **house** – the colour of the house is green* (adjective and noun)

4 Ned's talking about his house. Read what he says.
Choose the FOUR correct sentences from 1–7.

I'm very lucky
because I have a lovely big house.
On the first floor, there are four bedrooms and two
bathrooms. The bedroom at the front of the house is very big
and it has a balcony that looks out over the sea. I work from home, so I
have a desk at home in my study on the ground floor next to the kitchen.
On the ground floor, there's also the living room and a dining room. The
living room is big, but the dining room is small. There's a great view
of the garden from there. I don't have a garage. That's OK
because I don't have a car. I keep my bicycle in
the hall.

1 Ned's house has two floors.

2 Ned's study is on the first floor.

3 The big bedroom has a balcony.

4 Ned keeps his bicycle in the garage.

5 There is a bathroom on the ground floor.

6 There are ten rooms in the house.

7 There is a garden.

5 Listen to Dahlia, Eddie and Leanne talking about their
homes. Who lives: 🎧 1.6

* in Scotland?
* in Australia?
* in Mexico?

6 Listen again. Copy and complete the table. 🎧 1.6

Name	Number of floors	Number of rooms in home	Favourite place in home	Garden
Dahlia				
Eddie				
Leanne				

7 Complete the sentences about your home.

1 I live in a … in …

2 My home is very …

3 There are … floors.

4 There are … rooms. These are …

5 The biggest room is …

6 My favourite place in my home is … .
It's my favourite place because …

7 I don't have a …

> **Grammar**
>
> **Conjunctions 1**
> Conjunctions join two sentences together to make a longer sentence.
>
> To add a reason for something use *so*.
> *I work from home so I have a desk at home.*
>
> To add contrasting information use *but*.
> *The living room is big, but the dining room is small.*
>
> More? ➜ Grammar

> **Grammar**
>
> **Conjunctions 2**
> To give an explanation for something, or to say why, use *because*.
> *It's my favourite room because it has great views over the city.*
>
> To join two sentences and give more information use *and*.
> *It's my favourite place because it has lots of flowers and it's very beautiful.*
>
> More? ➜ Grammar

1.5 These are my hobbies

Learning aims

- Read an article about free time
- Post a comment online
- Listen to a radio show about hobbies
- Make questions and negative sentences in the present simple

1 **Discuss.** *What do you do in your free time? How often?*

2 **Read the online article. Find the hobbies in the photos a–j.**

The 10 most popular hobbies for teenagers

What do young people like doing in their free time? Hundreds of teenagers tell us about their hobbies. Let's find out what they say! What is the most popular hobby? Let's start with the tenth most popular hobby. At number ten, is riding a horse. Next, at number nine, teenagers say they like writing poems or short stories in their free time. At number eight, it's playing the drums. I'm not sure how many parents like that hobby! In seventh place, we have climbing. At number six, it's painting and drawing. At number five, it's singing. Some teenagers prefer to sing in the shower or in their bedrooms, but many sing in groups. In fourth place, teenagers say they like going cycling, especially in the spring and summer months. Number three is taking photos. Most teenagers have smartphones so they can use their phones to take photos. The second most popular hobby is doing yoga. Everyone wants to relax at the weekend and after school. And the most popular hobby for teenagers is … going SKATEBOARDING. Teenagers tell us they skateboard in parks near their homes. What do you like doing? Is your hobby one of the top ten for teenagers? Post a comment below and let us know.

3 **Read the article again and number the top ten hobbies.**

4 **Work with a partner. Ask and answer questions about the hobbies in the article.**

- *Do you like … ?*
- *Yes, I do./No, I don't.*

5 **Post a comment about the hobbies in the article.**

Name 4 months ago

I like going skateboarding too.

👍 148 👎   REPLY

Vocabulary

I like / don't like …
Do you like …?

climbing
doing yoga
drawing
going cycling
going skateboarding
painting
playing the drums
riding a horse
singing
taking photos
writing poems and short stories

Grammar

Grammar

Auxiliary verb *Do*
When you make a question or a negative sentence in the present simple tense, you need to use the auxiliary verb *do*.
Do you **like** playing the drums?
Does he **run** every day?
I **don't like** painting.
You use *do* for short yes/no answers too.
Yes, I **do.**   **No**, I **don't.**   **Yes**, he **does.**   **No**, he **doesn't.**
More? ➜ Grammar

Gerunds
A verb in the *-ing* form can be used as a noun. This is called a gerund.
I *like* **painting**.
I *like* **singing**.
More? ➜ Grammar

6 **Listen to a radio show about hobbies. Copy and complete the table.** 🎧 1.7

Name	Hobby	How often … ?	How long …?
Sophia	go running		
Izzy			
Amira			
Julia			

7 **Complete the questions using the words in the box.**

do (×2)   long   often   what

1 _____ are your hobbies?
2 What _____ you like doing in your free time?
3 _____ you have any hobbies?
4 How _____ do you go running?
5 How _____ do you practise for?

8 **Match the answers a–d to the questions 1–5 in activity 7.**

a About 45 minutes.
b Yes, I do.
c Twice a week.
d I go climbing and I like painting too.

9 **Ask a partner about their hobbies. Use the questions in activity 7.**

Study tip

Record phrases to help you remember hobbies. For example:
listen to music   watch films do yoga

Grammar

How often? / How long?
You use *How often …?* to ask how frequently you do something.
How often do you go running?
I go running once a month/ three times a week.

You use *How long … for …?* to ask about the length of time.
How long do you play guitar for every day?
I play guitar for twenty minutes every day.
More? ➜ Grammar

The International DofE Award

The International DofE, or Duke of Edinburgh, Award, is for young people who are 14-24 years old. They learn new skills and have new experiences. **The DofE believes that not all learning happens in school.** Thousands of young people in more than 130 different countries around the world take part in this award every year. There are three levels: Bronze, Silver and Gold. It usually takes about six months to do each level. For each level you complete different activities in four different areas: a physical activity, for example learning to play a new sport. The second part is a practical skill, for example learning to cook a meal. The third part is volunteering. When you volunteer, you help other people, for example looking after children, helping older people at home, or cleaning a beach or park. The final part is an expedition. You go hiking for a few days with a group of friends and you have to follow a map, cook for yourselves and sleep in a tent.

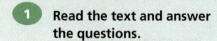 **Read the text and answer the questions.**

1 Who can do a Duke of Edinburgh award?

2 How many levels are there?

3 How long does each level usually take?

4 What do you do at the end of the award?

Glossary

skill ability to do something well
experience something that you do
take part in to do something with other people
complete to finish
expedition a journey made for a particular purpose

Discuss

What do you think the sentence in bold in the text means? Do you agree with it?

I think it means that …
What do you think?
I agree with this sentence because …
I don't agree with this sentence because …

Look at Gina. She is in Canada and this is her final DofE expedition. She is doing a 127-kilometre dog-sled ride across the snowy mountains of Ontario! Gina says, "DofE helps you to learn about yourself. You try new things and it shows you that you can achieve a lot. It makes you active and curious. It also gives you useful experiences and skills to put on your CV for university or work. I think the International Duke of Edinburgh Award is an amazing experience for everyone!"

2 **Read the text and choose A, B or C.**

1 The International DofE Award is for young people in …

A Canada.

B the UK.

C one of the 130+ countries where you can do the award.

2 Gina believes that the DofE award …

A helps students get better grades at school.

B can help you find a job.

C is good because you help other people.

3 **Do you help others? Write about your experience.**

- Who do you help?
- What do you do?
- Do you like doing it?

Find out

1 *Look on a world map. Where is Ontario?*

2 *Is there an International Duke of Edinburgh Award in your country?*

The same …

In most of Canada, there are two official languages: English and French. In Vancouver in the east of Canada, most people speak English, but in Quebec in the west, most people speak French. About 20% of Canadians can speak both languages. *What languages do people speak in your country?*

but different

Review

1 George is talking about himself. Listen and choose the correct answers. 1.8

1 George lives in ...

  a Australia   **b** England   **c** the United States

2 He has ... hair.

  a long blond   **b** curly brown   **c** straight black

3 His house has ... bedrooms.

  a two   **b** three   **c** four

4 George's family have pet ...

  a rabbits   **b** cats   **c** dogs

5 George's hobby is ...

  a growing plants   **b** playing tennis   **c** running

6 George does his hobby ...

  a three times a week   **b** once a week   **c** every day

7 His friend Matt is very ...

  a quiet   **b** funny   **c** boring

2 Read and complete the email from Zanie. Use the words from the box.

> animals biggest garden funny going old orange

Hi,

I'm Zanie. I love **1** _____, and I have a lot of pets! I have two fish. They're **2** _____ and white and very pretty. I also have a white rabbit called Benny. He's really **3** _____ and he makes me laugh, but my dad doesn't like him. Benny lives in the **4** _____. My cat is called Steve, and he's very **5** _____ – he's sixteen so he's older than me. My **6** _____ pet is my horse, Zack. I love **7** _____ horse-riding. He's a baby – he's only one year old but he's taller than me!

3 Talk about yourself to your partner. Answer the questions.

- *What do you look like?*
- *Who is in your family?*
- *Do you have any aunts, uncles or cousins? What are their names?*
- *What do you like doing with your friends?*
- *What pets do you have?*
- *What's your home like?*
- *What hobbies do you have? How often do you do them?*

How are you doing?

Read and copy the checklist below. For each 'I can … sentence'
think and decide: **very well, quite well,** or **OK, but I need
more practice**.

Use the checklist to help you improve your English.

I can …	Very well	Quite well	OK, but I need more practice
• describe myself and others			
• use the present simple tense			
• talk about my family and friends			
• describe what someone is like			
• use adverbs of frequency (never, always, rarely)			
• talk about why I like or don't like someone			
• talk about pets			
• use pronouns (he, she, they, his, her, them, etc)			
• talk about my home			
• talk about my hobbies			
• ask and answer questions			

How to improve

Get into good study habits. Choose the best options for you.

When?
I study English best in the **mornings / afternoons / evenings**.
I study English best **in the week / at the weekend**.

Where?
I study English best in **my bedroom / the kitchen / the dining room / the study**.

Who?
I study English best **with a friend / by myself / in a group**.

How?
I learn new words by **drawing pictures of the words / writing the meaning of the word / saying the word
many times**.

Words and phrases – Unit 1

Adverbs of frequency

always _____

never _____

normally _____

often _____

rarely _____

usually _____

once a week _____

twice a week _____

three times a week _____

How often …? _____

Body parts

beard _____

eye _____

face _____

hair _____

mouth _____

nose _____

I wear glasses. _____

He has a bald head. _____

Countries

Australia _____

Mexico _____

Scotland _____

Describing people

active _____

angry _____

boring _____

curious _____

famous _____

friendly _____

funny _____

greedy _____

happy _____

intelligent _____

interesting _____

kind _____

nice _____

pleasant _____

polite _____

quiet _____

rude _____

sad _____

sensible _____

serious _____

shy _____

very _____

to be called … _____

to be in a good /bad mood _____

to make someone laugh /
smile / cry / happy / sad
/ angry _____

He's my best friend. _____
We've been friends
for five years. _____

Family

baby _____

brother / sister _____

childhood _____

cousin _____

elderly _____

family _____

father / dad _____

friend _____

grandchildren _____

grandfather / granddad /
grandpa _____

grandmother / grandma /
granny _____

grandparent _____

grandson / granddaughter _____

guy _____

husband _____

marriage _____

married _____

mother / mum _____

nephew / niece _____

older / younger _____

parent _____

partner _____

relative _____

single _____

son / daughter _____

teenager _____

twin _____

uncle / aunt _____

wedding _____

wife _____

Hobbies

climbing _____

to do yoga _____

drawing _____

to go fishing _____

free time _____

to go cycling _____

going hiking _____

to go running _____

to go skateboarding _____

hobby / hobbies _____

to listen to (rock
classical / pop) music _____

painting _____

to play the clarinet
drums / flute / guitar /
piano / trumpet / violin _____

to ride a bicycle / horse _____

singing _____
to take photos _____
to watch a film _____
to write a poem /
  short story _____
How long for ...? _____
for two hours _____

Home
apartment / flat _____
back garden _____
balcony _____
bathroom _____
bedroom _____
bicycle _____
ceiling _____
dining room _____
door _____
downstairs _____
flat _____
floor _____
front garden _____
furniture _____
garage _____
ground floor _____
hall _____
house / home _____
kitchen _____
living room _____
neighbourhood _____
plant _____
stairs _____
study _____
upstairs _____
wall _____
window _____
to keep something
  somewhere _____

Pets
bird _____
cat _____
dog _____
fish _____
horse _____
mouse _____
pet _____
rabbit _____
rat _____
snake _____
spider _____
I'd like to have a ... _____

Physical appearance
beautiful _____
big _____
blonde _____
curly _____

dark _____
fair _____
fat _____
glasses _____
good-looking _____
handsome _____
long _____
old _____
pretty _____
short _____
slim _____
small _____
straight _____
tall _____
thin _____
ugly _____
young _____

Places where pets live
in my bedroom _____
in a cage _____
in a glass bowl _____
in a glass box _____

Verbs
to achieve / manage to _____
to agree _____
to believe _____
to clean _____
to complete _____
to cook _____
to do _____
to find _____
to finish _____
to follow _____
to give _____
to have to _____
to help _____
to learn _____
to like _____
to look after _____
to make _____
to mean _____
to play _____
to post a comment _____
to put _____
to show _____
to sleep _____
to speak / talk _____
to take (time) _____
to take part in _____
to try _____
to volunteer _____
There is / There are ... _____

2 My day

• Describe my daily routine • Listen to a teenager talk about her daily routine
• Use the present continuous to talk about what I'm doing now

1 **Match the words in the box with the pictures.**

> brush my teeth   do my homework   do sport   get dressed   get up
> go to bed   go home   go to school   have breakfast   have a bath   have a shower
> have dinner   have lunch   meet my friends   relax   watch TV

2 **Listen to Lara talking about her day. What activities does she mention? Write the letters of the pictures in activity 1 (a–p) in the order you hear them.** 2.1

3 **Listen again and answer the questions.** 2.1

1 What day is she talking about?

2 What time does Lara get up?

3 Who does she go to school with?

4 Who does she have breakfast with?

5 What time does she have lunch?

6 How long does she watch TV for?

4 Choose a day of the week. Use the pictures in activity 1 to make notes about the activities you do on that day. You do not need to use all the pictures.

5 Work with a partner. Talk about your routine for this day.

| Use *then* to say that one thing happens after another. | I go home and do my homework. ***Then*** I have dinner. |

Prepositions
Use the preposition *at* to talk about the time you do something.
We have lunch at half past twelve.
Use the preposition *for* to talk about how long you do an activity.
I watch TV for an hour.
Use the proposition *with* to talk about the other people also doing an activity.
I have dinner with my family.

More? ➜ Grammar

6 Listen to five teenagers. What are they doing? Number the activities in order. 🎧 2.2

a

b

c

d

e

7 Listen again and complete the sentences. 🎧 2.2

1 Dalia *is brushing her teeth* _____.
2 James _____.
3 Birta _____.
4 Kamal _____.
5 Leanne _____.

Grammar

Present continuous
Use the present continuous to talk about what you are doing now.
Use *am / are / is* + verb + *-ing*.
am / are / is are part of the verb to be.
*What **are** you **doing**?*
*I'm **having** a shower.*
*Is she **watching** TV?*
*No, she **isn't**. / Yes, she **is**.*

More? ➜ Grammar

8 Complete the sentences with the correct form of the verb *be*.

1 Hi Jeanette. What _____ you doing?
2 Mum and Dad _____ having breakfast.
3 Hassan _____ doing his homework.
4 I _____ not going to school today. It's Saturday.
5 _____ Tom getting dressed?
6 Mum, _____ we having dinner now?

9 Work with a partner. Play *What are you doing?*

- Student A: Choose one activity from Activity 1.
- Student B: Ask Student A *What are you doing*?
- Student A: Mime your activity.
- Student B: Guess the activity *Are you …?*
- Student A: Answer *Yes, I am* or *No, I'm not.*
- Student B: Guess again or your turn to choose and mime.

2.1 At home

Learning aims
- Describe jobs at home
- Talk about the jobs I do at home
- Give opinions about doing jobs at home

1 Discuss. *What jobs do you do at home?*

2 Read and listen to three teenagers talking about the jobs they do at home. Find the word or phrase for each job a–k. 🎧 2.3

1 I don't do many jobs at home but I cook dinner every day. My brother and I always lay the table before dinner. Then we clear the table after dinner and we do the washing up. **Lisa**

2 I don't do any jobs in the week because I do my homework. At the weekend, I clean the house with my parents and do the laundry. I tidy up my bedroom and I take the rubbish out. **Henry**

3 I like doing jobs in the garden. I do the gardening and in the spring I plant vegetables with my dad and my grandfather. I don't do many jobs in the house, but I iron my school uniform every weekend. **Eddie**

Vocabulary

I/You/We/They…	He/She…
clean the house/car	cleans the house/car
clear the table	clears the table
cook dinner	cooks dinner
do the gardening	does the gardening
do the laundry/washing	does the laundry/washing
do the washing up	does the washing up
iron clothes	irons clothes
lay the table	lays the table
plant vegetables	plants vegetables
take the rubbish* out	takes the rubbish* out
tidy up	tidies up
(*American English = trash)	

3 Work with a partner. Tell them what jobs you do and don't do at home.

- *I don't do many jobs at home but I …*
- *I do a lot of jobs at home, I …*
- *At the weekend, I …*
- *I always … I never … I sometimes …*

Study tip

Look for words that you know in a sentence to help you work out what any new words mean. For example, I always lay the table *before dinner*. Use 'before dinner' to help you work out what 'lay the table' means.

4 **Answer these questions.**

- What verb form is used in the texts in activity 2?
- In the last lesson you learnt about present continuous. What is the difference between present simple and present continuous?

5 **Read about the jobs Eva does at home. Answer the questions.**

I hate doing jobs at home. They're boring! But my mum makes me do the laundry and she makes me iron my clothes. At the weekend, my dad makes me clean his car. They give me 10 dollars a week but I still don't like helping! My parents say it's very important to do jobs at home because it teaches you good skills. I don't agree because the jobs aren't difficult and I know how to do them anyway.

1 Does Eva like doing jobs at home?

2 What jobs does Eva do at home?

3 Who asks Eva to clean the car?

4 When does Eva clean the car?

5 How much money does Eva get for the jobs she does?

6 Why do her parents think it's important to do jobs at home?

7 Does Eva agree with her parents that it's important to do jobs at home?

8 Does Eva think the jobs she does at home are difficult?

6 **Put the words in the correct order to make sentences.**

1 makes / the rubbish out / my dad / me / take

2 lay / him / his mum / the table / makes

3 the washing up / do / her / makes / her granddad

4 makes / my sister / us / the gardening / do

7 **Copy and complete the sentence for you.**

My parents make me _____ at home.

8 **Work in small groups. Read and discuss the sentences. Which do you agree or disagree with?**

I love doing jobs at home. I like tidying and cleaning the house.

My parents are great. They don't make me do jobs at home.

If I do jobs at home, my parents give me money. I think this is right.

> **Grammar**
>
> **make someone do something**
> To talk about obligation, when someone gives you a job that you must do use verb + object + infinitive without *to*.
>
> *My mum **makes me do** the laundry.*
>
> *My dad **makes me clean** the car.*
>
> The object can be: *me / you / him / her / it / us / them.*
>
> *My brother **makes her do** his homework.*
>
> **More?** ➜ Grammar

2.2 At school

1 **Discuss.** *What is your favourite school subject?*

What do you think are the most difficult subjects?

What are the easiest subjects?

2 **Work with a partner. What are the names of the subjects in the pictures? What other subjects do you study at school?**

Study tip

Draw a symbol or sign next to each subject word to help you remember the meaning.

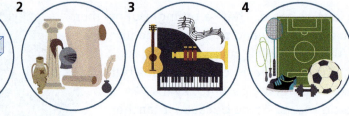

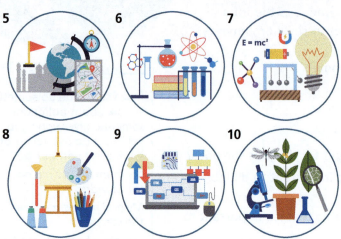

Vocabulary

I study …
art
biology
chemistry
computer science (IT)
drama
geography
history
languages
maths
music
physical education (PE)
physics
religious education (RE)
science

3 **Listen to Assad talking to his mum about his school timetable. Write the missing school subjects.** 🔊2.4

	Time	Monday	Tuesday	Wednesday	Thursday	Friday
Lesson 1	8.45 – 9.35	history	French	computer science	5 _____	English
Lesson 2	9.40 – 10.30	chemistry	2 _____	English	6 _____	7 _____
Break	10.30 – 11.00					
Lesson 3	11.00 – 11.50	1 _____	maths	PE	history	maths
Lunch	11.50 – 12.50					
Lesson 4	12.50 – 1.40	RE	physics	4 _____	RE	physics
Lesson 5	1.45 – 2.35	maths	geography	biology	geography	music
Break	2.35 – 3.00					
Lesson 6	3.00 – 3.50	art	3 _____	French	art	8 _____

4 **Look at Assad's timetable. How many times a week does Assad have …?**

a sports   **b** science   **c** maths

5 Work with a partner. Play *Guess the day*. Draw your timetable for a week and show your partner. Describe a day for your partner to guess.

- *In lesson … I have …*
- *In the morning, I have …*
- *Before / After break / lunch I have …*
- *On Mondays / Tuesdays … I have …*

Use *before and after* to talk about the order you do things and what happens first | *Before* lunch I have PE.

6 Tell your partner which is your favourite school day and why.

- *My favourite school day is … because I have / don't have / like / don't like …*

7 It's the evening and Assad's dad is asking Assad how his day at school was. Look at Assad's timetable in activity 2. Listen and say what day it is. 2.5

8 Listen again and complete the sentences with the words from the box. 2.5

was   had   did   didn't   have

Dad: How was school today?

Assad: It **1** _____ OK.

Dad: What lessons **2** _____ you have today?

Assad: I **3** _____ computer science, English and PE this morning.

Dad: What about science? Did you **4** _____ science?

Assad: No, I had physics yesterday but I **5** _____ have physics today.

Dad: What **6** _____ you **7** _____ in the afternoon?

Assad: I **8** _____ maths, biology and French.

9 With your partner, role-play the conversation between Assad and his dad.

10 Imagine today is Friday. Write sentences about your timetable.

Yesterday I had …

Yesterday I didn't have …

Before … I had …

After … I had …

Grammar

Past simple

Use the past simple tense to talk about a short finished action in the past (what happened before).

Regular verbs use the base form of the verb + *ed*.
walk → *Yesterday I **walked** to school.*
If the verb ends in an e, for example, phone, you only add a d. *phone* → *He **phoned** me.*

Some verbs have an irregular form.
Have → *I **had** physics yesterday.*
Be → *How **was** the physics lesson yesterday? It **was** fine.*

Use *did* to make questions and *didn't* to make negatives.
*Did you **have** science today? No, I **didn't have** science today.*

More? → Grammar

2.3 At the weekend

1 **Discuss.** *Look at the photos in the questionnaire. Which activities do you do at the weekend?*

2 **Do the questionnaire with your partner.**

It's the weekend!

go to the cinema

go out with friends

go to a restaurant

watch TV with my family

go shopping

go to the gym

① **What do you like doing at the weekend?**
 a relaxing at home
 b going out with friends
 c doing your homework
 d doing your hobbies

② **Who do you like spending time with at the weekend?**
 a your family
 b your friends
 c yourself
 d your sports team

③ **What's your favourite thing to do with friends or family at the weekend?**
 a eat in a restaurant
 b go shopping for clothes
 c go to the cinema
 d go for a long walk

④ **What did you do last weekend?**
 a I went shopping.
 b I went to the gym.
 c I stayed at home.
 d I watched a movie.

⑤ **For each sentence say if you do it always, sometimes or never.**
 1 always   **2** sometimes   **3** never
 a At the weekend I go out.
 b I see my friends at school in the week, so I don't see them at the weekend.
 c If it's the weekend, I don't do my homework.
 d If it's the weekend, I relax at home.

Vocabulary

to do my homework
to eat in a restaurant
to go for a walk
to go shopping
to go to the cinema
to go to the gym
to go out with my friends
to have a picnic
to have fun
to relax
to stay at home
to watch a film*
to watch TV
(*American English = movie)

Study tip

When you read or hear a word or phrase you don't know, look it up in a dictionary or ask someone what it means. Then write a new sentence using the word or phrase. Try and use the new word or phrase in your next conversation in English.

Study tip

Learn words that go together as phrases.

to spend time (doing something or with someone: *I spend time with my friends at the weekend.*)

to spend money (on something: *I spend money on clothes.*)

3 Read Poppy's email. Work with a partner and discuss why she loves weekends.

Hi!

I love weekends. In the week I do all my homework, I tidy my room and I do jobs at home after school, so at the weekend it's my time to relax and have fun. On Saturday I get up at 11 o'clock. Then I have a long bath and I have a big breakfast. I relax until lunchtime. Then I get dressed and I go out to meet my friends. If it's nice weather, we meet in the park and we have a picnic. Then we go shopping for new clothes. If it's not nice weather, we go to the cinema. When we have money, we go to a restaurant for dinner. On Sunday, I spend the day with my family. I get up at about 9 o'clock. I go shopping at the supermarket with my mum. Then, I go to the gym with my family. We have lunch at home together then we watch a film on TV. We often watch romantic films because my mum loves them!

What do you do at the weekend?

Poppy

4 Decide if the sentences about Poppy's weekend are true (T) or false (F).

1 Poppy does her homework. **T/F**

2 Poppy spends time with her family. **T/F**

3 Poppy sometimes goes to the cinema. **T/F**

4 Poppy always eats in restaurants. **T/F**

5 Match the zero conditional sentence halves.

1 When I have free time,

2 When you go shopping,

3 If you go to a friend's house,

4 When you go to the cinema,

5 If I don't have any homework,

a you are not at home.

b you spend money.

c I play football or go swimming.

d I can meet my friends.

e you watch a film.

6 Ask and answer the questions with a partner. *What do you do at the weekend …*

- … *when it is hot?*

- … *when it is cold?*

- … *if you have some money?*

- … *if you don't have any money?*

7 Write a reply to Poppy's email. Use the questions to help you.

- Do you like weekends?

- What do you do at the weekend?

- Who do you do different activities with at the weekend?

Grammar

Zero conditionals
To talk about the things that are generally true, present habits or scientific facts use the zero conditional.

The zero conditional uses *if* or *when*.

You can make the zero conditional with two present simple verbs: one in the *if / when* clause and one in the main clause. The *if / when* clause can come at the start or at the end.

When or *If* + present simple, present simple in the main clause.

OR: Present simple + *when* or *if* + *present simple*. (no comma needed)

If the weather's nice, we meet in the park.
When we have money, we go to a restaurant for dinner.
I don't go out at the weekend when I have homework.
I go to the gym if I have time.

More? ➜ Grammar

2.4 Around town

1 Discuss. *Is it easy to travel around town where you live? Why or why not?*

Learning aims
- Talk about how to get around town
- Read a short paragraph from a story
- Use the past continuous to talk about things that happened in the past

2 Match the forms of transport (1–11) with the pictures. There is one extra form of transport. What is it?

a  b   c   d   e

f   g  h  i   j

1	by train	5	walk / on foot	9	by taxi
2	by bicycle / bike	6	by bus	10	by metro / underground
3	by ferry	7	by boat	11	by motorcycle
4	by tram	8	by car		

3 Complete the sentences 1–6 with a form of transport from activity 2.

> How do you go to school? Why?

1 I go by … because it's good exercise, it's good for the environment and it's quicker than walking.

2 I go by … because the bus stop is outside my house.

3 I go … because I live very close to my school.

4 I go by … because my school is on the other side of the river.

5 I go by … because my dad is a teacher at my school so he takes me to school every day.

6 I go by … because my school is in a different town and there are no buses.

4 Ask and answer these questions with a partner.

- *How do you get to school?*
- *Why do you use this transport?*
- *How long does your journey take?*
- *How do you go shopping?*
- *What transport did you go on yesterday?*

To say why you use a form of transport use *because*.	I walk *because* I live close to my school.
To say what transport you used yesterday use past simple.	I *went* to the cinema by train. I *took* the bus home.
To talk about your journey time use *take* + time.	It *takes 20 minutes* to get to school by car.

Sometimes we can say things in two or more ways:	*How do you go to school?* I go by bus.
	How do you get to school? I take the bus.

5 **Read the beginning of a story. Answer the questions.**

Jade was sitting on the number 24B bus. It was raining. There was a man sitting in the seat in front of her. He was reading a book. There was a woman with a baby. The baby was crying and the woman was looking in her bag for something. Jade was bored. She was looking out of the window when she saw it. A light in the sky. It was a purple and orange light. What was it? And why was it getting closer?

1 Where was Jade?

2 Who was looking in a bag?

3 How was Jade feeling?

4 What was Jade doing?

5 What did Jade see?

6 **Copy and complete the sentences with the past continuous of the verbs.**

1 At one o'clock, Mr Thompson … a book. (read)

2 I didn't go for a walk because I … my homework. (do)

3 We … at 6.00. (not drive)

7 **Complete the sentences with the correct form of the verbs.**

1 I (watch) _____ TV when Sally (phone) _____ me.

2 Tim (eat) _____ his dinner when Pedro (walk) _____ into the room.

Grammar

Prepositions

To talk about where something is, use prepositions of place: in, in front of, on, out of, under.

*Jade was sitting **on** the number 24B bus.*

*There was a man sitting in the seat **in front of** her.*

More? ➔ Grammar

Grammar

Past continuous

To talk about a continuing action/s in the past use the past continuous.

You make the past continuous with the past simple form of the verb *to be* [was / were] + the *-ing* form of the main verb.

*Jade **was sitting** on the bus.*

*The baby **was crying**.*

To talk about a continuing action in the past before another often shorter action stops it, use the past continuous + *when* + past simple.

*She **was looking** out of the window **when** she **saw** it.*

More? ➔ Grammar

2.5 My time

1   **Discuss.** *What's your favourite time of the day and why?*

2   **With your partner, write the correct words using the words in the Vocabulary box.**

1   This word is the opposite of first. _____

2   Midday is 12.00 in the morning. This word is 12.00 at night. _____

3   What is the next word? yesterday, today, _____

4   This word means four weeks. _____

5   This word is the opposite of late. _____

Vocabulary

early	next
first	soon
last	today
late	tomorrow
midday	week
midnight	yesterday
month	

3   **Match sentences 1–7 with letters a–g on Mara's calendar.**

1   Mara went to the dentist last month.

2   She visited her grandparents yesterday.

3   It's her birthday next week.

4   It was her dad's birthday last week.

5   She has her first driving lesson next month.

6   The school holidays start tomorrow.

7   She goes to her book club on the first Monday of each month.

4   **Ask and answer with your partner.**

- *What did you do last week?*
- *What did you do yesterday?*
- *When is your next holiday?*

Grammar

Present simple to talk about the future

You can use the present simple tense to talk about the future for planned events, facts and timetables. You need to use a time phrase too.

*It's Mara's birthday **next week**.*

*She **has** her first driving lesson **next month**.*

*The school holidays **start tomorrow**.*

*My next holiday **is in December**.*

More? → Grammar

5 Look at the invitation. What is it for?

BARBECUE

When: _____

What time: _____

Where: _____

How to get there: _____

Grammar

Prepositions of time

To talk about dates and days use the preposition *on*.
My birthday's **on** *the 1st of May.*
I go to book club **on** *Mondays.*

To talk about times use the preposition *at*.
It starts **at** *2.00.*

To talk about months use the preposition *in*.
My next holiday is **in** *December.*

To talk about how long a journey is use *takes*.
It **takes** *15 minutes.*

More? ➔ Grammar

6 Listen and find the information to complete the invitation in activity 5. 🎧 2.6

7 Complete the sentences with the words from the box. Listen again to check your answers. 🎧 2.6

can   finishes   next   see   starts   that   to invite

1 I'd like _____ you to a barbecue.

2 It's _____ week, on Saturday.

3 Is _____ the 1st of May?

4 _____ you come?

5 It _____ at 2.00 in the afternoon and _____ at midnight.

6 _____ you next weekend.

8 Role-play with a partner.

Student A

You had a party last night. Student B is asking you questions about the party. Answer Student B's questions.

The party was …

The party started …

The party finished …

The party finished / didn't finish late.

We ate …

We drank …

People got to the party by car / on foot …

Student B

Ask Student A questions about his / her party.

- Where was the party?
- What time did the party start?
- What time did the party finish?
- Did the party finish late?
- What did you eat at the party?
- What did you drink at the party?
- How did people get to your party?

Children know that education is important. Some take amazing forms of transport or make difficult journeys to get to school.

In parts of the USA, there's often snow in the winter. Buses and cars can't travel because it's too dangerous. Many children can't get to school. This is called a '**snow day**'. However, in Makinac Island, USA, children ride **snow mobiles** so they can go to school in the snow.

In Indonesia, some children have a different problem to get to school. Their school is on the other side of a big river. So they **cross** the river by **rope bridge**. It isn't easy to cross the bridge when you are carrying a school bag and you're wearing a school uniform.

1   **Read the text and answer true (T) or false (F).**

1   All children have difficult journeys to school.   **T/F**

2   Makinac Island is in Indonesia.   **T/F**

3   A 'snow day' means children can't travel to school in the snow.   **T/F**

4   Children on Makinac Island travel on the snow to school in the winter.   **T/F**

5   Children in Indonesia take a boat to school.   **T/F**

Glossary

rope bridge a bridge made of rope you hold as you walk
snow mobile special type of transport for travelling in the snow
to cross to go from one side of something to the other

Discuss

Which of these journeys is the most fun/interesting/dangerous?

I think going to school by (snow mobile/rope bridge) is ...
What do you think?
I agree/disagree

Nathan is twelve years old. He lives in the Philippines. There are many islands and lots of water in the Philippines so people often travel by river. Every day Nathan walked with his friends through the river to school because there weren't enough boats. He got up early every day because the journey to school took a long time. "I didn't like it! I arrived at school at eight o'clock and I was wet and tired," says Nathan.

Then last year, a **charity** gave the school children boats to get to school. The boats are yellow because school buses are usually this colour. Now it takes less than one hour to get to school. So Nathan can get up later and he's not tired at school. On the journey home he does his homework on the boat. "It's fantastic!" says Nathan. "I'm learning more and I'm very happy. My parents are happy too because when I get home I can help them with jobs in the house."

2 **Read the text. Choose the correct option to complete each sentence.**

1 Nathan **liked** / **didn't like** walking to school with his friends.

2 Nathan's journey on foot was **long** / **short**.

3 When he arrived at school he was **late** / **tired**.

4 School boats and buses are **the same** / **a different** colour.

5 Buses are **more** / **less** useful than boats in the Philippines.

6 Now Nathan's journey to school is **quicker** / **slower**.

3 **Discuss with a partner.**

- *How do you get to school?*
- *How important is school to you?*
- *Does your journey to school change at different times of the year?*

Glossary

charity an organisation that helps people

Find out

1 *Look on a world map. Where are the Philippines?*

2 *How many islands are there in the Philippines?*

The same …

In the Philippines, many school students learn English as an *additional** language. However, there are more than 700 languages in the country! So English is useful to help people communicate.

What languages do you speak? Do you speak the same language at home and at school?

*additional= extra or other

but different

Review

1 **Dylan is talking about his life. Listen and choose the correct answers.**

1 Dylan likes …

   a languages   **b** history   **c** maths

2 On Saturdays, Dylan gets up at …

   a 10 o'clock   **b** half past ten   **c** eleven o'clock

3 On Saturdays, Dylan visits his …

   a grandmother   **b** grandfather   **c** dad

4 He …

   a does the laundry   **b** does the gardening   **c** takes the rubbish out

5 Dylan goes to the gym …

   a on foot   **b** by bicycle   **c** by bus

6 At the gym he …

   a meets a friend   **b** goes swimming   **c** has lunch

7 Dylan spends Saturday evenings with …

   a his mum   **b** his grandfather   **c** his friend

8 Dylan likes …

   a cleaning   **b** cooking   **c** relaxing

2 **Read and complete the email from Camila. Use the words from the box.**

> by bike   gym   made   maths   midnight   yesterday

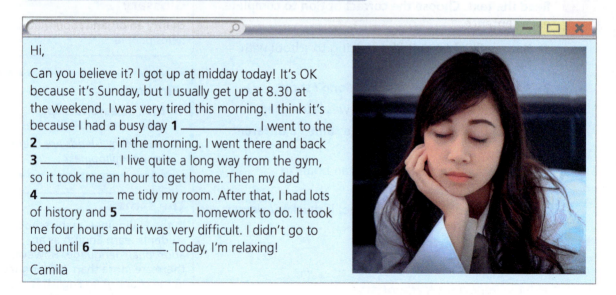

Hi,

Can you believe it? I got up at midday today! It's OK because it's Sunday, but I usually get up at 8.30 at the weekend. I was very tired this morning. I think it's because I had a busy day **1** ＿＿＿＿＿. I went to the **2** ＿＿＿＿＿ in the morning. I went there and back **3** ＿＿＿＿＿. I live quite a long way from the gym, so it took me an hour to get home. Then my dad **4** ＿＿＿＿＿ me tidy my room. After that, I had lots of history and **5** ＿＿＿＿＿ homework to do. It took me four hours and it was very difficult. I didn't go to bed until **6** ＿＿＿＿＿. Today, I'm relaxing!

Camila

3 **Which sentences are in the past simple and which are in the past continuous?**

1 Harry was washing the car.
2 Katy was playing her violin.
3 Li was in the kitchen.
4 Grace and Ola were doing the washing up.

4 **Talk about yourself to your partner. Answer the questions.**

- What are your favourite subjects at school?
- What school subjects don't you like?
- How do you get to school? How long does it take?
- What jobs do you do at home?
- What do you like doing at the weekend?
- Who do you spend time with at the weekends?
- What did you do yesterday?

> **How to improve**
>
> When you have questions to respond to in writing and speaking tasks, you can use the verbs in the questions in your answers.

How are you doing?

Read and copy the checklist below. For each 'I can … sentence' think and decide: **very well, quite well,** or **OK, but I need more practice**.

Use the checklist to help you improve your English.

I can …	Very well	Quite well	OK, but I need more practice
• describe my daily routine			
• use the present continuous			
• talk about jobs I do at home			
• talk about school subjects			
• use the past simple			
• talk about activities I do at the weekend			
• talk about things that are generally true with *When* or *If*			
• talk about transport where I live			
• use different time words and phrases			
• use the past continuous			

> **Study tip**
>
> Knowing what you are good at and what you need to practise more helps you to improve your English.

Words and phrases – Unit 2

Adverbs and prepositions of place

above _____
across _____
around _____
behind _____
below _____
beside / next to _____
between _____
down _____
everywhere _____
from _____
here _____
in _____
inside _____
nowhere _____
off _____
on _____
out _____
outside _____
over _____
over there _____
somewhere _____
there _____
to _____
under _____
up _____
upstairs _____
with _____

Around town

ambulance _____
bicycle _____
boat _____
bus _____
car _____
ferry _____
metro / underground _____
motorcycle _____
on foot _____
taxi _____
train _____
tram _____
to get in / out of _____
to get on / get off _____
to go by bus / car _____
to take the bus _____
to travel by bus / train _____
to get on / off the bus
    / train _____
to walk _____

At home

bottle _____
box _____
flower _____
(back / front) garden _____
gate _____
kitchen _____
path _____
plant _____
sink _____
tin _____
tree _____
wall _____
to clean _____
to clear the table _____
to cook _____
to do some gardening _____
to do the laundry _____
to do the washing _____
to do the washing up _____
to grow vegetables _____
to sew _____
to iron _____
to lay / clear the table _____
to plant _____
to take the rubbish out
    (American English –
    rubbish = trash) _____
to tidy up / clean the
    house _____
My mum / dad makes me
    do the laundry. _____

At the weekend

to eat in a restaurant _____
to go for a walk _____
to go shopping _____
to go to the cinema _____
to go to the gym _____
to have a picnic _____
to listen to music on
    headphones _____
to meet my friends _____
to relax _____
to spend time with
    my family / friends _____
to stay at home _____
to watch TV / a thriller
    / a romantic film /
    a comedy _____

Daily routines

daily / everyday _____
to brush / comb hair _____
to brush teeth _____
to do my homework _____
to do sport _____
to get dressed / undressed _____
to get up _____
to go to bed _____
to go home _____
to go to school _____
to have breakfast / lunch /
  dinner _____
to have a bath _____
to have a shower _____
to meet my friends _____
to relax _____
to wash your face _____
to watch TV _____

Education – studies

break _____
class (group of students) _____
classmate _____
homework _____
lesson _____
term _____
timetable _____

Invitations

invitation _____
I'd like to invite you to
  my birthday party. _____
Can you come? _____

School subjects

art _____
biology _____
chemistry _____
computer science / IT _____
drama _____
geography _____
history _____
languages _____
maths _____
music _____
physical education / PE _____
physics _____
religious education / RE _____
science _____
subject _____

Time

after _____
afternoon _____
(At) one / two o'clock _____
before _____
clock / watch _____
date _____
day / week / month _____
evening _____
half / quarter of an hour _____
(It's) half past seven /
  (a) quarter to seven /
  (a) quarter past seven _____
hour _____
midday _____
midnight _____
minute _____
monthly _____
morning _____
past _____
season _____
second _____
My birthday's on the
  1st of May. _____
It starts at 2 o'clock. _____
It only takes 15 minutes. _____

Time expressions

afterwards / later / then _____
again _____
at last _____
early / late _____
finally _____
first _____
firstly _____
future _____
immediately _____
last _____
meanwhile _____
moment _____
next _____
since _____
sometimes _____
soon _____
still / yet _____
suddenly _____
the day before yesterday _____
the following (week) _____
today _____
tomorrow _____
week – last week /
  next week _____
weekend _____
year _____
yearly / annual _____
yesterday _____

Reading

Read the email. For each question, choose the correct answer (A, B or C).

Hi!

I want to tell you about my school day. I get up at six o'clock in the morning. It's early! I have a horse called Chip so every morning before school I ride him and give him food. Then I come home, have a shower, have breakfast and run to the bus stop. I take the bus to school at quarter past eight. After school, I go to the library and do my homework. If my friend Max is in the library too, we walk home together. When she is not there, I get the bus. Then I go to see Chip again and clean him and his stable. My mum or dad cooks dinner and we always eat together at the table. My parents make me clear the table and do the washing up after dinner. I go to bed at about ten o'clock.

Write to me soon!

Luca

1 **Luca is writing to tell you about his …**

A routine.

B pet.

C friends.

2 **Before school Luca …**

A rides his horse.

B goes running.

C goes cycling.

3 **Luca goes to school …**

A on foot.

B by bus.

C by horse.

4 **Luca does his homework …**

A in the morning.

B in the afternoon.

C in the evening.

5 **Luca … walks home from school.**

A never

B always

C sometimes

6 **Luca goes to see his horse …**

A once a day.

B twice a day.

C three times a day.

7 **Before bed, Luca …**

A does some jobs.

B does his homework.

C rides his horse.

Listening

Listen and choose the correct answer (A, B, C or D).

You are at home.

1. You are with your mum. Your mum asks you something.

   What is your dad doing?

A   B   C   D

2. When you find your dad, he asks you to do something.

   What does your dad ask you to do?

  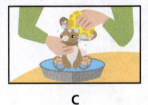 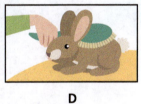

A   B   C   D

3. Dad tells you something.

   What time is dinner?

A   B   C   D

4. Your sister calls you on your phone. She tells you something.

   Where is your sister?

A   B   C   D

Speaking

Work with a partner.

Student A

Ask Student B these questions.

- Tell me about your family.
- Tell me about your house.
- Do you have any pets?
- How often do you do sport?
- What's your favourite school subject?
- How do you get to school in the morning?
- What did you do last weekend?
- When did you last go shopping?

Student B

Ask Student A these questions.

- Tell me about a friend you have.
- What are your hobbies?
- What jobs do you do at home?
- How often do you go to the cinema?
- What school subject don't you like?
- What time do you go to bed at the weekend?
- What did you do yesterday?
- When did you last tidy your bedroom?

Study tip

Record yourself speaking in English. Listen to the recording and try to improve your pronunciation.

Writing

Your name is Joe Hudson. You are looking for a penfriend from another country to write to.

Complete the form for the penfriend.

Your name	Joe Hudson
Number of people in your family	
How you travel to school	
Now give more information about your family. **Write about:** • the name and age of one person in your family • what they look like • why you like them. **Write 20–30 words.**	

3 My life

Are you ready?

- Talk about foods I like, don't like and prefer
- Use *would you like* and *can* to make offers and requests

1 Match the words in the box with the pictures.

apple   banana   carrot   coconut   cucumber   mango   onion   orange   pepper   tomato

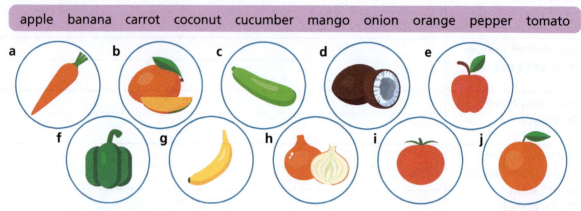

a   b   c   d   e

f   g   h   i   j

2 Copy and complete the table with the words from activity 1. Then add two more in each column. Find the words in English for your favourite fruits and vegetables.

Fruits	Vegetables
apple	

Study tip

Personalise your learning. Find out what your favourite things are in English so you can talk and write about yourself more easily.

3 Listen and answer the questions. 🎧 3.1

1 What fruits does Katie like?

2 What fruits doesn't Katie like?

3 Does Katie prefer carrots or peppers?

4 Ask and answer these questions.

What fruits do you like?   What vegetables do you like?

Use *and* to talk about more than one thing you like.	I like mangoes *and* apples.
Use *or* to talk about more than one thing you don't like.	I don't like bananas *or* coconuts.
Use *but* to make a contrast.	I like apples *but* I don't like oranges.

Vocabulary

I like …
I don't like …
Which do you prefer … or …?
I prefer …
apples
bananas
carrots
coconuts
cucumbers
green peppers
mangoes
onions
oranges
tomatoes

| Use *prefer* to talk about the thing you like more. | Which do you *prefer* carrots or peppers? |
| | I *prefer* peppers. |

Grammar

Nouns
Many nouns in English have singular and plural forms: *carrot* > *carrots*
These nouns are called *countable* nouns because you can count them.
one carrot, two carrots, three carrots, many carrots
You can use *a* or *an* with countable nouns: *an apple, a banana*
Use plurals with: I like…/ I don't like…/ I prefer…

More? ➜ Grammar

5 Look at the pictures. Listen and repeat the words. 3.2

6 Listen and write the letters a–s in the order you hear the words from activity 5. 3.3

7 With a partner, copy and complete the table with the words from activity 5. Then add the fruit and vegetables you learned in activity 1 to the table. Use a dictionary to help you.

Countable nouns	Uncountable nouns
biscuit/s	water

8 Read and listen to the dialogues in a restaurant. Complete the gaps with *would* or *can*. 3.4

Waiter: Good evening. **1** _____ you like a table for two people?

Customer 1: Yes. **2** _____ we have a table near the window, please?

Waiter: Yes, you **3** _____.

Customer 2: Excuse me!

Waiter: Yes, Madam. **4** _____ I help you?

Customer 2: Yes, **5** _____ we see the menu, please?

Waiter: **6** _____ you like some drinks?

Customer 1: Yes, please. **7** _____ I have some sparkling water, please?

Customer 2: And **8** _____ I have a cola, please?

Waiter: Yes, of course.

9 In groups of three, practise the dialogues in activity 8.

Grammar

Nouns
Some nouns in English do not have a plural form. These are *uncountable* nouns. You can't count uncountable nouns or use *a / an* with these nouns.

Water is an uncountable noun:
~~a water, one water, two waters~~

More? → Grammar

Grammar

Offers and requests
Use *would you like* to make offers.
Would you like a table?

Use *can* to make and reply to requests.
Can we have a table near the window, please?
Yes, you can.

But people working in shops and cafes use *can* for offers :
Can I help you?

More? → Grammar

3.1 Shopping for food

1 Discuss. *Where do you go shopping for food?*

2 Talk with your partner. What do you buy in these shops?

KIOSK BUTCHER'S MARKET FISH SHOP BAKERY

3 Match dialogues A–E with the shops in activity 2.
S is the shopkeeper and C is the customer.

A
S Hello. What would you like?
C I'd like some fish, please.
S How **1** _____ fish would you like?
C I'd like one kilo please.

B
S What would you like?
C I'd like some potatoes, please.
S How **2** _____ kilos would you like?
C Two kilos please.
S OK, here you are.
C Thank you.

C
C Hi! Can I have a bottle of water, please?
S Would you like still or sparkling water?
C I'd like still, please.
S Anything **3** _____?
C Yes, I'd like an ice cream, please.
S Would you like strawberry or chocolate ice cream?
C Chocolate, please. How much is that?
S That's $3.90, please.

D
S Good morning. What would you like?
C I'd like **4** _____ bread, please.
S How many loaves would you like?
C Two loaves, please.
S Here you are. Anything else?
C No, thank you.

E
C Hello, I'd like some beef, please.
S Of course. How much beef would you like?
C Um …
S This is two kilos. Is this enough?
C No, that's too much.
S This is one kilo. Is this **5** _____?
C Yes. That's enough. Thank you.

4 Listen and complete the dialogues in activity 3. Use the words from the box. (3.5)

> else   enough   many   much   some

5 With your partner read out the dialogues from activity 3.

6 Copy and complete the sentences with *much* or *many*.

1 How _____ apples would you like?

2 How _____ milk would you like?

3 How _____ chicken would you like?

4 How _____ cups of coffee would they like?

7 Role-play shopping with a partner.

Student A

1 With Student B, choose a shop from activity 2.

2 You are the customer. Decide what you want to buy.

3 Role-play with Student B.
- Hello.
- I'd like some / a bottle of … please.
- … grams / kilos, please.
- That's enough, thank you.
- How much is that?
- Thank you.

Student B

1 With Student A, choose a shop from activity 2.

2 You are the shopkeeper. What questions do you want to ask the customer?

3 Role-play with Student A.
- Hello. What would you like?
- How many / much …?
- Is this enough?
- Anything else?
- That's $…, please.
- Thank you.

To ask how much something costs:	How much is that?
To reply:	That's $5, please.

Grammar

Talking about quantity
Use: *much, many, some, any, enough, too much* to talk about how much of something you need.

Use *some* with uncountable nouns: *I'd like some white bread, please.*

Use *some* with plural countable nouns: *I'd like some potatoes, please.*

To ask about quantities, use *How much …?* or *How many …?*

Use *How much* with uncountable nouns: *How much beef would you like?*

Use *How many* with countable plural nouns: *How many potatoes do you want?*

Is this enough?

Yes, that's enough. / No, that's too much / not enough.

You can make uncountable nouns countable by adding a unit of measure: *a cup of …, a glass of …, a bottle of …:*

Bread is uncountable but a *loaf of bread* is countable; one loaf of bread, two loaves of bread, etc.

Water is uncountable but a *glass of water* or a *bottle of water* is countable.

More? → Grammar

Vocabulary

I work at …
the bakery.
the kiosk.
the butcher's.
the fish shop.
the market.

I'd like …
one loaf / two loaves of bread.
one kilo / two kilos of carrots.
two glasses of water.

3.2 Eating out

1 Discuss. *What food and drink do you like eating when you go to a restaurant?*

2 Ask and answer these questions with a partner.

- *What food can you see in the pictures?*
- *How often do you eat this food?*
- *Who do you go to a café or restaurant with?*
- *How much does it usually cost to eat or drink in a café or restaurant?*

3 Listen to a man and woman in a restaurant. Do they order food? Do they order drinks? 🔊 3.6

4 Listen again and tick the correct items for the waiter. 🔊 3.6

Menu	Woman	Man
STARTER		
Tomato soup		
Onion soup		
Green salad		
Chicken salad		
MAIN COURSE		
Chicken burger		
Beef burger		
Omelette		
Fish		
DESSERT		
cake		
fruit		
DRINKS		
sparkling water		
still water		

5 Listen again and complete the gaps with words from the menu. 🔊 **3.6**

Customer: For my starter, I'd like the **1** _____, please.

Waiter: Would you like the **2** _____ or the **3** _____?

Customer: I'd like the **4** _____, please.

Waiter: Of course. And what would you like for your main course?

Customer: Can I have the **5** _____, please?

Waiter: Oh, I'm sorry. I've just sold the last **6** _____. Is the **7** _____ ok?

Customer: Is it spicy?

Waiter: No, not at all.

Customer: That's fine then, thank you.

6 With your partner role-play the conversation between the waiter and the customer from activity 5.

7 Work in pairs. Write a new conversation between a customer and a waiter. You can use the menu from activity 4.

8 Role-play your conversation to another pair.

Grammar

Offers and requests

Use *would* + *like* to ask and answer questions about what you want. This is more polite than using *want*.

What *would* you *like* to drink?

Would you *like* the chicken salad?

I'd like the green salad, please.

More? → Grammar

Vocabulary

What would you like for your …?
starter
main course
dessert

I'd like the …
beef burger
cake
chicken burger
chicken salad
fish
fruit
green salad
omelette
onion soup
tomato soup

Is it spicy?

What would you like to drink?
I'd like a …
mineral water
sparkling water
still water

3.3 Shopping for clothes

1 **Discuss.** *How often do you go shopping for clothes? Where's your favourite place to buy clothes?*

- Learn new words and phrases for clothes and accessories
- Understand how we use gerunds to talk about people's shopping preferences
- Discuss shopping online
- Talk about clothes shopping

2 **Listen and match conversations 1–4 about shopping with the photos a–d below.** 3.7

a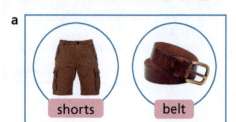

shorts   belt

b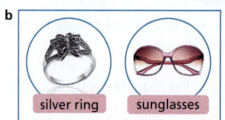

silver ring   sunglasses

c

trainers

d

skirt   shirt   jacket   bag   sandals

3 **Listen again. Number the conversations in order 1–4.** 3.7

A A person is buying a gift for a friend. ☐

B A person bought some clothes but he/she doesn't like them. ☐

C A person is buying some clothes for a wedding. ☐

D A person is trying on some clothes and they are too big. ☐

4 **Complete the conversation between a shopkeeper and a customer with the phrases from the box.**

> how much   would you like   looking for   size   try on

Shopkeeper: Hi. Can I help you?

Customer: Yes, please. I'm **1** _____ a smart jacket.

Shopkeeper: OK. What colour **2** _____?

Customer: I'd like a pink jacket, please.

Shopkeeper: OK, here you are.

Customer: Excuse me. Can I **3** _____ these shoes, please?

Shopkeeper: Yes, of course. What **4** _____ are you?

Customer: I'm a size 6. They're perfect.

Customer: **5** _____ are they?

Shopkeeper: They're $40.00.

Vocabulary

I'm looking for a / some …

gold	bag
leather	belt
plastic	coat
silver	dress
smart	earrings
	jacket
	jeans
	jewellery
	necklace
	ring
	sandals
	shirt
	shoes
	shorts
	skirt
	sunglasses
	tights
	trainers*
	socks
	tights
loose	trousers**
tight	(school)
	uniform

(*American English = sneakers)
(**American English = pants)

Study tip

Putting words into categories can help you learn useful vocabulary sets to talk about a topic.

5 Put the words in the Vocabulary box into the correct category. Can you add any words to each category?

clothes	accessories	material

6 Work with a partner. Practise the dialogue in activity 4 and make your own using the words from Vocabulary box.

7 Discuss. *Which do you prefer: shopping in shops or online?*

8 Read the texts. Who prefers shopping online? Who prefers shopping in shops?

> I don't like shopping online. There are too many websites. It takes a long time to look for things. If you order something online, it takes a long time to arrive. When you buy clothes in a shop, you take your new clothes home and you can wear them the same day. **Todd**

> Shopping online is very relaxing. I shop online at home in the evening and at the weekend. I like shopping online. Sometimes my friend Sophie and I shop online together. I don't like trying on clothes in shops. I like trying on clothes at home. **Lily**

> I like shopping online for socks, tights or my school uniform. But for other clothes I prefer shopping in the city. On Saturday, I went to Vancouver and I found an amazing clothes shop. It sold old clothes. I love buying old clothes! I don't like buying new clothes. In Vancouver I bought some amazing jeans and a coat. They are from the 1970s! **Rose**

9 Read the texts again and answer the questions.

1 Who thinks shopping online is relaxing?
2 Who likes buying new clothes and then wearing them on the same day?
3 Who doesn't like modern clothes?
4 Who thinks it's difficult to find clothes online?
5 Who found an amazing shop?
6 Who doesn't like trying clothes on in shops?

10 Ask and answer these questions with a partner.

- *Do you like shopping online? Why or why not?*
- *Do you like trying on clothes in shops?*
- *What did you buy at the weekend?*
- *Where did you buy it?*

Grammar

Gerunds
Use verbs + *ing* (gerunds) as nouns to talk about activities you like or don't like.

Shopping online is very relaxing.

I like shopping online.

I don't like trying on clothes in shops.

More? ➜ Grammar

How to improve

When you answer questions, use the same tense in your answer as you hear in the question.

3.4 Going out with friends

1 Discuss. *What do you like doing with friends?*

2 Listen and match messages 1–6 with pictures a–f.

1 Hello Eve
Would you like to go swimming tomorrow afternoon? Let me know!

2 Hi Justin
Would you like to come to the zoo with me and my parents this weekend?

3 Hi Flora
I'm going to go shopping with Ava and Nuria on Sunday. Would you like to come with us?

4 Hello Karim
Henry and I are going to go to the gym this afternoon. Would you like to come too?

5 Hi Jess
I finished my homework at 4pm so I'm going to go to the coffee shop now. Do you want to meet me there?

6 Hi David
Would you like to come to the cinema? The film starts at 8.00. Why don't we meet at 7.30?

a  **b** **c** **d** **e** **f**

3 Match messages 1–6 in activity 2 with replies a–f.

a Thanks for inviting me, but I'm going to go fishing with my dad this afternoon.

b How nice! See you tomorrow afternoon.

c What a pity! I'm still doing my homework! Let's do it another day!

d Sorry, but I can't because I'm going to visit my grandparents on Sunday.

e Yes, I'd love to. See you later.

f Thanks! I'd love to. See you at the weekend!

Vocabulary

I'm going to …
go to a coffee shop / café
go to a football match
go to a music festival
go to the beach
go to the cinema
go to the gym
go to the theatre
go shopping
go swimming
go to the zoo

Grammar

***Going to* to talk about plans**
To talk about plans use the verb *to be* + *going to* + main verb.
*Henry and I **are going to go** to the gym this afternoon.*
*I**'m going to visit** my grandparents tomorrow.*
*He**'s going to finish** his homework tonight.*

More? → Grammar

4 **Copy and complete the table with the phrases.**

How nice!   I'd love to.   Would you like to ...?   Sorry, but I can't.

What a shame! I'm busy then.   Do you want to ...?   What a pity! I'm having dinner with my dad.

Let's do it another day.   See you later.   Why don't we meet at ...?

To invite someone	To accept an invitation (say yes)	To turn down / refuse an invitation (say no)
	How nice!	

5 **Work in pairs. Practise saying the messages and replies in activities 2 and 3.**

6 **Copy and complete Eva's sentences.**

On Friday evening, I **1** ... with my friends Gina and Ellen.

On Saturday, I **2** ... for breakfast with my cousins, then we **3** ... .

On Sunday, I **4** ... with my dad.

7 **Make and accept or refuse invitations with your partner. Use the photos and the language in the text messages in activities 2 and 3.**

- *I'm going to ...*
- *Would you like to ...?*
- *Thank you, but I can't because ... / How nice. I'd love to.*
- *See you ...*

go to the beach   go to a football match   go to the theatre   go to a music festival

3.5 Going online

1 **Discuss.** *What activities do you do online? What social media do you use?*

Learning aims
- Talk about going online
- Write about using the internet
- Read a blog post about online safety
- Use imperatives to give advice

2 **Match photos 1–4 with types of technology a–d. Which types of technology do you use?**

1
2
3
4

a laptop   **b** computer   **c** tablet   **d** mobile phone

3 **With your partner, play *Guess the word* using words from the Vocabulary box.**

It's a kind of …

You use it to …

Vocabulary

blog
blogger
computer
laptop
mobile phone
printer
radio
selfie
tablet
text message
video game
website

4 **Do the questionnaire with your partner.**

1 Do you prefer …?
a listening to music online
b listening to CDs
c listening to the radio

2 Do you prefer … ?
a taking photos of other people
b taking selfies
c taking photos of places

3 What do you usually do with your photos?
a print them with a printer
b post them on social media
c keep them on your computer

4 Do you prefer … ?
a posting photos and videos online
b reading blogs
c writing a blog

5 What do you do most online?
a use social media
b watch films and TV shows
c play video games
d do homework or learn new things

6 How often do you go online?
a once a day
b less than once a day
c more than once a day

Use *prefer* + verb with *-ing* to talk about how you like to do things	I *prefer watching* films on my TV.

5 Listen to a radio interview with Jenny Green. How old is she?

6 Listen again and choose the two true statements.

1 Jenny doesn't like going online.

2 Jenny watches films on her phone.

3 Jenny buys clothes online.

4 Jenny is a blogger.

5 Jenny has a laptop, a mobile phone and a computer.

7 Write a paragraph about what you do and don't do online. Say what types of technology you use and don't use.

8 Read the blog post about online safety. Do you know this advice?

BE SAFE ONLINE

The internet is amazing, but you should use it safely. Here's some advice:

1 Think about what you post on social media. Don't use your real surname.

2 Never upload photos that show where you live.

3 Don't open a message from someone you don't know.

4 Always tell an adult if someone you don't know asks to meet or talk to you.

5 Never give anyone your bank details online.

Grammar

Imperatives

To give advice you can use the imperative.
Use the infinitive of the verb without *to*.

Think about what you post on social media websites.

You use *Do not* or *Don't* in the negative.

Don't use your real surname.

You can also use *never / always* + the imperative.

Never upload photos that show where you live.

Always tell an adult if someone you don't know asks to meet you.

More? ➜ Grammar

9 Choose the correct options to complete the advice.

---

1 Never / Always spend too much time online. Don't **2 spend / spending** more than two hours a day on your phone. **3 Always / Never** meet friends or do some sport! **4 Being / Be** safe online!

---

10 With your partner, give each other advice about being safe online. Choose *Do* or *Don't*, *Always* or *Never* to make sentences.

- … think about what you post on social media.
- … upload photos that show where you live.
- … use your real surname on social media.
- … open a message from someone you don't know.
- … agree to meet someone you met online.
- … tell an adult if someone you don't know asks to meet you.
- … give people online your bank details.

We all like shopping and buying new things, but we should look after our old things too! At a Repair Café you can fix or repair your broken things, for example if you tear your clothes, you can repair them. People also often repair things like bicycles, toys and watches. You can sew, glue, paint or do anything you need to. A Repair Café lends people the **tools** and the materials, for example, cotton or paint, they need but may not have at home. There are also people who can help you because they know how to fix things. You can also meet friends and have a coffee or something to eat at a Repair Café. A Dutch woman called Martine Postma **organised** the first Repair Café in 2009. It was in Amsterdam in the Netherlands. Now, there are more than 1500 Repair Cafes all over the world.

1 **Read the text and choose the correct answers True (T) or False (F).**

1 People can help you fix your old things.   T/F
2 At Repair Cafés people sell their old things.   T/F
3 There are tools and materials to help you repair things.   T/F
4 The first Repair Café was in Amsterdam.   T/F

Find out

1 *Look on a world map. Where is The Netherlands?*
2 *Is there a Repair Café in your country?*

Discuss

Are Repair Cafes a good idea? Why or why not?

I think Repair Cafes are / aren't a good idea because …

What do you think?

I agree / disagree …

Glossary

organise make happen
tool thing you use to fix or repair something

Justin is 12 years old. He and his family run a Repair Café in, Australia. 'I love fixing old things. My dad is a mechanic and we always spend time together at the weekends fixing old bikes and machines. We started our Repair Café because we wanted to teach other people how to repair their old things too. I posted about it on social media and all my friends and their families came along. Our first café had 85 visitors. People repaired bikes, lamps, speakers, alarm clocks, clothes, boots and shoes, and some people painted their old tables and chairs. My aunt and uncle made lots of cakes to sell, and they made tea and coffee for everyone. It was fantastic! Now we have a Repair Café every month.'

2 **Read the text and complete the sentences. Choose A, B or C.**

1 Justin started his Repair Café because he wanted to …

   A spend more time with his father.

   B teach other people how to repair things.

   C meet his friends at the weekends.

2 Justin … to get people to come to his Repair Café.

   A used social media

   B wrote a blog on his school website

   C sent text messages to all his friends

The same …

In Australia, children have to go to school from 6 years old to 16 years old.

What ages do children have to go to school in your country?

but different

3 **You decide to start a Repair Café in your school. Write an email to your friend about it.**

● Explain why you want to open the café and why you think it's important.

● Describe where and when the café is.

● Explain what happens at the café.

Write 80–90 words.

Review

1 Viv is talking about herself. Listen and choose the correct answers.

1 Yesterday Viv and her friends …

   a watched a film   **b** went shopping   **c** cooked a meal

2 Sophie bought …

   a some boots   **b** a jacket   **c** some jewellery

3 The girls had lunch …

   a in a café   **b** in a restaurant   **c** at home

4 They like …

   a listening to music   **b** taking selfies   **c** playing video games

5 They go to the cinema …

   a often   **b** sometimes   **c** rarely

6 They watch films at … house.

   a Viv's   **b** Sophie's   **c** Thalia's

7 Viv is going to go to …

   a the market   **b** Sophie's house   **c** the café

2 Read and choose the correct options.

At the market

1 How much meat would you like?

   A I'd like ten, please.   **B** I'd like a kilo, please.

At the restaurant

2 What would you like as a starter?

   A I'd like the soup, please.   **B** I'd like sparkling water, please.

At the clothes shop

3 Can I try on this jacket, please?

   A Yes, the changing room is over there.   **B** Yes, it's too loose.

Answering a text message

4 I'm going to go to the cinema this evening. Would you like to come?

   A How lovely!   **B** What a pity!

3 **Answer the questions about yourself.**

1 Which do you prefer: juice or milk?

2 Which do you prefer: burgers or pizza?

3 Which do you prefer: biscuits or cake?

4 Which do you prefer: pasta or rice?

5 Which do you prefer: eggs or fish?

4 **Talk about yourself to your partner. Answer the questions.**

- What's your favourite food?
- Do you have a favourite restaurant? How often do you go there?
- Do you like going shopping?
- Do you like shopping online?
- What do you like doing with friends?
- What social media do you use?
- How much time do you spend on screens a week?
- What do you do to stay safe online?

> **How to improve**
>
> When you are asked a question, use connectives, *and*, *but*, *or* to improve your sentences and to give more information.

How are you doing?

Read and copy the checklist below. Think and decide for each objective: **very well**, **quite well**, or **OK, but I need more practise**.

Use the checklist to help you improve your English.

I can …	Very well	Quite well	OK, but I need more practice
• talk about food and quantities			
• ask for food and drink in a café or restaurant			
• understand clothes and accessory words			
• ask and answer about how much something costs			
• talk about my how I like to shop			
• talk about plans to go out with friends			
• make and accept or turn down invitations			
• talk about the types of technology I use and what I do online			
• use imperatives to talk about online safety			

Words and phrases – Unit 3

Clothes shopping

bag _____

belt _____

boots _____

button _____

changing room _____

clothes _____

coat _____

dress _____

earring _____

fashion _____

fit _____

glasses _____

gold _____

jacket _____

jeans _____

jewellery _____

jumper / sweater _____

leather _____

loose _____

modern _____

necklace _____

old-fashioned _____

plastic _____

pocket _____

purse _____

ring _____

sandals _____

scarf _____

shirt _____

(a pair of) shoes _____

shopping _____

shopping online _____

shorts _____

silver _____

What size? _____

skirt _____

It is smart. _____

(a pair of) socks _____

suit _____

sunglasses _____

tie _____

tight _____

tights _____

to buy _____

to complain _____

to get a refund _____

to pay _____

to put on _____

to sell _____

to spend money _____

to take off _____

to try on _____

to wear _____

trainers (American English – sneakers) _____

trousers (American English – pants) _____

T-shirt _____

(school) uniform _____

watch / alarm clock _____

Can I help you? _____

Does it / Do they fit? _____

It fits / doesn't fit. _____

They fit / don't fit. _____

It's too loose / tight. _____

They're too loose / tight. _____

How much does it cost? _____

I'm looking for... _____

It's / They're perfect / too big / horrible / old-fashioned. _____

The trousers are comfortable. _____

It's / They're casual. _____

What a pity! _____

What size are you? _____

Food and drink

apple _____

banana _____

barbecue _____

beef _____

beef burger _____

biscuit _____

bread _____

burger _____

butter _____

cake _____

carrot _____

chicken _____

chicken burger _____

chicken salad _____

coconut _____

coffee _____

cola _____

cucumber _____

dessert _____

drinks _____

egg _____

fish _____

fruit _____

green salad _____

half _____

ice cream _____

juice _____

loaf / loaves (of bread) _____
main course _____
mango _____
meat _____
milk _____
mineral water _____
omelette _____
onion _____
onion soup _____
orange _____
pasta _____
pepper (green / red /
   yellow pepper) _____
pizza _____
restaurant _____
rice _____
salad _____
snack _____
sparkling water _____
spicy _____
starter _____
steak _____
still water _____
strawberry _____
sweets _____
tea _____
to cook _____
to cut _____
to grill / barbecue _____
tomato _____
tomato soup _____
yoghurt _____

Going online
app / application _____
blog (post) _____
blogger _____
computer _____
(group) chat _____
laptop _____
(mobile) phone _____
online safety _____
printer _____
radio _____
selfie _____
screen _____
social media _____
tablet _____
text message _____
to download _____
to post online _____
video _____
video game _____
website _____
wi-fi _____

Going out
to go to a coffee shop /
   café _____
to go to a concert _____
to go to a football match _____
to go to a music festival _____
to go to the beach _____
to go to the cinema _____
to go shopping _____
to go swimming _____
to go to the theatre _____
to go to the zoo _____

Making and responding to invitations
Do you want to …? _____
How nice! _____
I'd love to. _____
See you later / tomorrow. _____
Sorry, but I can't. _____
Thank you, but I can't.
   Let's do it another day. _____
What a pity! _____
What a shame! _____
Why don't we meet at …? _____
Would you like (to go to
   the cinema) _____
to accept an invitation _____
to invite _____
to turn down / refuse
   an invitation _____

Shops
bakery _____
butcher's _____
fish shop _____
kiosk _____
market _____
shop / store _____

4 Staying healthy

Are you ready?

- Name parts of the body
- Talk about school rules with *must* and *have to*
- Listen to people talking about sports
- Use reflexive pronouns

1 Do you remember the parts of the face? Play *This is my …* with your partner.

> ear eye face hair mouth nose

2 Listen and repeat. Now play *This is my …* using words for parts of the body.

- **a** head
- **b** shoulder
- **c** leg
- **d** knee
- **e** foot
- **f** arm
- **g** finger
- **h** hand
- **i** ankle
- **j** toe
- **k** back
- **l** neck
- **m** stomach
- **n** chest
- **o** throat
- **p** tooth

3 Ask and answer questions about sports.

Can you play … ?
Yes, I can. / No, I can't.

1 cricket 2 baseball 3 football 4 table tennis 5 badminton

4 Listen to conversations 1–3. Which part of the body has each person hurt? Name the sports. 🎧 4.2

5 **Complete the sentences with the words from the box.**

> myself   yourself   himself   herself   itself   themselves   ourselves

1 My baby brother can feed _____ now.
2 'Sorry, did you say something?' 'No. Don't worry. I was talking to _____.'
3 My grandparents taught _____ to speak Spanish with an app.
4 If you're hungry, make _____ some food.
5 We painted the house _____.
6 My little sister did her homework by _____.
7 Our new fridge cleans _____.

> **Grammar**
>
> **Reflexive pronouns**
> You can use a reflexive pronoun to show that you did something to, for or by yourself. (not involving another person)
> *I hurt **myself**.*
> *Have you hurt **yourself**?*
> *He taught **himself** to ride a bike.*
>
> **More?** ➜ Grammar

6 **Listen to Magda. Copy the table. Tick what she *has to* or *doesn't have to* do at school.** 🎧 4.3

	has to ✓	doesn't have to ✗
wear a school uniform		
do a lot of homework		
study a language		
do after school clubs		
stand up when the teacher comes into the room		
call the teachers Sir and Miss		
give her mobile phone to the teacher		
stay at school for lunch		

7 **Work in pairs. Use the information in activity 6 to talk about what students *have to do* and *don't have to do* at school.**

In our school we have to/don't have to wear a school uniform.

8 **Match the rules 1–6 to the signs a–f.**

1 You mustn't eat ice cream here.
2 You mustn't skateboard.
3 You mustn't take photos.
4 You mustn't swim here.
5 You must stop here.
6 You must wash your hands.

> **Grammar**
>
> ***have to / don't have to / must / mustn't***
> You use *have to* and *must* when you talk about something that must happen because someone else says it is necessary or important.
> *In our school we **have to** wear a school uniform.*
> *You **must** wash your hands.*
>
> You use *don't have to* to say that something is not necessary.
> *We **don't have to** stay at school for lunch.*
>
> You use *mustn't* to talk about what is not allowed.
> *You **mustn't** take photos.*
>
> **More?** ➜ Grammar

4.1 A healthy body

1 **Discuss.** *What things do you do to stay healthy?*

2 **Match the photos a–h to the words in the box.**

> cycling   drinking water   drinking coffee
> jogging   playing basketball
> playing rugby   sitting for a long time   smoking

Learning aims

- Learn new vocabulary to talk about healthy and unhealthy activities
- Listen to and read advice about how to stay healthy
- Write and talk about how to stay healthy using *should* and imperatives

a   b   c   d

e   f   g   h

3 **Which things in activity 2 are healthy and which are unhealthy? Copy and complete the table.**

healthy	unhealthy
cycling	

Grammar

should
You use *should* with a verb to talk about the right thing to do in a situation.
*You **should try** different sports and activities.*

More? ➜ Grammar

4 **Quickly read the magazine article on the opposite page and find the sports from activity 2.**

5 **Now listen and answer True (T) or False (F).** 4.4

1 Devina thinks we should do one sport well.   T/F

2 Devina says we should start running for thirty minutes.   T/F

3 She thinks rest is important for staying healthy.   T/F

4 She says moving is better for you than sitting.   T/F

Today we talk to top tennis star, Devina Macoy about staying healthy.

Interviewer: Devina, you are very healthy! What things should we do to stay healthy?

Devina: Walk everywhere if you can.

Interviewer: And obviously sport is important. Do you think it's best to just do one sport?

Devina: No, you should try different sports and activities. For example cycling, or team games, such as rugby, basketball and hockey are all good for us. These can all help you to stay healthy.

Interviewer: What other things should we do to stay healthy?

Devina: Do exercise. If you want to start a new sport, for example, jogging, first jog for five minutes. Rest the next day. If you can do five minutes, then try six minutes. Then after a month, you can maybe run for 30 or 40 minutes! Resting after exercise is good for you.

Interviewer: Anything else?

Devina: Yes. Drink lots of water! And keep moving! Don't sit for a long time. It's not healthy.

Interviewer: What about coffee? I hear that drinking coffee is healthy.

Devina: Drinking coffee can be healthy, but don't drink too much.

6 Read the article above again and write down all the imperatives.

7 Complete the advice using the verbs in the box. Some of the advice is negative.

| sit | try | drink | play | smoke | walk |

1 _____ tennis twice a week.
2 _____ a new sport.
3 _____ too much coffee.
4 _____ cigarettes.
5 _____ for a long time.
6 _____ to school.

8 Write some notes about things you can do to stay healthy. Use imperatives and *can*.

> You use *can* to talk about possibility.
>
> *Walk everywhere if you* **can**.
>
> *If you* **can** *do five minutes, then try six minutes.*

9 Work with a partner. Share advice on how to stay healthy.

- *What things should you do to stay healthy?*
- *What sports do you do?*

Grammar

Imperatives
Use *imperatives* to tell or ask people to do something or give advice. Use the infinitive of the verb without *to*.
Walk everyhere if you can.
Drink lots of water!

You use *Do not* or *Don't* in the negative.
Don't sit for a long time.

More? ➔ Grammar

4.2 Getting enough sleep

Learning aims
- Describe my bedroom
- Read an online post asking for and giving advice
- Give advice about sleep with *should* and *ought to*

1 Discuss. *How much sleep do you need every night? Do you sleep well?*

2 Write the correct word from the box for each photo 1–7.

> bed   bedroom   blanket   duvet   pillow   sheet   wardrobe

1

2

3

4

5

6

7

3 Listen to Greta talking about her bedroom. Choose the correct answers A, B or C. 4.5

1 Greta's bedroom is …

  A orange   **B** yellow   **C** red

2 Her duvet is …

  A orange   **B** yellow   **C** red

3 What is blue in Greta's bedroom?

  A the pillow   **B** the sheet   **C** the blanket

4 Where is her bed?

  A next to the window   **B** near the door   **C** next to the wardrobe

4 Describe your bedroom to your partner.

5 Hassan is asking for advice about sleep on an online chat. Read his post. Answer the questions on the opposite page.

Hassan

Hassan I don't know what to do. I'm 16 years old and I'm doing exams at school. The problem is that I feel tired all the time. I can't sleep at night. I stop studying at about 8 pm and I have a bath to relax. I go to bed at about 9.30 pm. I turn the light off in my bedroom and I lie down on my bed. I watch a film on my laptop and I turn it off at about 10.30 pm. But then I can't sleep. I don't go to sleep until about 1 am. I wake up at about 5 o'clock in the morning and I can't sleep anymore. I get up at 6.30 and start studying again. I feel ill and sleepy all day. Does anyone else have the same problem? What do you do to feel better?

       ◀ MESSAGES

---

1. What time does Hassan go to bed?
2. What time does Hassan go to sleep?
3. What two things does Hassan do before he goes to bed?
4. How many hours does he usually sleep?
5. What time does he wake up?
6. What time does he get up?

6 **Rewrite the questions in activity 5 to ask your partner.**

1. What time does Hassan go to bed?
   What time do you go to bed?

7 **Ask and answer the questions from activity 6 with a partner.**

| Remember use *for* to talk about how long you do something. | I sleep *for* eight hours. |
| Use *at* to talk about what time you do something. | I get up *at* seven o'clock. |

8 **Read the advice posted for Hassan. Complete the sentences using *should / shouldn't / ought to*.**

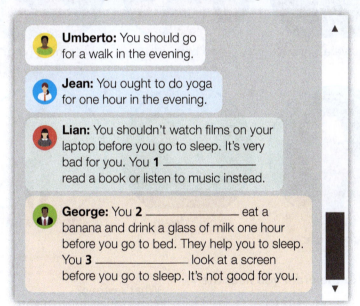

Umberto: You should go for a walk in the evening.

Jean: You ought to do yoga for one hour in the evening.

Lian: You shouldn't watch films on your laptop before you go to sleep. It's very bad for you. You **1** _____ read a book or listen to music instead.

George: You **2** _____ eat a banana and drink a glass of milk one hour before you go to bed. They help you to sleep. You **3** _____ look at a screen before you go to sleep. It's not good for you.

9 **Read the advice again and answer the questions.**

Who thinks that …

1. screens are bad before bed?
2. it's a good idea to do something physical in the evening?
3. some foods can help you to sleep?

10 **Write answers to the questions.**

1. What time do you think teenagers ought to go to bed?
2. How many hours do you think teenagers should sleep every night?
3. What do you think teenagers should do before they go to sleep?

4.3 Getting better

1 **Discuss.** *How often do you go to the doctor?*

Learning aims

- Describe common health problems and illnesses
- Listen to different conversations with a doctor.
- Understand the use of *could* for polite requests
- Write and talk about being ill and getting better

2 **Listen and repeat the phrases.** 4.6

a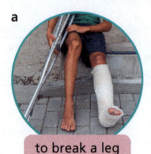
to break a leg

b
to cut your finger

c
to fall down

d
to have an allergy to something

e
to have a cold

f
to have a fever

g
to have a headache

h
to hurt (your knee, leg, etc)

i
to have a stomach ache

j
to have toothache

k
to lie down

l
to stand up

3 **Listen and write the letters a–l in the order you hear the phrases from activity 2.** 4.7

4 **Write answers to these questions. Use complete sentences. Share your answers with a partner.**

1 When did you last have a headache?

2 Do you have a stomach ache often?

3 What do you do when you have a fever?

4 Do you have an allergy to anything? If yes, what do you have an allergy to?

Vocabulary

What's wrong?
I have an allergy to plants.
I have a cold.
I have a fever.
I have a headache.
I have a stomach ache.
I have toothache.

What happened?
I broke my leg.
I cut my finger.
I cut myself.
I fell down.
I hurt my knee.
I hurt myself.

Could you lie down, please?
Could you stand up, please?

5 Listen to the conversations. What is wrong with Sam and Tom? What happened to the girl?

You use the verbs *to be* and *to feel* to say how you are:	I *am* / I *feel* tired / better / worse / hurt.
You use *to get* to describe a process:	*I am getting* better (= before ☹, now ☺)
You use *cut* + something	I cut my *finger* / *leg*
You don't say *I cut / hurt* 'me'	I cut / hurt *myself*

6 Write sentences about each person in activity 5.

1 Sam <u>has a fever. She doesn't have a stomach ache. She doesn't</u>_____

2 Tom _____

3 The girl _____

7 Read and listen to the boy talking to a doctor. What is wrong with the boy?

Doctor: Hello. How can I help you?

Boy: I don't feel well.

Doctor: What's wrong? Does anything **1** _____?

Boy: Yes. I have a **2** _____.

Doctor: When did it start?

Boy: It started yesterday.

Doctor: **3** _____ you lie down over there, please?

Boy: OK.

Doctor: Does it hurt here?

Boy: Yes.

Doctor: You **4** _____ rest today at home. If it **5** _____ worse, call me.

Boy: OK.

Grammar

Could for polite requests
You use *could* for polite requests. We often use *please* at the start or end of the sentence.
Could you lie down over there, please?

More? ➜ Grammar

8 Listen again and complete the conversation with the words from the box.

> could   gets   hurt   should   stomach ache

9 In pairs practise reading the conversation in activity 7.

10 Write a conversation between a teenager and a doctor.
Then role-play with a partner. Take turns to be Student A and B.
Student A is the doctor. Student B is the patient.

- *What's wrong?*
- *I have a …*
- *My … hurts.*
- *Could you … please?*
- *You should / ought to …*

4.4 A healthy mind

1 **Discuss. *Which words show a healthy mind?***

angry	calm	crazy

crying	happy	negative	positive

sad	smiling	unhappy	worried

Why is a healthy mind important?

Learning aims

- Read a magazine article about having a healthy mind
- Complete a summary of an article
- Use *need* and *needn't* to discuss problems and solutions

Vocabulary

active
to breathe
to cry
to laugh
to smile
to think
to worry

2 Read the article. Add titles a–e to paragraphs 2–6.

a Be positive.   d Keep active.

b Go to bed early.   e Have some fun.

c Don't study too much.

Study tip

Learn verb + noun collocations.
*to **make** a timetable*
*to **do** an exam*

How to be a teenager and have a healthy mind

1 What is the mind?

The mind is the part of us that thinks and tells us how we feel. It is an amazing thing, but sometimes it can think too much. And some of our thoughts can become negative and then we feel sad or angry. Here are some tips to look after your mind.

2 _____

Doing exams can make you cry, feel worried or a bit crazy. You need to do the right amount of study – not too much or too little – so make a timetable. Study for 45 minutes, then get up from your desk and move around for 15 minutes.

3 _____

You needn't study for 12 hours a day. It's a good idea to smile and laugh so why don't you go to the cinema and watch a comedy? Laughing puts you in a good mood.

4 _____

If you want a healthy mind, try to do sport or yoga every day. It can make you feel calm and ready to study again.

5 _____

Sleep is very important for your mind. Think of your mind as a computer. Sleeping gives your mind time to 'save' all the information you need for your exams.

Grammar

need to / needn't
You can use *need to* and *needn't* to say what is or is not necessary to do.

*You **need to** do the right amount of study.*
*You **needn't** study for 12 hours a day.*

You learned *don't have to* earlier in the unit. *Don't have to* means the same as *needn't*. Remember you use *to* with *need*, but not with *needn't*.

More? ➔ Grammar

6 _____

If you study, try not to worry about your exam. Instead, breathe, smile and tell your mind everything is OK.

3 **Complete the summary of the article in activity 2.**

To have a healthy mind you need to make a study timetable; take a break from studying every **1** _____ minutes; smile and **2** _____, do sport or **3** _____ regularly, and have enough **4** _____. You needn't study for **5** _____ hours a day.

4 **Complete the advice on studying for exams with *need to* or *needn't*.**

> **Studying for exams**
>
> 1 You _____ do the right amount of study.
>
> 2 You _____ be positive.
>
> 3 You _____ be worried about your exams if you study hard.
>
> 4 You _____ smile and laugh because laughing puts you in a good mood.
>
> 5 You _____ study for 12 hours a day.
>
> 6 You _____ go to bed early.

5 **Ask and answer these questions with a partner.**

- *Do you have a timetable for study?*
- *How many hours a day do you study for outside of school?*
- *How often do you take breaks and how long for when you are studying?*
- *What do you do that makes you laugh or smile?*
- *Do you do sport regularly? What do you do? How often do you do it?*
- *How many hours a night do you sleep for? Do you usually sleep well or badly?*
- *Are you usually a positive or a negative person? What or who helps you to think positively?*

> **Grammar**
>
> **Adverbs of manner**
> You use adverbs of manner to express how you do something.
>
> *Do you usually sleep **well** or **badly**?*
>
> *What helps you to think **positively**?*
>
> More? → Grammar

6 **Work in groups. Read the problem. What does Tadeo need to do? Write some advice for him.**

You need to / needn't …

I'm doing my exams this month. I have to drink lots of coffee and eat lots of snacks and sugar or I go to sleep at my desk. I'm not sure this is good for me. It's hard to feel positive about myself. But I need to study. What do I need to do?

4.5 Eating well

Learning aims
- Learn new words and phrases about eating well / badly
- Read about healthy and unhealthy food and drink and how we use passives to give facts
- Discuss food and drink choices

1 Discuss. *Do you think you eat well or badly? Why?*

2 Listen and repeat. 🔊 4.10

a cereal

b cream

c jam

d jelly

e lamb

f lemonade

g milk

h oil

i peach

j pear

k raspberries

l salt

m soft drink

n sugar

o vegetables

p watermelon

3 Are the foods and drinks in activity 2 healthy (H), unhealthy (U) or sweet (S)? Some foods might be more than one of these.

4 Read the article on the opposite page quickly. Which of these are not mentioned?

a coffee
b energy drinks
c sugar
d cream
e meat

Grammar

Passives
You use the passive
1 to talk about a process.
   *Often 250 mg of caffeine **is put** in an energy drink.*
2 to talk about facts where the thing is more important than the person doing the action.
   You make the passive by using the verb *to be* + the past participle.
   *Energy **drinks are** often **drunk** by students to help them study.*

More? ➜ Grammar

DR BOB says

Do you drink energy drinks?

CAFFEINE IN DRINKS

Energy drinks are very popular in the world now. They are often drunk by students to help them study. But are they healthy or unhealthy? Did you know you should only have an energy drink after you do a lot of exercise?

We should be careful about what is in energy drinks. You can find something called **caffeine** in these drinks. Caffeine is **natural**, and it is in coffee and tea. Sometimes caffeine is added to soft drinks. Often 250 mg of caffeine is put in an **energy** drink. That is a lot of caffeine! Too much caffeine can give you a headache, or make you feel unwell. So you should be very careful.

Another problem is sugar. We all love sweet food and drink, but in many drinks and food, sugar is added to make it sweet. We like it but it is not good for us. It is better to eat fruit because it already has sugar – natural sugar.

So what should you do? Next time you want an energy drink, make a drink yourself instead. Use fruit (such as raspberries, peaches) or raw vegetables, and milk or yoghurt.

> **Glossary:**
> **energy drink:** a drink that makes you feel awake and strong
> **natural:** from nature
> **caffeine:** a natural product - it gives you energy
> **milligram (mg):** a very small amount

30 mg of caffeine is put in a soft drink

There is 100 mg of caffeine in a cup of coffee

250 mg of caffeine is put in an energy drink

---

5 **Read the text again and answer True (T) or False (F).**

Dr Bob says …

1 it's best to have energy drinks before sport.   T/F
2 you can find caffeine in many drinks.   T/F
3 there is more caffeine in coffee than energy drinks.   T/F
4 sugar in fruit is healthier than food with added sugar.   T/F
5 you should make your own drinks.   T/F

6 **Write the words in the correct order to make passive sentences.**

1 put / is / bags / the food / in
2 soft drinks / to / is / often / added / sugar
3 drunk / is / by / coffee / many people / all over the world
4 added / is / to / sugar / breakfast cereals

7 **Discuss these questions.**

- *Is caffeine or sugar added to drinks you like?*
- *What other things are put in food and drink you like? Why?*
- *Is that a problem?*
- *Are these types of food healthy or unhealthy?*

English Summer Schools USA are a great way to practise your English! You can earn money and make new friends from around the world. If you are 18 or older and speak good English, maybe *you* can be one of our teachers!

Our children are aged 8-15, and they stay at summer school from one to six weeks. They come from many different places in the USA. Most of the children speak English but some of them don't, so you can help them learn!

How? Well, every day is different. The children do activities like sailing, climbing, walking, camping, and lots of other sports and fun things. And we do everything in English! The most important thing is there are no mobile phones or digital devices for the children so summer school is healthy in every way.

1 **Read the text and complete the sentences. Choose A, B or C.**

1 If you want to work at English Summer School you should ____
   A speak a little English.
   B be 18 or older.
   C practise your English.

2 The children at summer school ____
   A speak good English.
   B study English.
   C do all activities in English.

3 At English Summer School children ____
   A can't have mobile phones.
   B sit a lot.
   C are not healthy.

"My name is Christelle and I'm from France. That's me in the red jumper. Last year, after I finished school, I travelled to the USA to work in an English summer school. It was my birthday in June. I was eighteen when I arrived in the USA. I flew by myself to Los Angeles, in California. I met other teenage 'teachers' there. They were from all over the world: Africa, Australia, Europe, America. Everybody was really friendly. We spoke English all the time. It was the only language everyone understood. I think all young people should work at summer school because it is so much fun. We worked hard together from 8 in the morning until 8 at night. The girl at the front wearing the pink trousers in the photo is Nada. She is from Sweden. She is now a very good friend."

Find out

1 *Look on a world map. Draw a map and also draw a line following Christelle's journey from France to Los Angeles in the USA.*

2 *Are there English summer schools in your country?*

Discuss

Do you think summer schools are a good idea? Why /Why not?

Would you like to go to an English summer school? Why / Why not?

Is it healthy to have time without a mobile phone? Why / Why not?

I think summer schools are / aren't a good idea because ...
What do you think?
I agree / disagree ...
I would / wouldn't like to go to a summer school because ...
I think it is / isn't healthy to have time without a mobile phone because ...

2 **Read the text and answer True (T) or False (F).**

1 Christelle is from the USA.   **T/F**

2 She had her birthday at the summer school. **T/F**

3 She didn't travel with friends to the school. **T/F**

4 The work was quite easy.   **T/F**

5 She made a good friend at summer school. **T/F**

3 **Last summer you were a student at English Summer Schools USA. Write an email to your friend about it.**

- Explain where you went in the USA.
- Describe the teachers / the activities.
- Explain how it was healthy / good for your English.

Write 130–140 words.

The same ...

In Montreux, Switzerland, there is an English summer school just for girls.

In your country are there different summer schools for boys and girls, or not?

but different

Review

1 Complete what Minnie says about staying healthy with the phrases from the box.

> can sleep   do lots of   have enough sleep   is added   need to have
> ought to   shouldn't have   use their phones

a It's important for young people to _____.

b They don't do this because they _____ late at night.

c My friends _____ too many energy drinks.

d A lot of sugar and caffeine _____ and this is a problem.

e People _____ make drinks with fruit.

f I'm always tired after playing sport. Then I _____ easily.

g I _____ at least eight hours sleep every night.

h My advice is: _____ exercise.

2 Listen and check. 🔴4.11

3 Read and complete the email from Jackson. Use the words from the box.

> sleep   duvet   lie   pillow   positive   relaxing   rest   sleepy   worried   yoga

If I do a lot of sport, I always **1** _____ the next day! I love playing sports like rugby. It's good for your body. But I also like **2** _____. I really enjoy sleep. I like to **3** _____ down in bed under my **4** _____. It makes me feel very calm and **5** _____. I need to have **6** _____ thoughts before I go to bed, so I usually do some **7** _____. If I am **8** _____ about something, I write the problem on a piece of paper. Then I can relax. I put my head on the **9** _____ and usually go to **10** _____ in a few minutes.

4 Look at the groups of sentences A–C and D–F. Which sentence in each group is stronger? Which two sentences in each group mean the same?

A You must eat fruit and vegetables.

B You should eat fruit and vegetables.

C You ought to eat fruit and vegetables.

D We have to wash our hands.

E We should wash our hands.

F We must wash our hands.

5 Match sentences 1–2 to the meanings a–b.

1 You needn't tell her.

2 You mustn't tell her.

a She already knows.

b I don't want her to know.

6 Rewrite the sentences replacing the underlined word/s so that they have the same meaning.

1 You <u>needn't</u> do exercise on Saturday if you don't want to.

2 I <u>should</u> go to bed early.

3 He <u>must</u> stop smoking.

7 **Talk about yourself to your partner. Answer the questions.**

- What time do you go to sleep?
- How many hours a night do you sleep for? Do you usually sleep well or badly?
- What time do you get up?
- What time do people in your family wake up?
- Are you usually tired at school? Why or why not?
- How many hours do you study for at the weekends?
- What things make you laugh or smile?
- Do you do sport regularly? What do you do? How often do you do it?
- Are people in your family positive or negative people?
- Are the types of food you eat healthy or unhealthy? Give examples.

How are you doing?

Read and copy the checklist below. For each 'I can… sentence' think and decide: **very well**, **quite well**, or **OK, but I need more practice**.

Use the checklist to help you improve your English.

> **How to improve**
>
> When you learn a new verb or structure, try and use it in different tenses. I *fall asleep* at 10 pm > Yesterday I *fell asleep* at 9 pm.

I can …	Very well	Quite well	OK, but I need more practice
• Name parts of the body			
• Use *must* and *have to* to talk about what you are expected to do			
• Use reflexive pronouns			
• Listen to and read information about how to stay healthy			
• Write and talk about how to stay healthy			
• Use new vocabulary to talk about healthy and unhealthy activities			
• Describe my bedroom			
• Read and understand an online chat asking for and giving advice			
• Use *should* and *ought to* to give advice about sleep			
• Describe common illnesses, and getting better			
• Write and talk about being ill and getting better			
• Read and understand a magazine article about having a healthy mind			
• Read and understand a problem, and give advice			
• Talk about unhealthy and healthy drinks and food, and discuss how to eat well.			

Words and phrases – Unit 4

A healthy / an unhealthy mind

active _____
angry _____
calm _____
comedy _____
crazy _____
crying _____
exhausted _____
happy _____
lazy _____
mind (n) _____
negative _____
positive _____
sad _____
satisfied _____
smiling _____
tired _____
timetable _____
unhappy _____
worried _____
to breathe _____
to cry _____
to do an exam _____
to do sport _____
to do yoga _____
to get annoyed / angry _____
to laugh _____
to like / love _____
to save _____
to smile _____
to take a break _____
to think _____
to worry _____
unpleasant _____

Getting better

appointment _____
dentist _____
doctor _____
medicine _____
plaster _____
to be (un)healthy /
   in good health _____
to be ill / have an illness _____
to break (a leg / an arm) _____
to cut your finger /
   cut yourself / have a cut _____
to do exercise _____
to fall down _____
to feel ill / sick _____
to get better / worse _____
to have an allergy _____

to have a cold _____
to have a fever _____
to have a headache /
   a stomach ache /
   toothache _____
to have the flu _____
to hurt _____
to lie down _____

Getting enough sleep

bed _____
bedroom _____
blanket _____
duvet _____
lamp _____
pillow _____
sheet _____
closet / wardrobe _____
to be sleepy / tired _____
to feel tired / sleepy / ill _____
to feel better / worse _____
to get up _____
to go to bed _____
to go to sleep _____
to lie down _____
to rest _____
to sleep _____
to study _____
to wake up _____

Healthy and unhealthy food and drinks

apple _____
apricot _____
aubergine _____
banana _____
cabbage _____
cauliflower _____
caffeine _____
cereal _____
cherry _____
chocolate _____
cream _____
crisps _____
garlic _____
grape _____
jam _____
jelly _____
lamb _____
lemon _____
lemonade _____
lettuce _____
melon _____
mushroom _____
oil _____
peach _____

pear	————————————
pepper	————————————
pineapple	————————————
plum	————————————
potato	————————————
raspberry	————————————
raw	————————————
salt	————————————
soft drink	————————————
sugar	————————————
sweet	————————————
vegetables	————————————
vegan food	————————————
vegetarian food	————————————
watermelon	————————————
yoghurt	————————————

Healthy and unhealthy habits

drinking water	————————————
drinking coffee	————————————
sitting for a long time	————————————
smoking	————————————

Sports

ball	————————————
bat	————————————
champion	————————————
game / match	————————————
fan / supporter	————————————
football pitch	————————————
goal	————————————
golf course	————————————
medal	————————————
prize	————————————
(badminton / tennis) racket	————————————
(hockey) stick	————————————
team	————————————
tennis court	————————————
trainer / coach	————————————
to do athletics	————————————
to do gymnastics	————————————
to go skating / skiing / snowboarding / surfing	————————————
to play badminton / baseball / basketball / cricket / football / golf / hockey / rugby / table tennis / tennis / volleyball	————————————
to go cycling / jogging	————————————
to score a goal	————————————
to win a competition / race	————————————
to win a medal	

The body

ankle	————————————
arm	————————————
back	————————————
body	————————————
bone	————————————
chest	————————————
ear	————————————
eye	————————————
face	————————————
finger	————————————
(left / right) foot	————————————
hair	————————————
hand	————————————
head	————————————
heart	————————————
knee	————————————
leg	————————————
moustache	————————————
mouth	————————————
neck	————————————
nose	————————————
shoulder	————————————
skin	————————————
stomach	————————————
throat	————————————
toe	————————————
tooth	————————————
to see	————————————
to smell	————————————
to touch	————————————

Reading

Read the texts. For each question, choose the correct answer (A, B, C or D).

Jamal

Can you please go to the shop for me?
We need some fruit. I think we have enough
bananas and apples, but we don't have
any peaches. Don't get pears because
Granddad doesn't like them.

Mum x

1   What fruit should Jamal buy?

A bananas   **B** apples   **C** peaches   **D** pears

To: All students

This is important information about tomorrow's swimming competition. You need to be on
the coach outside the school gates at 4.00 and not at 4.30 as Mr Ford told you yesterday.

Mr Patel

2   What is Mr Patel telling students about the swimming competition?

A where it is   **B** when it is

C who is in the competition   **D** what time the transport leaves

Hi Dina
I saw you crying today at school after the English exam. I thought it was very
difficult. I have a headache now. Would you like to come to my house and watch
a comedy tonight? You could sleep here too.
Fiona

3   How was Dina feeling?

A unhappy   **B** unpleasant   **C** sick   **D** tired

Listening

Listen and choose the correct answer (A, B or C).

You will hear an interview with Ana. She is talking about food.

1 **What doesn't Ana eat?**

   A eggs

   B chicken

   C potatoes

Study tip

When you have to choose between answers, always make sure you read the questions and the answers properly before you listen.

2 **Ana … cooks at home.**

   A always

   B never

   C sometimes

3 **Ana eats out in restaurants …**

   A once a week

   B once a month

   C two times a month

4 **Ana recently went to a restaurant called …**

   A The Lemon Tree

   B The Green Tree

   C The Salt Room

5 **Ana ate …**

   A seafood

   B spicy pasta

   C steak

Speaking

Work with a partner.

Writing

Staying healthy

- Do you think you are healthy or unhealthy? Why?
- What do you eat to stay healthy?
- What activities do you do to stay healthy?
- What do you do to have a healthy mind?
- What do you think you should do to be healthier? Why?

Write 80–90 words in English.

Study tip

Write something for each question. Here you have five questions to respond to.

Study tip

Don't repeat. Try to use different words and phrases. For example, you could say:
Eating fruit is healthy.
Drinking water is also good for me.
The meaning of *healthy* and *good for me* is the same.

Are you ready?

- Talk about the town where I live • Write about the town where I live
- Use adverbs of degree

1 Complete the words.

a
mu — — — m

b
th — — — — —

c
bu — — — — —

d
t — — — — —
s — — — — — — —

e
sp — — — — c — — — — —

f
r — — — — — — — — — — —

g
z — —

h
s — — — — —

i
b — — — s — — —

j
s — — — — m — — — — —

Study tip

Remember to use a dictionary to help you find words you don't know.

2 Talk about the places where you live. Use the words from activity 1.

Use *There is / There are …* to talk about places where you live.	*There is* a restaurant. *There are* some shops.
Use *There isn't / There aren't …* to talk about places not found where you live.	*There isn't a market.*
If you use a plural noun with *There aren't*, use *any* (not ~~some~~).	*There aren't any shops.*

3 Match sentences 1–6 with town centre signs a–f.

a  OPEN

b  Station

c Monday–Friday 8:30 am–5:30 pm

d MONDAY–SUNDAY From 9 am–5:30 pm

e

f

1 You must not smoke here.
2 You can leave your car here.
3 You can go into the café now.
4 You can't go into the museum on a Saturday.
5 You can catch a train here.
6 You can buy a book in the bookshop on a Sunday morning.

4 Match the words from the box with their definitions.

> attractive boring busy crowded empty
> lively modern narrow wide

1 _____: not interesting; dull
2 _____: with no or few people
3 _____: nice to look at
4 _____: small in distance from one side to the other
5 _____: full of people
6 _____: with energy; a lot of fun things happening
7 _____: full of people who are doing things
8 _____: having a large distance from one side to another
9 _____: new

5 Complete the sentences with words from the box in activity 4.

1 The town centre has lots of old buildings. It isn't very _____.

2 It's quite _____ where I live. There aren't a lot of things for young people to do here.

3 I went shopping yesterday, but it was really _____ – I had to wait to go into my favourite shops.

4 The streets in my town are very _____. You can't drive a car down the streets.

5 Usually the town centre is very crowded, but last weekend it was _____ because it was very cold and rainy.

6 Work with a partner. Which adjectives from activity 4 can you use to describe where you live?

7 Listen to Sasha talking about where she lives. Decide if sentences 1–5 are true (T) or false (F). 🔴 5.1

1 Sasha lives in a big city.   T/F
2 There's a theatre in her town.   T/F
3 The town is empty on Saturday afternoons.   T/F
4 Sasha prefers going shopping on Sundays.   T/F
5 Sasha thinks her town is boring for young people.   T/F

8 Write a short paragraph about where you live. Share your paragraph with a partner.

Vocabulary

There is/There's/There isn't a/an …
bakery
bookshop
butcher's
fish shop
kiosk
market
museum
restaurant
theatre
school
sports centre
supermarket
train station
zoo

Grammar

Adverbs of degree
You use adverbs of degree in front of adjectives to show the intensity of the adjective.

not strong ─────────────→ strong

quite   very   too
           really

*It's **quite** lively.*

*It's **very** quiet in town today.*
You can also use ***really*** instead of *very*.

*It's **too** busy for me.*

More? ➜ Grammar

5.1 My neighbourhood

Learning aims
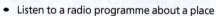
- Listen to a radio programme about a place
- Talk about what is on my street
- Read a magazine article about a famous bridge
- Use *used to* to talk about habits in the past

1 **Discuss.** *Do you live in a village, a town, or a city?*

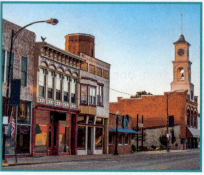

2 **Listen to a radio programme about a city in Australia. Write the letters of the things a–h you hear mentioned.** 🎧 5.2

a bridge

b bus stop

c car park

d metro/underground station

e pedestrian crossing

f roundabout

g traffic lights

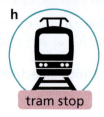
h tram stop

3 **Listen again and choose the correct options.** 🎧 5.2

1 What's the name of the road?
   - **A** Bridge Road
   - **B** Melbourne Road
   - **C** East Road

2 Why is it a popular road?
   - **A** There are no cars allowed.
   - **B** There are lots of shops.
   - **C** There's a pretty river.

3 What's at the end of the road?
   - **A** a shopping centre
   - **B** a bridge
   - **C** a roundabout

Grammar

Prepositional phrases
To talk about where something is you use prepositional phrases.

There's a bridge at the end of the road.

There's a car park on the left next to the traffic lights.

More? ➜ Grammar

Vocabulary

I live in a village / town/ city.
This is my neighbourhood / road / street.
on the left / on the right

4 Ask and answer. *What's on the street where you live?*

> Use *There is / isn't …* to talk about the things where you live.

> *There's* a metro station at the end of my street.
> *Is there* a bus stop? Yes, *there is*. / No, *there isn't*.

5 Read what the reporter is saying. Answer the questions.

Hi everyone! I'm here in Melbourne and I'm standing next to a river. This is the River Yarra. The River Yarra looks yellow but it's one of the cleanest rivers in the world. There are fish in the river and sometimes you can see dolphins.

And over there behind me you can see a bridge. That is the famous Hawthorn Bridge. That bridge is important because it's one of the oldest metal bridges in Australia. It's a wide bridge because it's used for vehicles. People used to go across the bridge on horses. Now people go across it on trams. Before they built that bridge, people used to go across the river by boat.

1 What colour is the River Yarra?
2 What is the bridge made of?
3 How did people use to go across the bridge?
4 How do people go across the bridge now?
5 How did people use to go across the river before they built the bridge?

6 What superlatives does the reporter use about the two things he sees on his trip?

1 The Hawthorn Bridge is one of the _____ metal bridges in Australia.
2 The River Yarra is one of the _____ rivers in the world.

7 Work with a partner. Ask and answer questions about things in the classroom.

> What is this?
> What is that?
> What are these?
> What are those?

8 Write. Answer the questions about you.

1 What did you use to drink when you were five?
2 What time did you use to go to bed when you were at primary school?
3 Did you use to be afraid of anything?

> **Grammar**
>
> **Demonstrative pronouns**
> You use the demonstrative pronouns *this* (singular) and *these* (plural) to talk about people or things near you, and to introduce or identify people and things.
>
> *This* is the River Yarra.
>
> *These* are the dolphins that live in the river.
>
> You use the demonstrative pronouns *that* (singular) and *those* (plural) to talk about people or things not so near you.
>
> *That* is the famous Hawthorn Bridge.
>
> *Those* are the buses that go over the bridge.
>
> More? ➔ Grammar

> **Grammar**
>
> **Used to**
> You use *used to* to talk about things that happened a lot (habits) in the past.
> *How did people use to go across the bridge?*
>
> *People used to go across the bridge on horses. They didn't use to travel in cars.*
>
> More? ➔ Grammar

> **Vocabulary**
>
> behind
> here
> there
> over there

> **Study tip**
>
> Find other words you can use to describe where you live.

5.2 My favourite places

1 **Discuss.** *What's your favourite place in your neighbourhood? Why?*

2 **Match the buildings on the map with the words.**

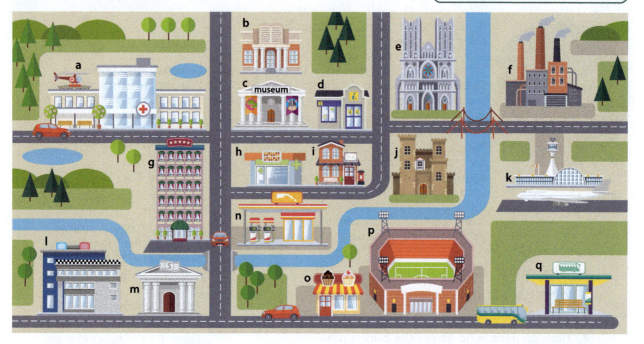

1 bakery	☐	**2** bank	☐	
3 bus station	☐	**4** cathedral	☐	
5 castle	☐	**6** clinic	☐	
7 factory	☐	**8** hospital	☐	
9 hotel	☐	**10** library	☐	
11 petrol station	☐	**12** police station	☐	
13 stadium	☐	**14** airport	☐	
15 post office	☐	**16** tourist information office	☐	
17 museum	☐			

Grammar

Prepositions

Use prepositions of place to say where something is.

*It is **next to / beside** the museum.*

*It is **behind** the museum.*

*It is **between** the bakery and the bus station.*

More? ➜ Grammar

3 **Use the map in activity 2 to answer the questions.**

1 Which building is opposite the factory?
2 Which building is next to the bank?
3 Which building is behind the museum?
4 Which building is beside the river: the hospital or the cathedral?
5 Which building is between the bakery and the bus station?

Study tip

Draw balls, squares and arrows to help you remember prepositions of place.

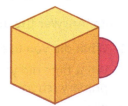

The ball is behind the box.

4 **Listen and complete the dialogue. Look at the map in activity 2 again. The tourist and the woman are in the museum.** 🔊 5.3

Tourist: Excuse me, could you tell me how to get to the
1 _____, please?

Woman: Of course. Leave the museum and turn
2 _____. Turn left and walk past the
3 _____. Go straight over the **4** _____
and turn left. The bus station is **5** _____
the road.

Tourist: That's great! Thank you.

5 **Work with a partner. Play *How do I get to the …?* Start at the hotel. Choose another building on the map in activity 2 and ask your partner for directions.**

Use imperatives to give directions:	*Turn right ./ Turn left.* *Go straight ahead.*

6 **Listen to three teenagers saying where they're going and why. Copy and complete the table.** 🔊 5.4

Person	Place	Reason
Marta		
Azza		
Cos		

7 **Choose two places from the map in activity 2. Write sentences to say why you're going to each place. Make dialogues in small groups.**

8 **Match speakers 1–3 to the places a–d. Then write a sentence for the other picture.**

1 I went to the camera shop to get my camera fixed.

2 I went to the hairdresser's to have my hair cut.

3 I went to the garage to have my car repaired.

Grammar

to + infinitive
You use *to* + infinitive to say why you do something. This follows another verb.

*I'm going to the restaurant **to have** dinner with Priya.*

More? ➜ Grammar

Vocabulary

camera shop
garage
hairdresser's
to cut
to fix
to repair

Grammar

get something done
To talk about something someone else does for us or another person you use a causative sentence: *have* or *get* + object + past participle.

*I went to the camera shop **to get** my camera fixed.*

*She went to the hairdresser's **to have** her hair cut.*

More? ➜ Grammar

a
b
c
d

5.3 Good neighbours

1 **Discuss.** *What is a good neighbour or a bad neighbour?*

2 **Read the notices about ways to help in a neighbourhood. Match the notices to the photos 1–8.**

Learning aims

- Talk about neighbours and helping in a neighbourhood
- Match speakers to activities
- Understand someone's plans and arrangements
- Use the present continuous to talk about the future

Vocabulary

neighbour
neighbourhood

a Coach needed for local girls football team. 4 hours a week.

b Can you play basketball? Join the neighbourhood team. We play at the weekend.

c Give two hours every Saturday to help us clean the streets in our neighbourhood.

d Artists wanted to paint a big picture on the wall of the old factory building.

e Come and do some gardening in the neighbourhood garden. Help us grow vegetables, fruits and flowers.

f Looking for good neighbours to visit and help older people in our neighbourhood. Jobs include doing their shopping, walking their dogs, and having a cup of tea with them.

g If you can cook, please come and make food for people without homes in our neighbourhood.

h Can you give an evening a week to teach English to people in our neighbourhood who don't speak it?

Study tip

Remember! When you read or hear a word or phrase you don't know, find out what it means. Then write a new sentence using the word or phrase. Challenge yourself to use the new word or phrase in your next conversation in English.

1

2

3

4

5

6

7

8

3 **Discuss the ways to help your neighbourhood in activity 2. Which activities would you like to do?**

4 Match the teenagers 1–4 to the best notice a–h for each of them from activity 2.

1 Miriam likes sports. She's happy to help for two evenings a week or at the weekend.

2 Lena wants to be a chef. She always cooks dinner at home for her family.

3 Paul plays basketball. He'd like to make some new friends.

4 Adam's favourite subject at school is art and he does a lot in his free time.

5 Listen to Rami talking about helping in his neighbourhood. What activities from activity 2 does he mention? 5.5

6 Listen again. Answer the questions. 5.5

1 What are Rami and the neighbours cleaning during the school holidays?

2 What are they doing with the rubbish?

3 What are Rami and the neighbours making?

4 What are they building for the local children?

5 What does Rami say about some of the old people?

7 Write the missing words. Then listen and check. 5.5

Well, a group of neighbours and I are **1** _____ a dirty area of land near the old railway station. We're **2** _____ up all the rubbish and we're putting it in the bins. We're also **3** _____ a small playground for the local children and we're **4** _____ a place for people to come and relax.

8 Ask and answer. Use the present continuous to talk about the future.

- *Who are you spending time with this evening?*
- *How are you getting to school next week?*
- *Where are you going next weekend?*
- *What are you doing in the summer?*

Vocabulary

to build
to do some gardening
to grow vegetables
to plant

Grammar

Present continuous to talk about the future
Remember you learned about the present continuous to talk about what you are doing now. You can also use the present continuous to talk about plans or arrangements in the future.

We're opening a small café next month.

More? → Grammar

5.4 My region

Learning aims
- Talk about the natural places in my region
- Read and understand an email about future plans
- Write an email about my future plans using *will* / *shall*

1 **Discuss.** *Do tourists visit your region? Why or why not?*

2 **Match the photos of nature with the words. Then listen and check.** 🔊 5.6

1 	2 	3 
4 	5 	6 
7 	8 	9 
10 	11 	12 

a beach	**b** coast	**c** desert
d forest	**e** hill	**f** island
g lake	**h** mountain	**i** river
j volcano	**k** waterfall	**l** wood

3 **What is there in your region? Discuss with a partner.**

There's a … but there isn't a … or a … .

We don't live near a / the …

Study tip

Some words in English have 'silent' letters (letters that you can't hear when you say the word). For example you do not pronounce the 's' sound in the word 'island' (*iland*). When you learn these words, write how to say the word next to the word in your word list.

4 Read and listen to Krish talking about his next holiday. Answer the questions. 🔴 5.7

I'm so excited about my next holiday. I'm visiting my cousin in Dubai for two weeks. I think it will be fun. We're going to go camping in the desert and we're going to go hiking in the mountains. Because Dubai is on the coast, we'll probably go swimming a lot. I think we'll go sailing too because my cousin has a boat.

I'll be home in August. Would you like to visit me? Shall I book some train tickets for you? Shall we go shopping in the city?

1 Where is Krish going?
2 Who is he visiting?
3 Where will they go?
4 What four things will they do?
5 When is he coming home?
6 What question does Krish ask his friend?
7 What does Krish offer to do?

5 Read the text in activity 4 again. Find:

- an example of the present continuous used to talk about future plans
- two examples of *going to* used to talk about future plans
- four examples of *will* used to talk about the future
- an example of *Shall I ...?* used to make an offer
- an example of *Shall we ...?* used to make a suggestion

6 Complete the sentences with *will*, *shall I* or *shall we*.

1 I think Jack ... be at the party.
2 ... come with you to the shops?
3 He ... probably get home at eight o'clock.
4 ... cook dinner tonight?

7 Copy the text from activity 4. Change the information in orange to talk about your holiday plans. Then read your text to your partner.

Vocabulary

I'm going to ...
Shall we ...?
We'll probably ...
I think we'll ...
go camping
go hiking
go sailing
go shopping
go swimming

Grammar

Future with will / shall
When you are guessing what will happen, you use *will*.

*I think it **will** be fun.*

*We'**ll** probably go swimming a lot.*

When you make an offer in British English, you use *shall I ...?*

***Shall I** book some train tickets for you?*

When you make a suggestion in British English, you can use *Shall we ...?*

***Shall we** go shopping in the city?*

More? → Grammar

5.5 I care about the environment

1 **Discuss.** *Is there a wind farm in your region? What is good about wind farms? What is bad about them?*

2 **Read the letter to the boss of the wind farm company, Mrs Mansour, and answer the questions.**

Dear Mrs Mansour

I am writing this letter to you because I am worried about the new wind farm. You want to build this new wind farm in the sea near our town. I care about the environment and climate change, but I also think wind farms are noisy and ugly. I also care about the view from my house.

Kind regards
Rebecca Van Heer

1 Where is the wind farm being built?

2 Does Rebecca agree with the plan to build it?

3 **Read three more letters to Mrs Mansour. Does each writer share Rebecca's opinion or not?**

Dear Mrs Mansour,

I am doing a project about the environment at school. A lot of my friends are doing their project on recycling, but I am interested in wind farms. I want to find out about the new wind farm. You are going to build the new wind farm in the sea near our town. I think this is a great idea because it will stop pollution. Please could you send me some more information about the wind farm?

Many thanks,
Josh Karmilo

Dear Mrs Mansour

Building a wind farm in the sea near our town is a good idea. I feel very positive about this. Building a wind farm in the sea is better than building it on the land.

The land is used for farming and farming is very important.

Best wishes,
Jessie Davis

Dear Mrs Mansour

I am an artist and I belong to a local painting group. We are excited about the new wind farm. We think wind farms are very beautiful. They're so tall and they look lovely in the sky with the clouds and the sun. I think I will paint the wind farm.

Many thanks
Carlos Lopez

4 **Read the letters in activities 2 and 3 again. Answer the questions.**

1 Who thinks it's better to build a wind farm in the sea than on the land?

2 Who thinks wind farms are beautiful?

3 Who thinks wind farms are ugly?

4 Who wants more information about the wind farm?

5 Ask and answer these questions with a partner.

- *Do you think wind farms are ugly or beautiful?*
- *Is it a good idea to have a wind farm in the sea? Why or why not?*
- *Which writer do you agree or disagree with? Why?*
- *Are you worried about climate change? Why or why not?*

6 Listen to Mrs Mansour talking about the wind farm. What month will they start building the wind farm? 5.8

7 Use the words in the box to complete the notes from Mrs Mansour's speech. Listen again to check your answers. 5.8

> build a wind farm   idea   climate change
> four months   the environment   pollution

I'm very happy to talk to everyone about the plans to **1** _____.
We are all worried about **2** _____.
We all care about **3** _____.
Wind farms are a good **4** _____.
Wind farms do not make **5** _____.
It will take **6** _____ to build the wind farm.

8 Change Mrs Mansour's speech in activity 7 into reported speech.

1 Mrs Mansour said that she …
2 Mrs Mansour said that they …
3 Mrs Mansour said that they …
4 Mrs Mansour said that wind farms …
5 Mrs Mansour said that wind farms …
6 Mrs Mansour said that it …

9 Complete the reported statements. Use the pronouns in brackets.

1 'I'm very worried about climate change.' (she) Sara
   Sara said that she was very worried about climate change.
2 'I don't like wind farms.' (she) Liv
3 'I recycle plastic bottles.' (she) Jules
4 'I'll go to the meeting.' (he) William
5 'There aren't enough wind farms.' (he) Wen
6 'The environment is the most important thing.' (she) Yash
7 'I won't travel by plane.' (he) Luke

Lowline is a project to build a beautiful new park in the Lower East Side neighbourhood of New York, USA. The place where the team want to build the new park used to be the Williamsburg Bridge tram station. The station closed in 1948 and nobody uses it now. The difficult part of the plan is that the old tram station is **underground** and the team are planning to fill the park with trees and plants because they want it to be a nice place for families to walk and spend time in. So they need to find a way to allow the light from the sun to get down into the park. The **architects** have used **software** to show what the park will look like and how they will get light into it. The people who live in the Lower East Side think it'll be amazing!

1   **Read the text and choose the correct answers.**

1   Where are the team planning to make the new park?

   A   In an old train station

   B   In an old tram station

   C   In an old bus station

2   What's the problem?

   A   It has lots of plants.

   B   It's not used.

   C   It's below the ground.

3   The people who live in the neighbourhood …

   A   are excited about the new park.

   B   are worried about the new park.

   C   want a shopping centre not a park.

Glossary

architect a person whose job is to design buildings and spaces
to plan to decide in detail what you are going to do
software computer programs
underground below the surface of the ground

Discuss

What do you think the underground park should be like?
I think it should look / have …
That's a great idea!
It could also have …

Rudee is fourteen years old. She lives in Bangkok, in Thailand. When she was a child, there were a lot of houses and flats in her neighbourhood but there weren't any parks or playgrounds. Rudee and her friends didn't have anywhere to play. But a few years ago, a new project was started. A team wanted to build some football pitches in Rudee's neighbourhood so the local children and teenagers could play football. But there was a problem. The streets are narrow and there were no rectangular spaces between the buildings. So the designers had a good idea – they built four football pitches but they were different shapes.

'The football pitches have changed our lives,' says Rudee. 'The football pitches are attractive. These spaces were dirty before and now they're clean. We have somewhere to go and meet our friends and play games. **We don't mind** if they aren't rectangles like other football pitches. Everyone loves them.'

2 **Read the text and answer the questions.**

1 Where does Rudee live?

2 What didn't she have in her neighbourhood when she was younger?

3 What did the new project build?

4 How are the football pitches different to other football pitches?

5 Does Rudee like the new football pitches?

3 **Discuss the questions.**

- *Where's the best place in your neighbourhood to go with friends?*
- *What do you and your friends do there?*
- *How often do you go there?*

Glossary

We don't mind It's not important to us

Find out

1 *Look on a world map. Where is Bangkok?*

2 *What nationality are people who live in Bangkok?*

The same ...

In Thailand, there are lots of English meet-up groups. English meet-up groups are for people who want to improve their English. They often meet in cafés. At an English meet-up group, people have conversations in English, sometimes they watch films in English and sometimes they play fun English games.

Are there any English meet up groups where you live?

but different

Review

1
Bianca is talking about herself. Listen and choose the correct answers. 🎧 5.9

1 Bianca lives in a …
  a village   **b** town   **c** city

2 The village is next to a …
  a volcano   **b** waterfall   **c** lake

3 The village didn't use to be …
  a empty   **b** busy   **c** nice

4 It's popular with tourists because there's a …
  a castle   **b** hotel   **c** restaurant

5 The cinema used to be a …
  a post office   **b** police station   **c** village shop

6 Bianca's favourite café is called …
  a The Coffee Shop   **b** The Cake Shop   **c** The Tea Stop

7 Bianca's band is playing at …
  a 7 pm   **b** 8 pm   **c** 9 pm

8 Bianca thinks it will be …
  a lively and fun   **b** boring and crowded   **c** relaxing

2
Read and complete the letter. Use the words from the box.

> behind   interested   neighbourhood   pick up   used to   will

Dear Mr Green,

I'm writing to you because my friends and I are
1 ＿＿＿＿＿＿ in improving our **2** ＿＿＿＿＿＿ and
we have a great idea. We want to make a zoo with
small animals for the children to visit. We think the
best place for this zoo is the car park **3** ＿＿＿＿＿
the old football stadium. The local football team
4 ＿＿＿＿＿＿ play football at the stadium every
evening and weekend. But now there is a new
stadium in the city centre and no one uses the one in
our neighbourhood. We'll clean up the car park and
5 ＿＿＿＿＿＿ all the litter. **6** ＿＿＿＿＿＿ you give us
some money to build the zoo, please?

Liam Parker

3
Which two sentences are in reported speech?

1 It rained yesterday in Hawaii.

2 David said that it rained yesterday in Hawaii.

3 I said that I don't like the rain.

4 Write the reported speech sentences 1–3 in direct speech.

1 Rachel said that she was worried about Lucien.

2 Orla said that she wasn't feeling well.

3 Vlad said that he was walking in the park.

5 Talk about yourself to your partner. Answer the questions.

- Do you live in a village, a town or a city?
- What buildings are there where you live?
- Do you like where you live? Why or why not?
- Do you help in your neighbourhood? How?

- What is there in your region?
- Do tourists visit your region? Why or why not?
- What will you do to help climate change?
- What are you doing next weekend?

How are you doing?

Read and copy the checklist below. Think and decide for each objective: **very well**, **quite well**, or **OK, but I need more practise**.

Use the checklist to help you improve your English.

I can...	Very well	Quite well	OK, but I need more practice
• name things in the place where I live			
• talk about my region			
• use *used to* to talk about the past			
• talk about what's on my street and in my neighbourhood			
• use demonstrative pronouns			
• ask for and give directions			
• use infinitives of purpose and causative sentences to talk about why I go somewhere			
• use the present continuous to talk about the future			
• use *will* to talk about the future			
• understand a writer's opinions and attitudes			
• give my opinion on climate change			
• use reported speech			

How to improve

Check back to your I can ... lists in units 1–4. Which sections did you tick **OK, but I need more practice**? What can you do to improve now?

Words and phrases – Unit 5

Adjectives

It is …
attractive _____
big _____
boring / dull _____
busy _____
close _____
cold _____
comfortable _____
cosy _____
crowded _____
dangerous _____
deep _____
dirty _____
dry _____
empty _____
enormous _____
free (available) _____
heavy _____
lively _____
lonely _____
loud _____
low _____
modern _____
narrow _____
new _____
noisy _____
old _____
popular _____
real _____
safe _____
(the) same (as) _____
silent _____
simple _____
small _____
tidy _____
typical _____
warm _____
wet _____
wide _____
wonderful _____

Adverbs of emphasis

certainly _____
even _____
quite _____
really _____
so _____
very _____

Being a good neighbour

neighbour _____
neighbourhood _____

to build _____
to do some gardening _____
to grow vegetables _____
to pick up litter / rubbish _____
to plant _____

Nature and the environment

air _____
beach _____
branch _____
climate _____
coast _____
desert _____
dust _____
earth _____
forest _____
grass _____
hill _____
island _____
lake _____
moon _____
mountain _____
nature _____
region _____
river _____
sand _____
seashore _____
shade _____
shadow _____
star _____
stick _____
stone _____
top _____
underground _____
volcano _____
waterfall _____
wave _____
wood _____
world _____
tourist _____
to book _____
to go camping _____
to go hiking _____
to go sailing _____
to go shopping _____
to go swimming _____
to visit _____

Places I go

airport _____
bakery _____
bank _____
bus station _____
café _____
camera shop _____

cathedral _____

castle _____

cinema _____

clinic _____

coffee shop _____

college _____

corner _____

factory _____

farm _____

garage _____

gym _____

hairdresser's _____

hospital _____

hotel _____

library _____

lift / elevator _____

motorway _____

office _____

petrol station _____

pharmacy _____

place _____

playground _____

police station _____

post office _____

service station _____

square _____

stadium _____

swimming pool _____

traffic _____

train station _____

tourist information office _____

to cut _____

to fix _____

to repair _____

to turn _____

Go straight over the
bridge. _____

to go straight ahead _____

Turn left/right _____

It's on the left/right. _____

It's on the other side
of the river. _____

It's across the road from
the post office. _____

It's next to the
police station. _____

It's behind the hospital. _____

It's beside the hotel. _____

It's over there. _____

What's good for the environment?

climate change _____

cloud _____

environment _____

farming _____

land _____

landscape _____

pollution _____

recycle / recycling _____

sea _____

sky _____

sun _____

view _____

wind farm _____

Where I live

bookshop _____

bridge _____

bus stop _____

car park _____

metro / underground
(station) _____

museum _____

neighbourhood _____

pedestrian crossing _____

restaurant _____

river _____

roundabout _____

school _____

sports centre _____

(bus / train / tram) station _____

street / road _____

supermarket _____

theatre _____

town / city _____

traffic lights _____

tram stop _____

village _____

zoo _____

There is a post office at
the end of the road. _____

People used to travel
across it on horses.
They didn't use to _____
travel in cars. _____

6 A big world

Are you ready?

- Name parts of the world
- Do a quiz about the world
- Talk about where I live, where I was born and what language I speak
- Use the present perfect to talk about my experiences

1 Look at the photos 1–9 and match them to the parts of the world a–i. Then listen and check. 🔴 6.1

a Africa
b North America
c Central America
d South America
e Antarctica
f Asia
g Australia
h Europe
i The Arctic

Grammar

Superlatives

You use a superlative to say that one thing or person has more of a particular quality than all the others in a group.

You use the adjective + -est for short adjectives of one syllable.

cold > *the coldest*
the coldest part of the world

You change the y to an i and then add -est when the adjective ends in a y.

happy > *the happiest*
She's *the happiest* person I know.

For most other longer adjectives of two or more syllables that don't end in y, you add *the most* before the adjective.

important > *the most important*

More? ➔ Grammar

2 Do the world quiz.

1 **Which is the largest continent?**
a Africa
b Antarctica
c Asia

2 **Where are the countries Uruguay and Chile?**
a South America
b Africa
c Europe

3 **Which part of the world is this city in?**
a Asia
b Australia
c North America

4 **Which part of the world are the capital cities Bangkok, Singapore and Manila in?**
a Europe
b South-East Asia
c North America

5 **Which part of the world is Japan in?**
a East Asia
b Europe
c The Middle East

World Quiz

3 Match the countries to the parts of the world they are in,
the nationalities and their languages.

Countries	Parts of the world	Nationalities	Languages
1 France	Asia	Egyptian	Arabic
2 China	Central	Honduran	English
3 Australia	America	Chinese	French
4 Egypt	Africa	French	Spanish
5 Brazil	Europe	Brazilian	Portuguese
6 Honduras	South America	Australian	Chinese
	Australia		

4 Listen and complete the information about Carolina. 6.2

Country born in: _____

Part of the world she lives in now: _____

Country lives in: _____

Nationality: _____

First language: _____

5 Listen and answer the questions about you. 6.3

6 Listen to the conversations and then ask your partner
questions about where they have been. 6.4

Have you been to …?

Yes, I have been to …

No, I haven't been to …

6 Which part of the world does this animal live in?
a Australia   b Central America   c Africa

7 Which part of America is the Amazon Rainforest in?
a North America   b Central America   c South America

8 Which part of the world is Saudi Arabia in?
a Africa   b The Middle East   c South-East Asia

9 Which is the coldest part of the world?
a The Arctic   b Antarctica   c North America

10 Which continent is the highest mountain in?
a Asia   b Antarctica   c Europe

6.1 The natural world

Learning aims
- Read an article about animals.
- Understand new words in an article.
- Express possibility and probability in a discussion using modals of possibility and adverbs of probability.

1 **Discuss.** *What animals are there in your country?*

2 **Match the words in the box to the animals a–l.**

> bear chicken cow dinosaur duck elephant
> fly lion monkey sheep snake tiger

a b c d e f

g h i j k l

3 **Divide the animals in activity 2 into groups.**

> **farm animals**   **wild animals**

> **insects**   **animals that used to live on Earth**

Vocabulary

about / around / approximately …
10,000 years ago
on Earth
in the earth
on the farm
to be excited / sure
it's (not) …
heavy / large / long / old

4 **Complete the sentences using superlatives of the adjectives in brackets.**

1 Elephants are _____ land animals in the world. (**large**)

2 The Siberian tiger is _____ cat in the world. It weighs about 400 kg. (**heavy**)

3 Are monkeys _____ animals in the world? (**intelligent**)

4 The python that lives in South-east Asia is _____ snake in the world. It is more than 6 metres long. (**long**)

5 Nyasasaurus is _____ dinosaur in the world. It lived approximately 243 million years ago. (**old**)

6 Some people think flies are _____ animals in the world. (**annoying**)

5 Quickly read the article below and find four animal words.

Is it a dinosaur?

Giles Redwood was working on his farm in Minnesota, USA when he found something in the earth. 'It was big and I thought it might be the bone of a horse, but I wasn't sure,' he told a newspaper reporter. Giles sent a photo of the bone to his friend, Mona, and she thought that the bone was possibly from a dinosaur. Giles sent the photo to a museum. People from the museum came to the farm and they found more bones. They said that these bones could be from a dinosaur. After a while, they found a very long bone. They were very excited. This long bone showed the people from the museum that these bones were definitely not from a dinosaur. Instead, this long bone showed them that these bones were definitely the bones of a mammoth.

Mammoths were enormous animals. They used to live on Earth but they don't live on Earth any more. Mammoths looked like large elephants and they had lots of hair. They lived in woods and forests and they ate trees and other plants. Mammoths lived in North

mammoth bones

and Central America, but they did not live in South America. This is probably because the plants in South America were very different. Mammoths stopped living on Earth around 10,000 years ago. This may be because people caught lots of mammoths and ate them. Or perhaps it might be because of climate change.

6 Answer the questions about the article.

1 Where does Giles Redwood live?
2 What did he find in the earth on his farm?
3 What did he send to his friend Mona?
4 What animal did Mona think the bone could be from?
5 What animal was the bone from?

7 Work with a partner. Discuss what the photo shows.

This may be …
But it could be …
Perhaps it's a …
It's probably a … because …

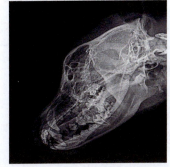

Study tip

Think about the meaning of the whole sentence, and the sentence before and after it, to work out the meaning of a word you don't know.

Grammar

Modal verbs of possibility
You use *may* or *might* to talk about something which is possible, but you are not 100% sure of.
*I thought it **might** be the bone of a horse.*
*This **may** be because people caught lots of mammoths and ate them.*
You use *could* to say you are not completely sure if something is possible:
*They said that these bones **could** be from a dinosaur.*

More? → Grammar

Grammar

Adverbs of probability
You use adverbs of probability to say how sure you are about something.
You use *definitely* to say you are sure that something is true.
*This long bone showed them that these bones were **definitely** the bones of a mammoth.*
You use *probably* to say you think something is true but are not sure.
*This is **probably** because the plants in South America were very different.*
You use *possibly* to say you are less sure.
*She thought that the bone was **possibly** from a dinosaur.*
You can also use *perhaps* or *maybe* instead of *possibly*. They mean the same. *Perhaps / Maybe* are usually at the start of the sentence.
***Perhaps** it might be because of climate change.*

100%		30%
definitely probably		possibly perhaps maybe

More? → Grammar

6.2 What's the weather like?

Learning aims
- Learn words to describe the weather
- Read online comments about weather conditions
- Use the first conditional to talk about things that might happen in the future

1 **Discuss.** *What's your favourite season or weather? What's the weather like today?*

2 **Read the comments. Match comments 1–3 to photos a–c.**

Leave us a comment about your holiday!

1 Ski France
It's spring here in the mountains. Usually the weather in spring is lovely. There is usually sunshine and lots of snow, but this year the weather is terrible! It's cold and there's lots of fog so we can't see where we are skiing. There's lots of ice under the snow so it's dangerous to ski in some places. If the weather conditions don't get better, we'll go home on Saturday.

2 Forest Walk in Central America
It's August, so it's the rainy season here. It's very hot and humid and the temperatures are around 35 degrees. There was a storm last night with thunder and lightning and a lot of rain. It was amazing to watch! It's really hot, but I'm carrying on walking because the forest is very beautiful.

3 Surfing on the Gold Coast, Australia
It's beautiful here. The sea shore is clean and very pretty, but unfortunately the surfing isn't very good. The waves were too small on Monday and Tuesday so we couldn't surf. On Wednesday we did some surfing but on Thursday the wind was too strong so we couldn't surf. The weather forecast says it'll rain tomorrow and over the weekend. I don't think we'll be able to surf again until next week.

> You use *too* when something is more than enough or more than necessary.

> The waves were *too* small so we couldn't surf.
> The wind was *too* strong so we couldn't surf.

3 **What's the weather like? Find the weather words in the comments in activity 2. Then match them with the symbols a–l.**

 a b c d e f

 g h i j k l

4 **Ask and answer these questions with a partner.**

- *Do you like the activities in activity 2?*
- *Which would you like to try? Why?*
- *Where would you like to go / visit? Why?*
- *What type of weather do you like? Why?*

5 **Read the comments again. Decide if each statement is true (T) or false (F).**

1 In France they can't ski because it's too hot. T/F

2 The weather conditions were dangerous for surfing on Monday and Tuesday on the Gold Coast. T/F

3 There was a storm in the forest. T/F

4 The skiers might leave the mountain because of the weather. T/F

5 The walker in Central America had to stop because of the weather. T/F

6 It will be sunny on the Gold Coast at the weekend. T/F

6 **Complete the first conditional sentences using the verbs in bold.**

1 If the weather _____ **(be)** good tomorrow, we _____ **(have)** a picnic.

2 If my grandparents _____ **(go)** on holiday this summer, they _____ **(go)** to Italy.

3 If you _____ **(not go)** to bed now, you _____ **(feel)** tired tomorrow.

4 If Karim _____ **(not arrive)** in the next five minutes, we _____ **(miss)** the start of the film.

5 If I _____ **(cook)** dinner, _____ you _____ **(do)** the washing up?

6 If she _____ **(want)** to be in the team, she _____ **(have to)** come to the meeting after school.

7 **Listen and answer the questions.** 6.5

1 Where is the group going?

2 How long is the walk for?

3 What will they do if someone feels sick?

4 What will they do if they see any interesting birds or animals?

5 What will they do if they see a tiger?

8 **Write answers to the questions. Use the first conditional.**

1 What will you do if it is hot and sunny this weekend?

If it is hot and sunny this weekend, I'll …

2 What will you do if there is a storm this weekend?

3 If you go on holiday this summer, where will you go?

4 If you go on holiday this summer, who will you go with?

5 If you don't go on holiday this summer, what will you do?

9 **Read your sentences from activity 8 to your partner.**

Grammar

First conditional
You use the first conditional to talk about things which might happen in the future. The first conditional has two parts to the sentence: *if* + present simple, … *will* + infinitive. One part of the sentence is the likely result of the other part of the sentence being true.
*If the weather conditions **don't get better**, **we'll go** home on Saturday.*

More? ➜ Grammar

Vocabulary

What's the weather like?
It's …
30 degrees
cold
hot
humid
sunny
There's lots of …
fog
ice
lightening
rain
snow
sunshine
thunder
wind
There are lots of …
clouds
There's a …
storm
What season is it?
It's …
spring, summer, autumn, winter
It's the dry/rainy/wet season
weather conditions
weather forecast

6.3 Where would you like to go?

1 **Discuss.** *Where would you like to go in the world?*

2 **Listen to Jon and Ryan talking about where to go on holiday. Match countries 1–5 with their opinions a–e.** 6.6

1 The Caribbean	**a** It's very windy.
2 The west coast of Portugal	**b** There are storms in July.
3 Thailand	**c** There's lots of rain in July.
4 The east coast of Scotland	**d** There's a fantastic festival in the summer.
5 Edinburgh	**e** There are too many insects in July.

3 **Complete the parts of the conversation from activity 2 with the words from the box. Listen again to check.** 6.6

> but let's look into look up point out
> ring up shall sort out take up unless

Jon: Hey Ryan, shall we **1** _____ our holiday in July?

Ryan: **2** _____ have a look at the holiday website.

Jon: Ok... oh **3** _____ we go to the Caribbean?

Ryan: Can I **4** _____ that there are storms in the Caribbean in July?

Ryan: Isn't it very windy on the west coast?

Jon: I don't know. But if it is windy, we'll **5** _____ sailing.

Ryan: Let's **6** _____ what the weather in Thailand is like in July.

Ryan: Shall we go on a city holiday? That might be nice, **7** _____ you want to sit on the beach.

Jon: I like beach holidays, **8** _____ I'd also like to go to the Edinburgh Festival.

Jon: **9** _____ your manager and ask her if you can change your holiday to August.

Ryan: OK. Shall we **10** _____ apartments?

4 **Match the phrasal verbs from activity 3 to their meanings.**

1 contact by telephone

2 tell someone a fact or information

3 organise

4 find a fact or information about something

5 start doing an activity

6 see if something is possible to get or make happen

Grammar

Phrasal verbs

Remember some verbs in English consist of more than one word. They are called phrasal verbs. Usually they have a verb + a particle (*in/out/on/up* etc.). A phrasal verb does not have the same meaning as the verb does on its own.

look into
look up
point out
ring up
sort out
take up

More? → Grammar

Vocabulary

I want to …
go sailing
play golf

5 **Role-play with your partner.**

- Use a map of the world or a holiday website.
- Student A: Suggest a place and month to go on holiday.
- Student B: Look up the weather and some interesting facts about the place. Make notes.
- Student B: Suggest a different place for Student A to look up facts about.
- When you have notes for four places, choose one you both want to go to.
- Share your reasons with another pair.

You use *Shall* and *Let's* to make suggestions:	***Let's*** *look at the holidays website.* ***Shall*** *we go to the Caribbean?*

6 **Match the words in the box to the pictures a–p. What do we use each one for? Then listen and check.** 🔴 6.7

air conditioning barbecue cooker dishwasher electricity freezer fridge gas heating iron microwave oven television washing machine telephone wi-fi

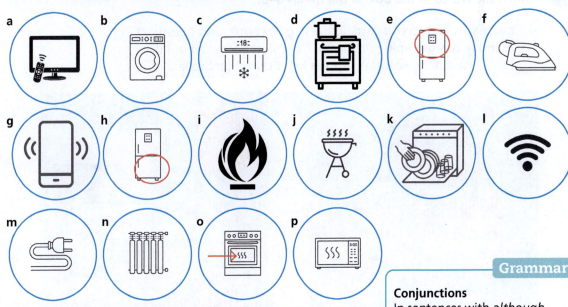

a b c d e f

g h i j k l

m n o p

You can give short answers to 'do' questions:	***Do*** *you have a microwave in your home?* *Yes, I do. / No, I don't.* ***Did*** *you have wi-fi in your last holiday home?* *Yes, I did. / No, I didn't.*

7 **Listen to Jon and Ryan talking again. What items doesn't the holiday apartment have?** 🔴 6.8

8 **Complete the sentences with *although* or *unless*.**

1 I'm going to go swimming _____ it rains.

2 I still want to go _____ I'm not feeling well.

6.4 A school trip

Learning aims
- Understand information about a school trip
- Use relative pronouns to say who, what or where I am talking about

1 **Read the notice. Answer the questions about the school trip.**

1 How long is the school trip going to be?

2 Which two continents are they going to go to?

3 Which two sports are they going to do?

4 When is the meeting about the trip?

Vocabulary

We are going to …
fly back to Europe
go on a trip
go skiing
play hockey
visit schools

> Year 10 school trip for girls
>
> This year the school trip is going to be a two-week trip. In the first week we are going to visit schools in Ghana, in Africa and we are going to play hockey there. In the second week we are going to fly back to Europe and we are going to go skiing in Andorra.
>
> If you are interested, come to the meeting in Room D2 on Friday at 4.30 pm.

2 **Match the words in the box to the things a–p.**

> backpack cap credit card gloves guidebook hat passport
> phone charger plug raincoat school uniform school tie
> swimming costume sports kit tickets umbrella

3 **Discuss.** *Which of the items above do you think students will need for the trip? Why? What other things do you think they will need?*

I think they'll need … because …

4 **Match sentences 1–6 with the students' photos from the school trip a–f.**

1   This is the hockey team that we played against in Ghana.

2   This is the view that we could see from our hotel room in Andorra.

3   This is the bus driver who drove us around Ghana.

4   This is the hotel where we stayed in Ghana.

5   This is Gerard who taught us how to ski.

6   This is the restaurant where we had dinner on our last night in Andorra.

a    b    c

d    e    f

5 **Complete the sentences with *who*, *where* or *that*.**

1   What's the name of the hotel _____ we stayed in Ghana?

2   Is this the new jacket _____ you bought for this trip?

3   Students _____ go on school trips are lucky.

4   Maria has a cousin _____ lives in Canada.

5   Thanks for the photos _____ you sent us.

6   I did all the homework _____ my teacher gave me last week.

7   This is the street _____ I lived until I was twelve.

8   That's the man _____ was sitting in front of us on the bus this morning.

6 **Work in pairs. Take turns to use photos on your phones to make sentences using relative pronouns.**

- *This is my cousin / sister / friend / the person who …*
- *This is the place / restaurant / hotel where …*
- *This is the holiday / trip / book / jumper / umbrella that …*

> ### Grammar
>
> **Relative pronouns**
> You use clauses with relative pronouns to say exactly who or what you are talking about, or to add more information about them.
>
> You use the relative pronoun *that* to talk about things; *who* to talk about people; *where* to talk about places.
>
> *This is the hockey team **that** we played against in Ghana.*
>
> *This is the bus driver **who** drove us around Ghana.*
>
> *This is the hotel **where** we stayed in Ghana.*
>
> More? ➜ Grammar

6.5 Let's go!

1 Discuss. *How do you prefer to travel? Why?*

Learning aims
- Read emails about travel plans
- Write an email about travel plans
- Use the present simple tense to talk about the future

2 **Read the email. Choose the correct answers.**

> Hi Aunty Nell,
> I'm looking forward to seeing you on Saturday. What time does your flight arrive? There's a train station at the airport. The last train leaves the airport at 8 pm. So if your plane arrives before 8 pm, you can get the train to our house. The trains to Whitehaven leave from platform 6 and take around 40 minutes. If you have a lot of baggage or if your plane arrives later in the evening, I'll drive to the airport and pick you up. There's a car park opposite the main entrance, so I can meet you there. You have to cross the road when you come out of the airport.
> Let me know what you prefer.
> See you soon,
> Austin

1 Which day is Aunty Nell arriving?

   A Saturday   **B** Sunday   **C** Monday

2 What time is the last train?

   A 4:00   **B** 6:00   **C** 8:00

3 Which is the correct sign that Aunty Nell needs to look for when she leaves the airport?

   A   **B** ENTRANCE   **C** EXIT

3 **Complete Aunty Nell's reply. Use the words from the box.**

> airport   baggage   car park   get lost   maps   train

> Hi Austin,
> How are you? I'm looking forward to seeing you on Saturday, too! I don't like flying but I want to see you all very much. Our flight arrives at the **1** _____ at 6.30 pm, so we may be able to get the train, but we do have quite a lot of **2** _____ – five suitcases! The suitcases are full of presents, of course! ;) If the plane is delayed, we'll miss the last **3** _____.
> We could rent a car and drive, but we're very bad at reading **4** _____ and we might **5** _____! Can you come and pick us up from the airport, please? We can meet you at the **6** _____. We're on flight number TH548. Please send me your mobile number so I can call you if there's a problem. My mobile number is 77645 8903031.
> See you very soon,
> Aunty Nell

Grammar

Present simple to talk about the future

You use the present simple to talk about future plans that are part of a timetable or something arranged at a definite time in the future. There is usually a time expression in these sentences.

*Our flight **arrives** at the airport at 6.30 pm.*

More? → Grammar

---

4 Read Aunty Nell's postcard to her friend, Gina. Find all the verbs in the present simple tense. Which ones refer to the future?

Dear Gina,

We're having a wonderful holiday in England with my nephew Austin. Austin lives in a typical English house with a big garden. We went to London yesterday and I bought you a lovely hat. I'll give it to you when we get home. Our flight leaves London on Friday the 18th in the morning, and we arrive on Saturday afternoon on the 19th.

When does Jim start his new job? Please say 'Good luck' from us.

See you soon,
Nell

Gina Brown
1005 Main Street
Toronto
Canada

Vocabulary

airport
baggage
entrance
exit
flight
map
passenger
plane
platform
postcard
railway station
suitcase
train
to arrive
to be / get lost
to cross the road / street
to be delayed
to depart / leave
to drive
to fly
to look forward to (something)
to miss (a train / plane / bus)
to park
to rent a car
What time does the plane depart / leave / land / arrive?
What time is your flight?
The flight is delayed.
Where is the entrance / exit / platform / station?

5 Write answers to these questions about the future.

1 When is your next holiday?

2 What time does school finish today?

6 Your friend is coming to visit you by plane. Write an email to discuss how your friend will get from the airport to your home.

● Ask for information about their flight.

● Explain two or three ways they could get from the airport to where you live.

● Ask them to let you know what they prefer.

● Suggest an activity you can do on their visit.

Country: UGANDA

Location: East Africa

Largest city: Kampala

Population: 34.8 million people

Nationality: Ugandan

Official language: English

Other languages: Luganda, Swahili, Bantu, Nilotic

Climate: Rainy seasons: March – May , October – December
        Dry seasons: December – February, June – September

Money: Uganda shilling

Best university: Makerere University, Kampala

Animals: gorilla, chimpanzee, hippo, crocodile, giraffe, rhino, lion,
        elephant, leopard, buffalo, zebra, antelope, snakes, mongoose

Exports (things they sell to other countries): cotton, gold, fish, tea,
                                               coffee, flowers

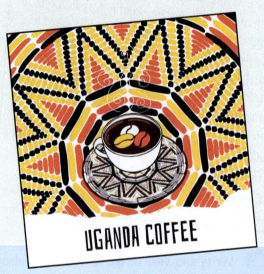

UGANDA COFFEE

1 **Decide if the sentences are true (T) or false (F).**

1 Uganda is not a country in Asia.   T/F

2 The best university in Uganda is in the largest city.   T/F

3 Uganda has a cold season and a hot season.   T/F

4 Most people in Uganda speak French.   T/F

5 There are tea and coffee farms in Uganda.   T/F

2 **Work in pairs. Discuss. How is your country the same as or different from Uganda?**

3 **Write about your country. Follow the example above.**

"My name is Samuel and I'm Ugandan. I'm a tourist guide and I take groups of tourists into the Bwindi Impenetrable Forest to look for gorillas. Gorillas are an endangered species. This means that there are not many gorillas left in the world and one day soon there may not be any. Fifty percent (50%) of all the world's mountain gorillas live here in Uganda. They live in two places in the mountains: the Mgahinga Gorilla National Park and here in the Bwindi Impenetrable Forest. There are twelve families of gorillas in Bwindi and my job is to take tourists to meet them. This gorilla is called Mwirima. He's one of my favourite gorillas. It took two years to make friends with Mwirima. I think it's important for people to learn about the gorillas and understand them better. I teach tourists about the gorillas and why it's important to look after their home. We can only stay for one hour with the gorillas so that the gorillas can continue with their routines. Tourists can take photos and videos but they mustn't touch or try to hug the gorillas because the gorillas will get annoyed. They also mustn't give them food. Gorillas are such beautiful animals and I think it's very important that we keep them safe."

4 **Read the text and answer the questions.**

1 How many places in Uganda do the gorillas live in?

2 How many gorilla families live in the Bwindi Impenetrable Forest?

3 How long did it take Samuel to make friends with Mwirima?

4 How long can tourists stay with the gorillas for?

5 What can't tourists do with the gorillas?

5 **What does the verb *continue* in the text mean? Can you guess by reading the other words in the sentence?**

We can only stay for one hour with the gorillas so that the gorillas can continue with their routines.

6 **Last month you went to Uganda and visited the mountain gorillas. Write an email to your friend about it.**

- Say what month you went.
- Explain how you travelled to and around Uganda.
- Describe the climate and weather.
- Describe what the walk in the forest was like.
- Describe what it was like to meet the gorillas.

Write 130–140 words.

Find out

1 *Which other places can you find gorillas?*

2 *What do gorillas eat?*

3 *Is there an endangered species in your country?*

Discuss

Is it important to look after the animals in our countries? Why or why not?

I think it is / isn't important because …
What do you think?
I agree / disagree …
I think we should / ought to …

The same …

In September, there is a three-day festival in Kampala called the Bayimba International Festival. At the festival there is Ugandan music, films, dances, theatre and art.

Is there a festival about culture in your country?

but different

Review

1   **Kang is talking about himself. Listen and choose the correct answers.** 🎧6.9

1   Kang lives in …

   a   China   **b**   France   **c**   The USA

2   He was born in …

   a   The USA   **b**   England   **c**   France

3   He speaks …

   a   English, Chinese and French   **b**   English and Chinese   **c**   English, Chinese and Spanish

4   His mother is …

   a   Chinese   **b**   American   **c**   French

5   His favourite season is …

   a   winter   **b**   spring   **c**   summer

6   If he has enough money next summer, he'll go to …

   a   England   **b**   Spain   **c**   South America

7   He's learning to speak …

   a   Spanish   **b**   Portuguese   **c**   Italian

2   **Read and complete the email from Freda. Use the words from the box.**

> backpack   cold   flight   French   fridge   south   who   winter

Hi Mum

How are you? I'm having a great time here in Turkey in the **1** _____ of Europe. It's **2** _____ here so it's warm and sunny in the day, but it's **3** _____ at night. The people **4** _____ work in the hotel are lovely but they don't speak English and I don't speak Turkish, so we have to speak in **5** _____! My room is very comfortable. I have heating, a small **6** _____ and a big television. I usually get up late, but tomorrow I have to get up at 6 am, because I leave at 8.00 to get my **7** _____ home. I need to pack my **8** _____ now. If I don't pack tonight, I'll miss my plane tomorrow!

See you very soon!

Freda

3 **Talk about yourself to your partner. Answer the questions.**

- What part of the world do you live in?
- Where were you born?
- What nationality are you?
- What languages do you and your family members speak?
- What is your favourite animal in your country? Why do you like it?

- What's the weather like today? What do you think the weather will be like next month? Why?
- What will you do if the weather is good next weekend?
- Where would you like to go in the world? What would you like to see or do there?
- What are the four most important things to take with you when you travel? Why are they important?

How are you doing?

Read and copy the checklist below. Think and decide for each objective: **very well, quite well,** or **OK, but I need more practise**.

Use the checklist to help you improve your English.

I can...	Very well	Quite well	OK, but I need more practice
• Name my own and some other countries, nationalities and languages			
• Use superlatives to talk about the *most* of something			
• Name different animals			
• Use modal verbs and adverbs to express possibility and probability			
• Work out the meaning of unknown words in a text			
• Talk about the weather			
• Use the first conditional to talk about things which might happen in the future			
• Listen to and understand a conversation about planning a holiday			
• Understand the meaning of some phrasal verbs to do with holidays and travel			
• Use *Shall* and *Let's* to make suggestions			
• Use co-ordinating and subordinating conjunctions when speaking and writing			
• Name things in the home			
• Understand information in a notice about a school trip			
• Discuss items needed for a school trip			
• Describe photos on my phone using relative pronouns			

Words and phrases – Unit 6

Animals
animal _____
bear _____
chicken _____
cow _____
dinosaur _____
duck _____
elephant _____
fly _____
insect _____
lion _____
monkey _____
sheep _____
snake _____
tiger _____

Countries
Australia _____
Brazil _____
China _____
Egypt _____
England _____
France _____
Honduras _____
Portugal _____
Spain _____
Uganda _____
to be born: Where were
   you born? What country
   were you born in? I was
   born in … _____
to live: Where do you live?
   What country do you
   live in? I live in … _____

Going on a school trip
backpack _____
battery _____
cap _____
(phone) charger _____
credit card _____
(a pair of) gloves _____
guidebook _____
hat _____
passport _____
plug _____
raincoat _____
school tie _____
school uniform _____
sports kit _____
swimming costume /
   trunks _____

tickets _____
umbrella _____

Household appliances
air conditioning _____
barbecue _____
cooker _____
dishwasher _____
electricity _____
freezer _____
fridge _____
gas _____
heating _____
iron _____
microwave _____
oven _____
television / TV _____
washing machine _____
telephone _____
wi-fi _____

Languages
Arabic _____
Chinese _____
English _____
French _____
Portuguese _____
Spanish _____
What language do you
   speak? What is your first
   language? I speak… _____

Nationalities
Australian _____
Brazilian _____
Chinese _____
Egyptian _____
British _____
French _____
Honduran _____
Portuguese _____
Spanish _____
Ugandan _____
What's your nationality?
   What nationality
   are you? I'm… _____

Parts of the world
Africa _____
America Central / North /
   South America _____
Antarctica _____
Asia _____
Europe _____
The Arctic _____

north _____

south _____

east _____

west _____

East Asia _____

South-east Asia _____

Middle East _____

Which part of the
world ... ? _____

Phrasal verbs

look into _____

look up _____

point out _____

ring up _____

sort out _____

take up _____

Seasons

autumn _____

spring _____

summer _____

winter _____

Travelling

adventure _____

airport _____

baggage / suitcase _____

delay / delayed _____

direction _____

driver _____

entrance _____

exit _____

flight _____

hot _____

journey _____

map _____

passenger _____

plane _____

platform _____

postcard _____

railway station _____

train _____

(return / one way) ticket _____

to approach _____

to arrive _____

to ask for _____

to be / get lost _____

to cross the road / street _____

to depart / leave _____

to drive _____

to fly _____

to look forward to
(something) _____

to miss (a train /
plane / bus) _____

to park _____

to rent (a bike) _____

trip _____

visit _____

Weather

cold _____

degree _____

fog _____

heat _____

humid _____

ice _____

lightning _____

night _____

rain _____

snow _____

storm _____

sunshine _____

thunder _____

weather _____

weather conditions _____

weather forecast _____

wind _____

What's the weather like? _____

Reading

Read the text and complete the gaps 1–7. For each question, choose the correct answer (A, B, C or D).

The Lake District

The Lake District is a region in the north-west of England with **1** _____ of lakes and mountains. It's very popular with tourists and is often **2** _____ in the summer months from July to September. The best **3** _____ to start your holiday is at the tourist information office, **4** _____ you can find lots of ideas for activities to do. If you are **5** _____ in watersports, you should try sailing on Lake Windermere or you could **6** _____ waterskiing. If you **7** _____ walking, don't forget to take a map as it's easy to get lost.

1
A many
C a lot
B much
D enough

2
A lonely
C typical
B crowded
D empty

3
A place
C area
B neighbourhood
D town

4
A where
C when
B who
D that

5
A care
C worried
B excited
D interested

6
A point out
C look up
B take up
D ring up

7
A be
C have
B go
D take

Listening

You will hear an interview with Tayo Agbani, who is a young surfing champion.

For each question choose the TWO true statements (A–E). You now have some time to read the questions.

1
- **A** Tayo's parents are both Nigerian.
- **B** Tayo was born in Australia.
- **C** Tayo feels Nigerian.
- **D** Tayo's family moved to Australia for the surfing.
- **E** Tayo's father flies planes for his job.

2
- **A** Tayo likes snakes.
- **B** Tayo wants to live in Nigeria when he's older.
- **C** Tayo has family in the UK.
- **D** Tayo likes the weather in Australia.
- **E** Tayo doesn't like the summer.

3
- **A** Tayo is going to compete in a surfing competition in America.
- **B** Tayo has friends who also like surfing.
- **C** Tayo thinks surfing is more important for him than school.
- **D** Tayo says it's expensive to travel to surfing competitions.
- **E** Tayo is stopping surfing.

Speaking

Work with a partner.

Student A

You are going on holiday today. Ask Student B these questions.

- What do I need to pack?
- What time does the plane leave?
- How will we get to the airport?
- How long is the flight?
- What time do we arrive?
- What shall we do when we get there?

Study tip

Improve your fluency by using conjunctions and relative pronouns to make longer sentences.

Student B

You are calling a holiday apartment in Cardiff, Wales. Ask Student A these questions.

- How do I get from the railway station to the apartment?
- How long does the journey take?
- What equipment does the apartment have?
- What things can I do in Cardiff if it rains? And what things can I do if it's sunny?
- What time do I have to leave the apartment on my last day?

Writing

A holiday abroad

Last month you went on holiday to another country. Write an email to your English friend about this.

- Tell him / her where you went and who you went with.
- Explain how you travelled.
- Describe the weather on your holiday and give your opinion of it.
- Say what you did on your holiday.
- Tell your friend if it was a good holiday or not, and explain why.
- Say what country you would like to visit next, and why.

Write 100–110 words in English.

7 Education

• Make statements about my school • Name different types of schools and talk about the differences • Use adjectives to talk about school

1 Complete the sentences with the words from the box.

> class   classroom   homework   lessons   students   subject

1 Our teachers give us one hour of _____ to do every week.
2 My _____ has six computers in it.
3 This school is quite big: it has more than 800 _____.
4 We have three _____ before lunch, and two in the afternoon.
5 My favourite _____ is biology.
6 My English _____ has 18 people in it.

d

2 Rewrite the sentences in activity 1 so that they are true for you and your school.

3 Match each word to the correct photo.

> nursery school   primary school   secondary school   university

a

b

c

4 Discuss. *What are the differences between each of the schools in activity 3?*

Think about:

- the age of the students
- the size of the school
- the hours in the school day
- the number of year groups

- the school subjects that students study
- homework
- lessons
- classrooms

Use comparatives to talk about differences between people and places:	*Students at nursery school are **younger than** students at primary school.* *The school day is often **longer** at nursery school **than** it is at primary school.*

5 Match each adjective in Box A with the opposite adjective in Box B.

A	B
clever	bad
correct	boring
easy	difficult
fun	stupid
good	useless
useful	wrong

6 Which box in activity 1 has positive adjectives and which box has negative adjectives?

7 Choose the correct adjective to complete each sentence.

1 I don't like Ms Pick. I think she's a **good / bad** teacher.

2 I love our history lessons – they're always **boring / fun**.

3 'Is maths hard for you, David?' 'No, it's quite **easy / difficult** for me.'

4 Holly is going to university because she's a very **stupid / clever** girl.

5 The answer was America but I wrote Africa, so I got that question **correct / wrong**.

6 I don't know why we have to do art at school; It's a **useful / useless** life skill.

7 Enrico is the **best / worst** student in our science class. He always gets 100% for his homework.

8 Discuss. Work in small groups.

- *What is the most useful school subject? Why? Which is the most useless?*

- *What classroom activities do you think are fun? Which are boring?*

- *Which of these are easy or difficult to do in English?*
  - *learn vocabulary*
  - *learn grammar*
  - *speak in English*
  - *write in English*
  - *read in English*
  - *listen in English*

When an adjective comes after a noun, we use the verb *to be*:   *I think science is fun.*

7.1 I'm good at English

- Understand someone talking about what school subjects and activities they are good at.
- Have a conversation about what I am / am not good at using adverbs of manner.
- Read and understand an email about something that happened at school.
- Use *can* and *could* to talk about my abilities.

1 **Discuss.** *What are your favourite school subjects? Which are your best subjects?*

2 **Match each verb in Box A with a noun in Box B. You can use some nouns more than once.**

A
ask   answer   fail   pass   read   take   write

B
an essay   an exam   a question   notes   a text

3 **Listen to Shan talking about his school subjects. Copy and complete the chart to show what Shan is and isn't good at.** 🔊 7.1

subjects	good at ✓	bad at ✗
English		
Biology		
Chemistry		
History		
PE		
Geography		
Maths		
Music		

4 **Complete Shan's sentences with the phrases from the box. Listen again and check.** 🔊 7.1

answer the questions   do experiments   play an instrument   remember all the information   understand   write essays

1 I can't _____ English and often I can't _____.

2 I can't _____ in biology.

3 I can't _____ well in chemistry.

4 History is interesting, but I can't _____ easily and I get low marks.

5 I like music but I can't _____.

Grammar

can / can't
You use *can / can't* to say that someone knows how to do something or has the ability to do something.
Can / can't is a modal verb so it comes before the main verb in the sentence.
Can / can't + main verb without *to*.
I can't sing.

More? ➜ Grammar

5 **Read the email on the opposite page. Answer the questions.**

1 What lesson is Heidi writing about?

2 Where did the teacher write the instructions?

3 What did Heidi hear?

4 What did Heidi's classmate do?

5 What did Heidi do wrong in the lesson?

Hi Grandma,

How are you? I had a terrible day at school today. Everything was fine until chemistry. We were experimenting with some gas. Our teacher wrote what we had to do on the board, <u>but she didn't write them clearly</u> and <u>I couldn't read her writing very well</u>. <u>I mixed two gases together slowly</u> and then I carefully added a third gas. There was a 'pop' sound, and then I smelled something strange. My partner Luisa breathed in the gases. The teacher ran over to us and asked me what the gases were. She told me that these were not the correct gases and they were very dangerous. Luisa had a headache and she went home early. I hope she's OK.

Love you,

Heidi

6 **Complete the sentences using** *can / can't / could* **and** *couldn't.*

1 I _____ do the final exercise in my physics lesson today. It was very hard.

2 Shannon doesn't like art because she _____ draw.

3 We _____ hear the supporters at the football pitch every time there is a football match.

4 My dad _____ drive when he was my age.

7 **Read the three <u>underlined</u> sentences in Heidi's email. Choose the correct meanings.**

1 A The teacher's writing was good.

  B The teacher's writing was bad.

2 A Heidi was able to read the teacher's writing.

  B Heidi wasn't able to read the teacher's writing.

3 A Heidi took some time to mix the gases together.

  B Heidi didn't take much time to mix the gases together.

8 **Choose the correct word to complete each sentence.**

1 Ben finished his homework **quick / quickly**.

2 The presentation was good – Azza spoke very **clear / clearly**.

3 I did **bad / badly** in the maths test.

9 **Ask and answer with a partner. Talk about the activities from activity 2 and school subjects.**

● *What subjects are you good at / bad at?*

● *Are you good at ... ?*

● *Can you ... ?*

● *When you were in primary school could you ... ?*

Use the verb *to be* + *good at / bad at* + noun to talk about what you can and can't do well. Sometimes we use *not good at* + noun too.

I'm good at PE.

I'm not good at I.T.

Grammar

Past ability

You use *could / couldn't* to say that someone knew how to do something or had the ability to do something in the past. *Could* is a modal verb so it comes before the main verb in the sentence.

Could / couldn't + main verb without *to*.

*I **couldn't read** her writing very well.*

More? → Grammar

Grammar

Adverbs of manner

Most adverbs of manner are formed by adding *–ly* to an adjective. Some are irregular.

*bad – **badly***

*good – **well***

You use adverbs of manner to say how someone does something, or how something happens. So adverbs give information about a verb.

*I **mixed** two gases together **slowly**.*

More? → Grammar

Vocabulary

Gabe spoke English ...
badly
carefully
clearly
easily
quickly
slowly
well

7.2 How to be a good student

1 **Discuss.** *What makes a good student?*

Learning aims

- Read a blog post about how to be a good student
- Use the present perfect to ask and answer questions about the past up to the present
- Play a game using the present perfect

2 **Read the blog post about how to be a good student. Decide if sentences 1–4 are true (T) or false (F) according to the post.**

1 It's possible for everyone to get 100% in a test.   **T/F**

2 It's good to ask questions in class.   **T/F**

3 You should never answer a question if you won't get the answer right.   **T/F**

4 It's not good to revise for many hours at a time.   **T/F**

Top Tips on How to be a Good Student

Have you ever thought about why some students are better than other students? And have you worried that you are not a good student? Remember – a good student is not always the student who gets top marks for their homework or in a test. Sure, you might be able to get better marks – but we can't all get 100% for everything we do. A good student tries their best at school and knows how to study well. Here are five top tips to be a good student and get the best results you can.

1 Always ask questions if you don't understand. Teachers are there to help you and they are happy to explain something to you.
2 Don't worry if you get an answer wrong. It's important to try, and if the answer is wrong, you will learn the correct answer.
3 Write clear and complete notes – this will help you to revise.
4 Revise often and for a short time. It's a good idea to read your notes from your lessons in the evening or at the weekend.
5 Practise exam-style questions and activities. Then you will feel more relaxed in your exams.

3 **Ask and answer the questions with a partner. Share your ideas with the class.**

- *Which of the top five tips do you do?*
- *What other tip can we add to the list?*

Vocabulary

to explain
to get good marks / results
to know (how to)
to practise
to revise
to study
to try (your best)
to understand

Grammar

Present perfect
The form of the present perfect is:
have / has + past participle

You use the present perfect to ask questions about a finished event that happened in the past but we don't know when it happened or it's not important – it happened at some time in the past before now. You often add *ever* to these questions.
*Have you **ever** played sport for your school?*

You can use short form answers.
Yes, I have. No, I haven't.

To make negative statements with the present perfect you can use *never*.
*I've **never** ridden a horse.*

More? ➜ Grammar

4 **Complete the present perfect sentences using the verbs in bold.**

1 Annie _____ **(see)** the new James Bond film.

2 My grandparents _____ **(not meet)** my new baby brother.

3 Abdul _____ **(not take)** any English exams.

4 I _____ **(never travel)** abroad.

5 My friends _____ **(plan)** a birthday party for me.

6 _____ you _____ **(ever play)** chess? No, I _____.

5 **Listen to two students playing the *Good student* game and complete the dialogue.** 🎧 7.2

> Your turn!

> Number **1** _____.

> OK. Have you ever got 100% in a test or exam?

> Yes, I have.

> What was the **2** _____?

> It was **3** _____. Your turn!

6 **Play the *Good student* game. Work with a partner.**

Have you ever …

1 played sport for your school? If you have, what sport did you play?

2 read a book in English? If yes, what was the book? Did you enjoy it?

3 given a presentation in English? If yes, did you do it well? What was the presentation about?

4 studied another language that wasn't English? If yes, what was it?

5 got 100% in a test or exam? If yes, what was the subject?

6 said you were ill so that you didn't have to do a test or exam? If yes, what test or exam was it?

7 not done your homework. If yes, explain why?

8 taught a lesson at school? If yes, what lesson was it?

9 stayed up all night before a test or exam to study? If yes, what test or exam was it? Did you get a good result?

10 helped a friend to study for a test or exam? If yes, what subject was it for? Did your friend pass or fail?

7 **Work with a different partner. Talk about your partner from activity 6.**

Ricardo hasn't read a book in English. / Ricardo has never read a book in English.

Grammar

Past participles
The past participle of many verbs is formed by adding -ed to the verb.
answer – answered
ask – asked
play – played
Sometimes you need to add another letter:
plan – planned
stop – stopped
travel – travelled
Sometimes the verbs are irregular:
be – been
do – done
get – got
meet – met
say – said
see – seen
take – taken
teach – taught
More? → Grammar

7.3 A great school

1 **Discuss.** *What is important for a school?*
What shouldn't a school have or do?

2 **Can you remember? Which words in the box are compound nouns?**

after-school activities   canteen   computer room
director/headteacher   exam results   library
schoolyard/playground   school building
sports equipment   school uniform

3 Match the words in the box in activity 2 to photos a–j.

4 **Discuss. Use some of the sentences and phrases below.**

a Imagine the best school. Put the things in activity 3 in order from 1 (most important) to 10 (least important). Add you own ideas.

b Are the following things important for a good school?

the neighbourhood   the size of the school and the classes   the subjects you can study

school trips   how much money a school has   its language department

- *I think very good teachers are important.*
- *Do you think that … is important?*
  Yes, I do. / No, I don't.
- *I think it's more / less important for a school to be / have … than for it to be / have …*
- *In my opinion …*

5 **Find five compound adjectives in the text below.**

> My school is a private school, so my parents pay money for me to go there. It's an English-speaking school and there are lots of students who are American, British, Canadian and Australian. I like it because I'm very interested in other cultures. We have four six-week terms and a two-month summer holiday every year. It's a girl's school and we wear a uniform with a purple skirt, a white shirt, a purple tie and a purple long-sleeved jacket. My older sister and I both go to the same school and next year our ten-year-old sister will start there too. I think it's a good school because the classes are quite small – there are no more than 16 students in a class. The teachers are very kind and helpful and we go on lots of interesting school trips.

6 **Complete the sentences using the correct –ing or –ed adjective.**

1 a I'm going to a new school in September and I'm very _____.

b My aunt and uncle told us some _____ news – they're going to have a baby! (excited/exciting)

2 a Our science lesson today was _____.

b The sports teacher looked _____ during the cricket game this afternoon. (bored/boring)

3 a The school trip to the museum was _____.

b I'm too _____ to do my homework tonight. (tired/tiring)

7 **Write a paragraph about your school. Use the questions below and the paragraph in activity 5 to help you.**

- Do you go to a private school or a state school?
- Do you go to an English-speaking school?
- What are the nationalities of the students?
- How long are the terms and the holidays?
- Do you wear a uniform? If yes, what is it?
- Are any family members at the same school as you?
- Do you think your school is a good school? Why or why not?

Grammar

Compound adjectives
Some adjectives have more than one word in English. These are called compound adjectives. We usually use a hyphen (-) to connect the two words.
after-school activities

More? → Grammar

Grammar

-ing and -ed adjectives
You use –ing adjectives to describe what something is like.
We also go on lots of interesting school trips.
You use –ed adjectives to describe how you feel.
I'm very interested in other cultures.

More? → Grammar

Vocabulary

It's …
boring, exciting, interesting, tiring.
I'm …
bored, excited, interested, tired.
I go to a … school.
nursery/primary/secondary/ private
I go to university.

7.4 Different types of schools

Learning aims

- Talk about different types of schools
- Listen to and understand people talking about their schools
- Use the present perfect with *for* and *since* to talk about how long I have done something
- Use subordinating conjunctions to express how two ideas or events are connected by time
- Design a perfect school

1 Discuss the photos. Talk about:

- the students
- the school uniform
- the classrooms / learning spaces
- what it might be like to go to this school

online school

military school

performing arts school

2 Listen to Marta, Kane and Ju talking about their schools. Match them to the schools in activity 1. 7.3

3 Listen again. Answer the questions. 7.3

1 What is her uniform like?
2 What do the students do after school everyday?
3 What job does Marta want to do when she is older?

Marta

1 Does Kane wear a uniform to school?
2 Where does he do his learning?
3 What doesn't Kane like about his school?

Kane

1 What do students at Ju's school call their teachers?
2 How does Ju describe the school day?
3 What does Ju want to study at university?

Ju

4 Listen again and complete the sentences with *for* or *since*. 7.3

1 I've been at this school _____ four years now.
2 I've been at the online school _____ 2020.
3 I've been at a performing arts school _____ I was 11.

Grammar

Present perfect with *for* and *since*

You use the present perfect with *for* and *since* for something which started in the past and is still going on now.

You use *for* to talk about the length of time:
*I've lived here **for** five years.*

You use *since* with a specific time or date in the past.
*I've lived here **since** I was eleven years old.*

*My grandma has lived here **since** 1994.*

More? ➜ Grammar

5 Complete the sentences with *for* or *since*.

1 My mum has worked at the airport _____ six months.

2 My sister has been married _____ two years.

3 I've known my best friend _____ we were three.

4 We've had our rabbit _____ we moved to this house.

5 James has had a bike _____ June.

6 The shop has been closed _____ two weeks now.

6 Ask and answer the questions.

How long have you been at this school for?

I've been at this school for …
I've been at this school since …

7 Match the clauses to make sentences from activity 2.

1 **Marta:** Some of my friends want to be pilots or mechanics

2 **Kane:** I went to a normal secondary school

3 **Ju:** As soon as I finish my exams,

a before I came to this school.

b I will go to university.

c when they are older.

8 Answer the questions about the sentences in activity 7.

1 Are Marta's friends pilots and mechanics now?

2 Which school did Kane go to first: a normal secondary school or forest school?

3 Will there be any time between Ju finishing her exams and Ju going to university?

9 Make sentences using the subordinating conjunctions in brackets.

1 Kitty can stay here. Henry gets home. **(until)**

Kitty can stay here until Henry gets home.

2 Please do the washing up. You go to the cinema. **(before)**

3 George held the baby. Mary put the shopping in the car. **(while)**

4 Mr and Mrs Patel went out. Sami arrived to look after the children. **(as soon as)**

5 Rita was in the kitchen. She heard the phone. **(when)**

6 Mabel tidied the house. Mabel had a party. **(after)**

10 Work in small groups. Design a perfect school. Think about:

type of school | location | places in the school

classrooms | subjects or main subject | students

after-school activities | timetable | uniform

equipment | teachers | why this is a great school

Grammar

Conjunctions
Remember that conjunctions are words that link two sentences or clauses together. Subordinating conjunctions link a main clause with a subordinating clause (a clause that adds information to the main clause or explains the main clause). Some subordinating conjunctions refer to time.

*Some of my friends want to be pilots or mechanics **when** they are older.*

*I went to a normal secondary school **before** I came to this school.*

***As soon as** I finish my exams, I will go to university.*

More? → Grammar

Vocabulary

after
as soon as
before
until
when
while

7.5 Online lessons

Learning aims
- Read texts about online school
- Use the present perfect tense to talk about recent events

1 **Discuss.** *Have you done any online lessons?*
What do you need for online lessons?
What's good (or bad) about online lessons?

2 **Read and listen to the texts. Look at the definitions a–m and find the words in the texts.** 🎧 7.4

Vocabulary
document
email
folder
keyboard
laptop
memory stick
screen
tablet
touchscreen
printer
speakers
to download
to upload

a a small piece of equipment that can be joined to a computer and allows you to put information on it.

b a computer screen that allows you to give commands to the computer by touching parts of the screen rather than using the keyboard or the mouse.

c the set of keys that you press in order to operate a computer, tablet or mobile phone.

d a machine that you can connect to a computer, tablet or mobile phone in order to make copies on paper of a document or other information on the technology.

e a piece of text, for example a letter, that is kept on a computer and that you can read or change.

f a flat surface on which pictures or words are shown.

g move something, such as files to another device through the internet.

h a small flat computer that you operate by touching the screen.

i to move something to your computer or mobile phone from the internet.

j a way to send written messages electronically from one computer to another.

k a group of files that are stored together on a computer.

l a small computer you can carry around with you.

m a piece of electrical equipment through which sound comes out.

My school has been online for six months. It's awful. I use my tablet to do the lessons because it has a larger screen than my phone. But when I have to type something, for example when I have to fill in answers on a form or a test, it takes a long time to type and I make lots of mistakes because it is touchscreen. I miss parts of the lesson because I'm so slow. I really need a keyboard. **Lola**

Our school has had online lessons for a year and a half now and I hate it. It's really boring and it's very hard to be interested in the lessons. I don't have a PC or a laptop so I have to use my mobile phone and the screen is very small. My eyes get very tired. My school told me they would give me a computer but I still haven't received one. **Jed**

We haven't started online school yet, but we're going to have two days a week of online lessons next term. I'm looking forward to it. I like computing lessons so I think online lessons will be easy for me. I have a laptop and I will be able to work at the table in the dining room. If I need to print documents out, I can put them on a memory stick and use my dad's printer. **Max**

I've just started online school. I think it's much easier than walking to school every day. I work on my computer at my desk in my bedroom. The school uses a website and it's very clear. I can see if I have mail or if there are documents that I need to download. We do video lessons, but I don't have my camera on. I have new speakers so I can hear my teacher very clearly. We keep our work in folders and email it to our teachers. I've already uploaded all my work for today. It's great. **Fern**

3 Answer the questions about the people in activity 2.

1 Which two people have problems with online lessons?

2 Who isn't doing online lessons at the moment?

3 Who does their lessons on a tablet?

4 Who finds online school easy?

5 What type of technology will Max use for his online lessons?

6 Whose eyes get tired from online lessons?

7 What does Lola need to help her with her online lessons?

8 What new equipment does Fern have that helps her?

4 Find these words in the texts in activity 2. Read the sentences they are in. What tense is used?

already   just   still   yet

5 Use the words from activity 4 to complete these definitions.

1 The word … is used to say that something is continuing to happen now.

2 The word … is used to describe something that someone is waiting for and expecting, but that hasn't happened so far.

3 The word … is used to describe something that happened earlier than expected.

4 The word … is used to describe something that happened very recently.

6 Complete the sentences with *already*, *just*, *still* or *yet*.

1 Tammy _____ hasn't called me.

2 I haven't received the tickets for the concert _____.

3 I haven't downloaded the documents _____ because I've _____ turned the computer on.

4 That was quick – Heather has _____ replied to the text I sent two minutes ago.

5 You don't need to book a table at the restaurant because I've _____ booked one.

6 Have you finished painting the bedroom _____?

7 Sophie's _____ had her hair cut. It looks great.

8 I've looked in my bag, in the car and in the garage but I _____ haven't found my purse.

7 Write answers to these questions.

1 What lesson have you just had?

2 What exams have you already taken?

3 What tenses in English have you already learned?

4 What homework for this week haven't you done yet?

5 What film have your friends seen but you still haven't seen?

Grammar

Present perfect with *already*, *just*, *still* and *yet*.

You use the present perfect with *already* to refer to something that happened earlier than expected.
*'Go and do your homework, Lisa.' 'Don't worry, Mum, I've **already** done it.'*

You use the present perfect with *just* to refer to an action in the very recent past.
*I've **just** finished my homework.*

You use the present perfect with *still* in negative sentences to talk about something that should have happened by now but hasn't.
*I **still** haven't received my new laptop.*

You use the present perfect with *yet* for something that still hasn't happened but is expected to happen soon.
*I haven't finished my homework **yet**.*

More? ➔ Grammar

My school in India

This is Meera. Meera's school is an English-speaking private school in Gurugram in India. The school does not have normal classrooms. It has big open spaces. There are also smaller areas for individual study and group activities. Students can move around and talk to each other. Lessons are not traditional either. They are all about solving problems. Students work together to find out information about global problems and to think of possible answers to them. At the end of a piece of work, the students think and talk about how well they did the task and what they could do differently. The teachers at Meera's school believe this way of learning gives students the necessary skills they need for life.

1 **Read the text and choose A, B or C.**

1 At Meera's school, classrooms are …

   A outside.

   B small.

   C open spaces.

2 In lessons students …

   A try to solve problems.

   B teach other students what they know.

   C do lots of tests.

3 At this school, it's important to …

   A think about what you can improve in your studies.

   B get good grades.

   C speak more than one language.

Study tip

When you read a text, use everything on the page to help you work out the meaning of words you don't know, for example, headings, photos and the questions you are asked, may all help you.

2 **Find words in the text that mean …**

1 a behaviour or belief that has existed for a long time.

2 finding an answer to a problem or a question.

3 relating to the whole world.

This is Tanvi. She's been a student at the same school in Gurugram for four years. 'Before I came to this school, I was very worried,' she says. 'It's very different to my old school. My first day wasn't good. I didn't know anyone and I didn't understand what to do in the lessons. No one has their own desk, so I didn't know where to sit. I went home and cried. I told my mother that I didn't want to go back to this school. But she said I had to try for at least a week. So I came back the next day. The teachers were very kind and helped me. Then I met my friend Upma and I felt better. Now I love the way we learn. We talk a lot and we do lots of work online to find out information, so I now have very good computer skills. I feel more curious about the world and I am happy to say what I think and to make suggestions. I've made lots of friends and I've learned many things.

3 Read the text and decide if the answers are true (T) or false (F).

1 Tanvi is a student at the same school in Gurugram.   T/F

2 She didn't like her first day at the school.   T/F

3 She didn't make any friends at the school.   T/F

4 She doesn't like working on computers.   T/F

5 She preferred her old school.   T/F

4 You have recently moved to Gurugram and started at the same school. Write an email to your friend back home about it.

- Explain how long you have been at the school for.
- Describe how it is different to your old school.
- Say what are the good and bad things about the school for you.

Write 130–140 words.

The same …

There are lots of international companies in Gurugram, for example, Siemens, Coca-Cola, Pepsi, BMW and Hyundai.

Are there any international companies where you live?

but different

Find out

1 *Look on a world map. Where is Gurugram, India?*

2 *What's the population of Gurugram? What's the population of India? What's the population of your town or city? And your country?*

Discuss

Do you think learning by solving problems is a good idea? Why or why not?

I think learning by solving problems is / isn't a good idea because …
What do you think?
I agree / disagree …
I would / wouldn't like to go to a school like this because they teach by solving problems …

Review

1 **Leo is talking about himself. Listen and choose the correct answers.** 🎧 7.5

1 Leo has been at his school for …

   a one year   **b** two years   **c** four years

2 Leo's school is … than his old school.

   a bigger   **b** smaller   **c** about the same size

3 When Leo first went to his school, he …

   a loved it   **b** wasn't sure if he   **c** hated it
                           liked it

4 He made some friends …

   a in lessons   **b** in the neighbourhood **c** at an after-school club

5 He's good at …

   a languages   **b** sciences   **c** sports

6 Leo thinks online learning is …

   a good   **b** bad   **c** OK

7 Leo has a … at home.

   a laptop   **b** tablet   **c** PC

8 It's in …

   a his bedroom   **b** the living room   **c** his parent's office

2 **Read and complete the advertisement for Hazelwood School. Use the words from the box.**

> after-school   canteen   classes   director   exam   laptop   private   students

At Hazelwood School we believe that every child can achieve. Hazelwood is a **1** —————— school for 11–16-year-olds. We have 100 **2** —————— in each year group and our **3** —————— are small – up to 15 students. The school's **4** —————— results are excellent every year. There are many **5** —————— clubs and activities so your son or daughter will find something to enjoy.

We have a lovely new **6** —————— where our students can eat good food for breakfast and lunch. In year 5, our students do some online learning and we give them each a **7** —————— to take home for this.

Please come and visit our school. As soon as you come into the school building, you will see that this is the right place for your child.

Luisa Mayhew, **8** ——————

3 **Complete each sentence with a word from the box.**

> ever   for   never   since   still   yet

1 Have you had lunch —————?

2 Have you ————— been to America?

3 Maya and Rose have been friends ————— eight years.

4 Fred ————— hasn't called me.

5 I've ————— been to Australia.

6 My mum and dad have been married ————— 2004.

4 **Talk about yourself to your partner. Answer the questions.**

- Did you go to a nursery school when you were younger? Did you enjoy it?
- What can you do now that you couldn't do when you were at primary school?
- How long have you been at your school for?
- What school subjects are you good at? What are you bad at? Why?
- Where have you been this week? Who have you seen?

- What haven't you done yet this week that you need to do?
- Do you think school uniform is a good idea? Why or why not?
- Do you want to go to university? If you go to university, what will you study?
- What is your opinion on online learning? Is it easy, fun, difficult … ?

How are you doing?

Read and copy the checklist below. Think and decide for each objective: **very well, quite well,** or **OK, but I need more practise**.

Use the checklist to help you improve your English.

> **How to improve**
>
> Use your voice (intonation) to make what you are saying clear. Remember
> - our voices go up at the end of a question.
> - we stress the important words in our sentences.

I can…	Very well	Quite well	OK, but I need more practice
• Talk about my school			
• Say what school subjects I am good at			
• Use *can* and *could* to talk about abilities			
• Use adverbs of manner to talk about how someone does something			
• Read and understand a blog about being a student			
• Use the present perfect tense to ask and answer questions about the past to the present, and about recent events			
• Take part in a discussion about what makes a school good			
• Recognise compound nouns and compound adjectives related to school			
• Write a paragraph about my school			
• Listen to and understand people talking about their different schools			
• Use the present perfect with *for* and *since* to talk about how long I have done something for			
• Use some subordinating conjunctions to express how two ideas or events are connected by time			
• Give my ideas in my group on how to design a perfect school			
• Read and understand texts about online school, understanding the writers' opinions and feelings			
• Use the present perfect with *already*, *just*, *still* and *yet* to talk about recent events			

Words and phrases – Unit 7

Adjectives

It's … _____
amazing _____
bad _____
brilliant _____
clear _____
clever _____
correct _____
difficult / hard _____
early _____
easy _____
exact _____
excellent _____
extra _____
fantastic _____
final _____
fun _____
general _____
good _____
great _____
horrible _____
important _____
lucky _____
necessary _____
possible _____
poor _____
quick _____
ready _____
recent _____
rich _____
slow _____
soft _____
strong _____
stupid _____
sure _____
terrible _____
true _____
useful _____
useless _____
worse _____
wrong _____
It's the … _____
best _____
worst _____
It's … _____
boring, exciting,
  interesting, tiring. _____
I'm …
bored, excited,
  interested, tired. _____
I'm good at / bad at maths. _____
I'm not good at maths. _____

Adverbs of manner

badly _____
carefully _____
clearly _____
easily _____
especially _____
quickly _____
slowly _____
well _____

Online school

document _____
email / mail _____
file _____
folder _____
information _____
internet _____
keyboard _____
laptop _____
list _____
memory stick _____
menu _____
mouse _____
news _____
online _____
page _____
password _____
PC _____
printer _____
screen _____
speaker _____
tablet _____
to click _____
to copy _____
to download _____
to email _____
to fill in _____
to find _____
to go online _____
to make a call _____
to save _____
to send _____
to upload _____
touchscreen _____

School

after-school activities _____
bell _____
(black / white / interactive)
  board _____
canteen _____
classmate _____
computer room _____
course _____
department _____
desk _____
dictionary _____
director / headteacher _____
education _____
eraser _____
exam / test _____
exam results _____
example _____
exercise _____
library _____
mark _____
notice _____
nursery school _____
(sheet of) paper _____
pen _____
pencil _____
pencil case _____
poster _____
primary school _____
private school _____
project _____
ruler _____
school _____
school building _____
school report _____
school year _____
schoolyard / playground _____
secondary school _____
sports equipment _____
student _____
subject _____
to experiment _____
uniform _____
university _____

Subordinating conjunctions related to time

after _____
as soon as _____
before _____
during _____
till _____
until _____
when _____
while _____

Verb phrases related to school

to answer a question _____
to ask a question _____
to explain _____
to fail an exam _____
to get good
  marks / results _____
to know (how to) _____
to pass an exam _____
to practise _____
to read a text _____
to revise _____
to study _____
to take notes _____
to try (your best) _____
to understand _____
to write an essay _____

8 When I am eighteen

Are you ready?
- Revise future forms
- Talk about my plans
- Listen to people discussing plans

1 **Discuss.** *What are your plans after you finish school?*

2 **Listen and read. Answer the questions about each conversation.** 🎧 8.1

1 When is the game?
2 When is the party?
3 When will Sonya's friend be 18?
4 What time does the film start?

1
_____ the game tomorrow night?
Yes, I've already bought my ticket and I'm really excited!

2
_____ a party on Saturday afternoon. Can you come?
Sorry, I can't. I'm playing in a football match in the afternoon.

3
How old will you be in August, Sonya?
_____ seventeen. How about you?
I'll be eighteen. My birthday is in July.

4
What time does the film start tonight?
_____ at 8.30. So, let's meet at the cinema at 8.20.
OK, great. See you there.

3 **Complete the conversations with the correct phrases. Then listen again and check.** 🎧 8.1

> I'll be   I'm having   It starts   Are you going to see

4 **Choose the correct option to complete each sentence about the future.**

1 *I'm going to be / I am* a doctor when I'm older.
2 What time *is the flight to Paris leaving / does the flight to Paris leave* on Tuesday mornings?
3 *I'm meeting / I will meet* Julia tonight for dinner. We've booked a table at Gregory's Restaurant.
4 Oh no, *the train is cancelled. I'm arriving / I'll arrive* late for class.

Grammar

Future forms
You use different tenses to talk about the future:
going to + verb + *ing*
present simple
present continuous
will + verb

More? → Grammar

5 **Talk about these things with a partner.**

- *something you are definitely going to do next year*
- *when you will have your next birthday*
- *something that is happening tomorrow*
- *an event on your timetable*

I'm going to go to Spain next summer.

I'm playing tennis tomorrow.

I'll be sixteen on August 5th.

My piano lesson starts at 10 o'clock on Saturday.

6 You will hear some short recordings. Listen and choose A, B or C. 8.2

1 What is the girl doing tomorrow?

A

B

C

2 What time does the meal start?

A

B

C

3 How old will the boy be in August?

A

B

C

4 What time are they going to meet?

A

B

C

7 Ask and answer the questions with a partner.

- *What are you doing tomorrow / at the weekend / next month?*
- *What time does school start in the mornings next week?*
- *When do the summer holidays end?*
- *Are you going to go to university / college when you finish school?*
- *What are you going to study?*
- *How old will you be on 1st January next year?*
- *What won't you do next week? Why not?*

8.1 Jobs

1 Discuss. *What jobs do your family members or friends do?*

2 Match the jobs in the box to definitions a–t.

actor architect artist baker builder bus driver
businessman/businesswoman chef cleaner engineer
farmer firefighter flight attendant lawyer
manager mechanic nurse photographer pilot
police officer

a a person who builds or repairs houses and other buildings

b a person who uses scientific knowledge to design, build and look after engines and machines

c a person who cleans the rooms and furniture inside a building

d a person who acts in plays or films

e a person who flies an aeroplane or a helicopter

f a person who designs buildings

g a person who draws or paints pictures as a job

h a person who looks after the passengers on an aeroplane and serves them their meals

i a person who works in business

j a person who cares for people who are ill

k a person who advises people about the law

l a person who bakes and sells bread and cakes

m a person who owns or manages a farm

n a person who is responsible for running part of or the whole of a company

o a person who cooks in a restaurant or hotel

p a person who drives a bus

q a person who works in the police and who makes sure that people obey the law

r a person who puts out fires

s a person who repairs and looks after machines and engines, especially cars

t a person who takes photographs as a job

3 Listen and check.

4 Look at the phrases in the box. Do you know what they mean? Look up any words you don't know.

> **In his / her job he / she …**
> works outside / inside   makes phone calls   works long hours
> helps people   has a lot of responsibility   uses technology
> is well paid / badly paid   creates or makes things
> **His / Her job is …**
> dangerous   difficult   exciting   boring   fun

5 Talk about the jobs that your parents / family members do. Ask and answer the questions.

- *What job does your dad / mum / uncle / aunt do?*
- *He's / She's a …*
- *In his / her job he / she … His / Her job is …*

6 With a partner, make sentences about the jobs in activity 2 with the words and phrases from activity 4.

> Farmers work outside.

> Nurses work long hours. Their job is difficult.

> Pilots have a lot of responsibility. Their job is exciting.

7 Listen to some friends playing a game called *What's the job?* Which job are they describing? 🎧 8.4

8 With a partner, play *What's the job?* The student answering the questions can only answer *Yes / No*. Remember to use *you* to talk about the job in a general way.

9 Ask and answer the questions with your partner.

- *What job would you like to do in the future?*
- *Why?*

Grammar

General use of *you*
Sometimes you can use *you* to talk in a general way about something, especially when you are **speaking**.
- *So do **you** do this job inside?* = (do people do this job inside?)
- *Yes, **you** do.* = (yes, they do)
You can also use present passive, but this is more formal. You often find this in **writing** instead of speaking.
*This job **is** usually **done** outside.*

More? → Grammar

You use *would + like / love / hate* + infinitive to talk about things you do or don't want to do in the future.	I *would* **love** to be a doctor.	☺☺☺		*because …*	I like helping people.
	I *would* **really** *like to be* a doctor	☺☺☺			I like working outside.
	I *would like to* work with animals	☺			I don't like sport.
Use **really** to say how much you would *like / not like* to do something	I *wouldn't like to be* a footballer.	☹			
	I **really** *wouldn't like to be* a footballer.	☹☹			
	I *would* **hate** *to be* a footballer.	☹☹☹			

8.2 The world of work

Learning aims

- Use phrasal verbs to describe jobs
- Use verb patterns to describe plans
- Write about a part-time or summer job I would like to do.

1 **Discuss.** *Which jobs are dangerous?*

2 **Match the descriptions with the photos. Then write the name of each job. There are two extra photos.**

1 Colette fixes cars and bikes in her garage. She puts on gloves and boots to protect herself when she is working. She needs a lot of different tools to do her job. She works for herself.

2 Sami's job is to put out fires. If there is an emergency, he turns on the flashing lights and drives at full speed. He wears a uniform. He also goes to schools to talk about the dangers of fire.

3 Tina picks up passengers and takes them where they want to go. Sometimes she goes to the station and then drives back from the station. On Friday night and at the weekends there is a lot of work. She earns money for each trip. She knows the city very well.

4 Guy works in a clinic. He looks after sick people and finds out what is wrong with them. He gives them medicine and helps them to get better. His hours are Monday to Friday and Saturday mornings.

a

b

c

d

e

f

3 **Find six phrasal verbs in the texts in activity 2.**

4 **Match the definitions below to the phrasal verbs in the texts in activity 2.**

(care for) (collect) (discover) (stop) (switch on) (wear)

5 **Complete the sentences with the correct form of the phrasal verbs in the box.**

look after   put on   put out   pick up   turn on   find out

1 What's that strange noise? I need to _____ _____ what it is.

2 The bus driver _____ _____ passengers from the airport.

3 You should _____ _____ your lights, Dad! It's getting dark.

4 Don't forget to _____ _____ a hat. It's really cold tonight.

5 Mum _____ _____ Grandma if she doesn't feel well.

6 Please _____ _____ that cigarette, Madam. You can't smoke here.

Grammar

Phrasal verbs
Remember some verbs in English consist of a verb + a particle (*in/out/on/up* etc). These are called phrasal verbs. A phrasal verb does not have the same meaning as the verb does on its own. You have to learn these verbs together with the particles.

*Colette **puts on** gloves and boots to protect herself.*
*Sami's job is to **put out** fires.*

More? ➜ Grammar

6 **Read and match the people searching for a job 1–6 to the adverts A–F.**

A International summer school workers needed! Must speak at least two languages, including English, and like working outside. Must be polite and friendly.

1 I worked at a kids' club last summer. I played lots of sports and games and helped with meals. I have a first-aid certificate so I know what to do if there is an accident.

B Are you friendly and good at talking to customers? Summer salesperson job available for young person in local shoe shop. Must love footwear and be free during July and August.

2 I am looking for a job to earn money while I study. I get along well with people and I am reliable and hard-working. I can work weekends and a night job will be perfect.

C Part-time hours available in 24-hour café. Must be flexible, and happy to work weekends and evenings.

3 I would like to be a chef because I love cooking, but I need experience. I am a friendly person and I know that I will work well in a team.

D Are you good at working with children? Can you cook? Are you happy to learn how to look after people in an emergency? Free training is provided.

4 I studied French and Spanish at university. I am searching for a job in Spain with a good salary. I would like the opportunity to use my languages. On my gap year, I volunteered in a primary school.

E We are looking for graduates in languages to work as classroom assistants around Europe. Must have some experience working with children. You will be well-paid and you will receive holiday pay.

5 I'm going to college in September to study fashion design. I can work all summer, and I would like to get some experience in a shoe store. I am great at talking to people.

F Is food your passion? Do you love travel? Then join us as a volunteer on the International Food Programme. No experience is necessary – we provide training. Work with others and learn about other cultures!

6 I am a sociable and friendly person. I am really interested in working with people. I am fluent in English and Spanish, and I would like to use my languages.

7 **Write a short paragraph about a part-time or summer job you would like to do. Use the plan to help you. Write about:**

- What jobs you are interested in and why: *I'm searching for a job in Spain.*
- Your skills: *I am fluent in English and Spanish.*
- Your personality: *I am reliable and hard-working.*
- Any experience or qualifications you have: *I have a first-aid certificate.*
- Reasons for your choices: *I am looking for a job to earn money while I study.*

Grammar

Infinitive of purpose
You use an infinitive to explain *why* you are doing something.
I am looking for a job *to earn money* while I study.
I'm going to college in September *to study* fashion design.

More? → Grammar

8.3 Applying for jobs

Learning aims
- Complete a job application form
- Complete information in a CV
- Understand advice about jobs
- Write a short CV
- Review modal verbs

1 **Discuss.** *Have you ever applied for a job? Did you write an email, or complete an application form?*

2 Read the application form for a job. Complete the gaps 1–10 with the correct headings from the box.

> Address   Date of Birth   Education   Email   Experience
> Name   Nationality   Skills   Title   Qualifications

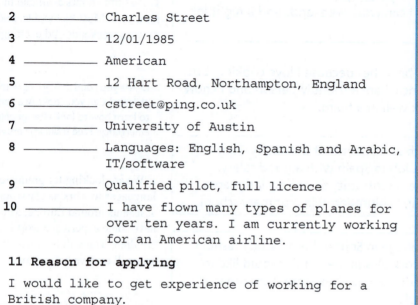

Application Form

Job Title: Pilot for New World Airways

1 _____ Mr

2 _____ Charles Street

3 _____ 12/01/1985

4 _____ American

5 _____ 12 Hart Road, Northampton, England

6 _____ cstreet@ping.co.uk

7 _____ University of Austin

8 _____ Languages: English, Spanish and Arabic, IT/software

9 _____ Qualified pilot, full licence

10 _____ I have flown many types of planes for over ten years. I am currently working for an American airline.

11 Reason for applying

I would like to get experience of working for a British company.

3 Read and listen to a teacher giving advice to young people about getting a job. What are the main sections you need in a CV? (8.5)

Hello everyone! Welcome to my 'World of Work' workshop. Today I'm going to give you some advice about how to get a job. Let's start with your CV or resumé. This is a document that provides a lot of information about you. In your CV, you need to include several sections.

Firstly, you should clearly write your Personal Details, such as your name, email address and phone number.

Next you ought to have a section called Skills. In this section, you can write things like: computer skills, works well in a team, etc. You can put examples in the third section called Experience. For example, you could write: 'Last year I helped my uncle in his shop selling vegetables', or 'Recently I helped organise a school party. I sold tickets and made food.' This is important even if you have never had a job before. Next you could add information on your Education and Qualifications.

Finally, you could explain your Reasons for applying. For example: 'Since I was a child, I have wanted to be a doctor.' 'I would like to get experience working in a hospital'. If you put all these things on your CV, you can send it to an employer. You can also use the information in a letter or an application form for any job. Good luck!

4 Choose the correct answer a, b, c, or d about the text in activity 3. The writer says writing a good CV …

a … means you will get a good job.

b … means you can easily use the information again.

c … is not helpful for application forms.

d … is very difficult for young people.

5 Put the words in order to make sentences using modal verbs.

1 this video / about / you / to get a job / should / watch / how

2 write / you / could / them / or phone / write a letter /

3 volunteer / think / everyone / I / as / work / should for free / a

4 minutes / can / ten / cycle to / in / I / work

5 my CV / on Friday / I / this job / send / need / for / to

6 Find all the examples of modal verbs in the text in activity 3.

7 Write a short CV for yourself. Use the sections in the box.

> Personal details
> Skills
> Experience
> Education
> Qualifications
> Reasons for applying

8 Read your partner's CV. Discuss your CVs and give advice on getting a job.

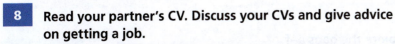

*So, you would like to be a lawyer? You **should** write to a law office, and say you want to do work experience.*

That's a good idea.

*First, you **could** earn some money working in a café, for example. **Then** / **Next** you **could** work for free in a different job to get experience.*

Great idea! / I like this idea.

Grammar

Modal verbs

We use: **subject +**   **modal verb +**   **infinitive without *to***

You use **should** when you give advice. In formal British English, you also use **ought to**.

| *Firstly,* | *you* | **should** | **write** *your personal details.* |
| *Next,* | *you* | **ought to** | **have a** *section called Skills.* |

You use **can** when you talk about what is generally possible:

| | *You* | **can** | **put** *examples in the third section.* |

You use **could** when you talk about what is possible but not certain when there is more than one option:

| | *You* | **could** | **write**, *'Recently, I helped organise a school party.'* |

You use **need to** to say what is necessary.

| *In your CV,* | *you* | **need to** | **include** *several sections.* |

More? ➜ Grammar

We use **adverbs of sequence** to describe the order of things.

Firstly, you should clearly write your Personal Details.

Next, you ought to have a section called Skills.

You can put examples in the third section called Experience OR Thirdly, you can put the examples in a section called Experience.

Finally, you could explain your Reasons for applying.

8.4 Starting a business

1 **Discuss.** *Would you like to start a business? What would you sell?*

Learning aims

- Understand an article about how to start a business
- Understand an interview about the world of work
- Understand and use reported commands
- Read a text and choose the correct headings

2 **Read the magazine article and match the correct headings A–F with paragraphs 1–5. There is one heading you do not need.**

A Rent or Buy?   **B** How to pay   **C** Happy customers?

D An important piece of paper   **E** Always smile!   **F** How to start

A new business

Jenni Logan, a businesswoman, gives some tips on running your own business.

Jenni was **unemployed** for six months, so she decided to start her own business. She says "I think it is really important for employers to look after their employees. Everyone needs to go on holiday and earn a good salary. And everyone would like to retire with enough money when they are too old to work. I'm going to retire when I'm fifty-five."

1 _____

If you want to start a business, it's important to understand how business works. First you need to decide what to do, for example what you would like to sell, and then you need to sell things at the right **a** _____.

2 _____

When customers buy something, always give them a **b** _____ This explains what they bought, when they bought it, and how much they paid.

3 _____

Sometimes customers change their minds and ask for a **c** _____. You must give them their money back if there is something wrong or they are not happy.

4 _____

Customers sometimes prefer to **d** _____ something to use it for a short time instead of buying it. For example, they pay $10 to use a bicycle for one hour.

5 _____

Most customers today pay with a **e** _____. However, some people prefer to use cash. So, you should make sure that you have enough notes and coins to give them the correct **f** _____.

3 **Read the text again and complete the gaps a–f with the correct words.**

refund   change   receipt   price   rent   credit card

4 **Read and discuss with a partner.**

Jenni said that that she was going to retire when she was fifty-five. What age do you want to retire at? Why?

Grammar

Reported speech
Remember to report what someone said, you normally change the tense of what they say.
Jenni says '*I'm going to retire when I'm fifty-five.*' > *Jenni said (that) she was going to retire when she was fifty-five.*

More? → Grammar

Vocabulary

5 Discuss these questions.

- *Are there many unemployed people in your country?*
- *How much is a good salary?*
- *Which jobs have the longest holidays?*

6 Listen to a radio show about jobs. Which question in activity 5 does Sammi Maketa answer? 8.6

7 Listen again. What advice does she give about jobs? 8.6

Grammar

Reported speech: commands
You use reported commands to say what someone told you to do.
You make these using *told* + *me / you / him / her / it / them / us* + (*not*) infinitive.
'Save money.' > *She **told me to save** money.*
'Become a teacher.' > *She **told him to become** a teacher.*
'Don't stay in the job for too long.' > *She **told us not to stay** in the job for too long.*

More? ➜ Grammar

8 Change the sentences into reported commands.

1 "Be careful" he said to me.

He told _____.

2 "Help me!" he said to me.

He told _____.

3 "Don't be late!" she said to them.

She told _____.

4 "Don't worry" my boss said to my friend.

My boss told _____.

8.5 Thinking about the future

1 **Discuss. *What are your plans for next year?***

2 **Listen and read the conversation. Are Sally and Jane going to university this year?** (8.7)

Sally: Finally! It's the summer holidays!

Jane: Yes! No more school.

Sally: I just **1** _____ sleep for a week.

Jane: Me too! What are your plans for next year?

Sally: Next year I'm going to university.

Jane: What are you going to study?

Sally: I'm not sure. I think **2** _____ study business.

Jane: Which university do you want to study at?

Sally: Umm, I don't really know yet but I **3** _____ in this city. I'd like to go somewhere new.

Jane: Do you want to stay in the United Kingdom?

Sally: Actually, I **4** _____ to university in another country.

Jane: Which one?

Sally: Well … I think the USA might be cool.

Jane: Yeah, it would!

Sally: How about you?

Jane: I'm going to work for a year and then go to university.

Sally: What job would you like to do?

Jane: I already have a job.

Sally: Great!

Jane: I'm going to work for my aunt in her factory. I'm going to build computers.

Sally: Amazing!

Jane: Yes, **5** _____ next week. So this week I'm having a break!

3 **Read the conversation again and complete the gaps with phrases from the box.**

> I will   don't want to stay   might go   want to   I start

4 **Listen again and check your answers.** (8.7)

Grammar

Future plans

You use *think + will* to talk about a possible decision.
*I **think I'll study** business.*
After *I think* you usually use a contraction: *I **think I'll …***
*I **think I'll study** English* = I'm not sure but it is very likely.
***Do** you **think you will** study English? **Yes, I do** / **No I don't**.*

You use *want* with the infinitive form of the verb to talk about a personal choice or preference.
*Which university **do you want to study** at?*
*I **(don't) want to stay** in this city.*

You use *would like* with the infinitive form of the verb to talk about future ideas.
*I**'d like to go** somewhere new.*
*Where **would you like to go**?*
*What job **would** you **like to do**?*

You use *might* with the infinitive form of the verb without *to* to talk about things that are possible but you are not sure about:
*I **might go** to university.*
*Where **might you go**?*
*I think the USA **might be** good.*

You use *going to* when you have a very strong idea:
*I**'m going to work** for a year.*

You use the present simple to talk about something that is arranged or timetabled and so is certain to happen.
I have a new job.
*Great! When **do** you **start**?*
*I **start** next week.*

More? → Grammar

5 Choose the correct option in sentences 1–7.

1 What job *will / would* you like to do in the future?

2 Where *will / would* you like to work?

3 *Do / Are* you want to stay in this city?

4 Would you *like / to like* to be a soldier?

5 *Do you think you / Do you* will study English in the future?

6 Will you *to get / get* a part-time job next year?

7 When *the job does / does the job* start?

6 Write your own answers to the questions 1–7 in activity 5.

7 Read the conversation in activity 2 again and find the fillers.

When you are not sure of your answer or you need more time to think, you use short phrases or 'fillers':	*That's a good question …* *Let me think …* *Umm …* *I don't really know …* *Well …* *Actually, …*	You use 'fillers' when you describe possible plans:	*Well*, I **want** to stay in this city. *I don't really know*, but I **don't want to** stay in this city. *That's a good question.* I **might get** a part-time job in a café. *Let me think …* **I'd really like to** live in a different country. *Umm …* **I think I'll** get a job using languages.

8 Look at these photos of jobs and the jobs in activity 3 in lesson 8.1. Work in small groups and do the following activity. Remember to use fillers to give yourself thinking time.

1 Choose five jobs you might like to do.

2 Say why you would like to do them.

3 Put them in order of preference 1–5.

4 Compare your lists.

5 Which job is the favourite in your group?

1
postman / postwoman

2
receptionist

3
salesperson

4
architect

5
singer

6
soldier

7
teacher

8
waiter / waitress

Would you like to be a vet?

What job do you think you'll do?

1 **Read the headline. What do you think the text is about?**

Success Stories: Young Business People

This is an amazing story about a little girl and nature. One day, when Mikaila was just four years old a bee **stung** her and she became very scared of bees. However, she decided to learn more about bees. And then another thing happened. Mikaila had a grandma who lived in another part of America. She sent a book to Mikaila's family, with an old family **recipe** for making lemonade. Mikaila had a great idea. She decided to make her own lemonade. But she didn't put sugar in the drink; she decided to put honey in the lemonade to make it sweet. Mikaila and her family really liked this new drink. So she entered a young person's business competition. Everyone loved it! Mikaila called her drink *Me & The Bees* because she wanted to help the bees, and she gives 10% of all the **sales** of her drink to help bees. The drink has been very successful. Now Mikaila is a teenager, and she has written a book about her experience of starting a business.

2 **Read the text and decide if the sentences are true (T) or false (F).**

1	Mikaila has always loved bees.	T/F
2	Her grandma sent her a book.	T/F
3	Mikaila made a drink with sugar.	T/F
4	Mikaila helps bees with her business.	T/F
5	She wrote a book about her idea.	T/F

3 **Work with a partner and tell Mikaila's story. Draw a timeline of Me and the Bees. Use the time adverbs of sequence on page 167:** *Firstly, Next, Then*.

4 **Discuss the questions.**

- *Do you think it is easy to start a business?*
- *What is most important thing you need to start a business. For example, money, time, a very good idea.*
- *What do you think Mikaila will do next?*

Glossary

to sting when a bee, or insect hurts you
a recipe you use this information to make a meal or a drink
sales all the money you get when you sell a product

The same ...

There are lots of big shops and supermarkets who now sell Mikaila's lemonade, such as World Market, Whole Foods Market and The Fresh Market.

Which are the biggest supermarkets near where you live?

but different

Kanu Zhang: King of Tech

When Kanu Zhang was just a small child, he always enjoyed playing with his parents' mobile phones. At first, they told him not to do this. However, when he was 10 years old, they realised he was very good at using technology. At the age of 12, Kanu won a national competition for designing a mobile phone app. Today, at the age of 17, he is a very rich young man. He has designed over 20 games and apps for mobile phones. "Anyone can be successful if they find something they love doing", he says.

5 Read the text. Answer the questions with full sentences.

a What did Kanu like doing when he was young?

b What happened when Kanu was ten years old?

c What did he win and how old was he?

d How old is he now, and does he have much money?

e What has he created for mobile phones?

6 Work with a partner. Design a poster for a business idea you have.

- Explain what the idea is.
- Say what the business will do.
- Say why your product / idea is so good.
- Include drawings.

Write 50–75 words.

Find out

1 *Are there any famous young business people in your country? What are they famous for? How old were they when they became business people?*

Discuss

Kanu says: 'Anyone can be successful if they find something they love doing'. Do you agree?

I agree / disagree …

I would / wouldn't like to go to be a young business person because …

I think you need a lot of money / to work very hard to be successful.

Review

1 Paolo is talking about himself. Listen and choose the correct answers. 🎧 8.8

1 Paolo …

  a has many shops   **b** has many friends   **c** sells online

2 Paolo's friends told him

  a not to sell pens   **b** not to sell online   **c** not to change jobs

3 Paolo thinks the most important rule in business is …

  a to sell the right thing **b** to advertise what you sell well   **c** to have a great name for your company

4 Paolo says it should be easy for customers …

  a to be happy   **b** to get the best price **c** to get a refund

5 In the future Paolo might …

  a get promoted   **b** start a new company **c** work with friends

6 Paolo … sell his businesses.

  a won't be able to   **b** won't ever   **c** would like to

7 When he is older, Paolo plans to …

  a retire   **b** have a party   **c** open a pen museum

8 At the moment he doesn't think he …

  a wants to stop working   **b** is rich enough   **c** could start another business

2 Read and complete the sentences about money with the correct answers.

1 If you want to start a business, you need a bank *refund / account*.

2 Don't forget to sell things at the right *price / credit card*.

3 Always give customers a *receipt / refund*, saying what they bought, when they bought it, and how much it cost.

4 Give customers a *price / refund* if they are not happy, or they change their mind.

5 Sometimes it's better to *rent / refund* a car, or a bike, for example, if you don't want to buy one.

6 Some people use notes and coins, but many people prefer using a *bank account / credit card*.

3 Match the jobs 1–6 with the actions A–E .

1 An artist   **A** picks up people.

2 A firefighter   **B** makes food.

3 A chef   **C** takes pictures.

4 A taxi driver   **D** puts out fires.

5 A flight attendant   **E** makes things.

6 A photographer   **F** looks after people.

4 **Talk about your future plans to your partner. Answer the questions.**

- What are you going to do next after school finishes?
- Do you think you will go to college?
- Will you get a job when you finish school? What job might you do?

- What would you like to do in the future?
- Where might you live?
- What things ought you to do to get a good job? e.g. To get a good job you should …

How are you doing?

Read and copy the checklist below. Think and decide for each objective: **very well, quite well,** or **OK, but I need more practise**.

Use the checklist to help you improve your English.

How to improve

How to improve
Listen carefully to the words and phrases at the end of each unit and take notes on any difficult pronunciation. For example, *photographer* has the stress here: pho**tog**rapher.

I can …	Very well	Quite well	OK, but I need more practice
• Remember how to use future forms			
• Listen to people discussing plans			
• Talk about my plans			
• Learn names of different jobs			
• Talk about jobs people do			
• Use *you* to talk in general about jobs			
• Write about a part-time or summer job I would like to do			
• Use phrasal verbs to describe jobs			
• Use would like / love / hate to talk about things in the future			
• Use verb patterns to describe plans			
• Complete a job application form			
• Complete information in a CV			
• Understand advice about jobs			
• Write a short CV			
• Use adverbs of sequence to describe the order of things			
• Use *ought to* give advice			
• Listen to and give advice about getting a job			
• Understand an article about how to start a business			
• Use business vocabulary			
• Understand a talk about jobs			
• Understand and use reported commands			
• Read a text and choose the correct headings			
• Learn and use 'fillers' when thinking about what to say			

Words and phrases – Unit 8

Jobs

actor _____
architect _____
artist _____
baker _____
boss _____
builder _____
businessman /
   businesswoman _____
chef _____
cleaner _____
cook
(bus / taxi) driver _____
engineer _____
farmer _____
firefighter _____
flight attendant _____
guide _____
hairdresser _____
lawyer _____
manager _____
mechanic _____
nurse _____
photographer _____
pilot _____
police officer _____
postman / postwoman _____
receptionist _____
salesperson _____
secretary _____
shop assistant _____
singer _____
soldier _____
teacher _____
vet _____
waiter / waitress _____

Describing jobs

creates or makes things _____
has a dangerous job _____
has a lot of responsibility _____
has an exciting / boring /
   fun job _____
helps people _____
is well paid / badly paid _____
makes phone calls _____
uses technology _____
works long hours _____
works outside / inside _____

Work

advert / advertisement _____
bank account _____
bill _____
business _____
cash _____
change _____
cheap _____
coin _____
closed _____
company _____
customer _____
employee _____
employer _____
job _____
office _____
on sale _____
open _____
price _____
receipt _____
salary _____
sales _____
to be unemployed _____
to earn _____
to find / search for a job _____
to get a job _____
to get promoted _____
to go on holiday _____
to rent _____
to retire _____
work _____

CVs and forms

address _____
application form _____
date of birth _____
education _____
email _____
experience _____
name _____
nationality _____
personal details _____
qualifications _____
reasons for applying _____
skills _____

Mass and units

centimetre _____
gram _____
kilogram _____
kilometre _____
litre _____
metre _____

Phrasal verbs

find out _____
look after _____
pick up _____
put on _____
put out _____
turn on _____

Verbs

to achieve / manage to _____
to agree _____
to approach _____
to arrange _____
to change _____
to check _____
to complete _____
to contact _____
to cover _____
to copy _____
to decide _____
to decrease _____
to describe _____
to discuss _____
to encourage _____
to end _____
to follow _____
to happen / take place _____
to increase _____
to keep _____
to lend _____
to let _____
to lie / tell lies _____
to lose _____
to miss _____
to mix _____
to move _____
to order _____
to pull _____
to push _____
to put _____
to receive _____
to remember / remind _____
to repeat _____
to return _____
to share _____
to show _____
to shut _____
to stay _____
to steal _____
to stop _____
to tear _____
to thank _____
to think _____
to throw _____
to try _____
to use _____
to visit _____

to want _____
to worry _____

Reading

Read the email and answer the questions.

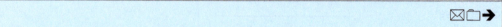

Hi Louis ✉️ 📁 ➡️

In your last email, you said that you aren't old enough to have a summer job in your country. That's a shame. We're the same age but I've worked for my dad for nearly three years. However, I've never earned money for working because I am also too young. He buys me things I want instead of paying me. I'm going to get a new bike soon for all the work I've done. That's cool, isn't it?

My dad has a garden centre business and I help him in the shop. I sell plants and flowers to the customers. I think it's interesting because I meet lots of different people. I try to make sure the customer is always happy. I'm quite good at it.

I usually work on Saturday afternoons and Sunday mornings. My dad would like me to help on Sunday afternoons because it is very busy, but that's when I play for my local football team.

I'd like to work in the garden café because it's much warmer than being outside. Maybe next year I will. In the future I don't want to work for my dad. I think I'll study business and I then I might start my own company.

Let me know your news. Write back soon ☺

Simon

1   Why can't Louis have a job?

2   How long has Simon had a job for?

3   Who does he work for?

4   Where does he work?

5   What does he do in his job?

6   How much does he earn?

7   When does he work?

8   Why would Simon's dad like him to work on Sunday afternoons?

9   Why can't Simon work on Sunday afternoons?

10 a   What would Simon like to do at the garden centre?

    b   Why?

11 What job might Simon do in the future?

Listening

Listen and choose the correct answers (A, B, C or D).

You will hear a talk for students about school. You now have some time to read the questions.

1 The problem with the canteen is …

A

B

C

D

2 Students will get to the sports field entrance by …

A

B

C

D

3 The café is near …

A

B

C

D

4 If there is a fire, students should go to …

A

B

C

D

Speaking

Work with a partner.

Student A

Ask Student B these questions.

- What is your favourite subject at school?
- What subject don't you like? Why?
- How much homework do you do every day?
- What did you learn last week?
- Would you like to go to university in the future?
- What would you like to study? Why?

Student B

Ask Student A these questions.

- What was your favourite subject at school when you were younger? Why?
- What subject did you not like? Why?
- How much homework do you think you will get each week next year at school?
- Tell me about something you have learned at school recently.
- In your opinion, how important is it to do after-school clubs?
- Is it important to do sport at school? Why? / Why not?

Study tip

In normal conversation, the speaker pauses to give the other person time to think before they answer. Practice pausing briefly between questions to give your partner time to think! Count to five ....

Writing

A holiday job

During the summer holiday, you worked in a café. Write an article for your school magazine about your job.

- Describe the cafe where you worked.
- Explain what jobs you had to do.
- Describe someone you worked with at the café.
- Say what you learned from the experience.
- Say what job you would like to have next summer, and why.

Write 120–130 words in English.

Study tip

Use past tenses to describe an experience: *I **learned** a lot in this job.*
Use time adverbs: *Firstly, …/ Secondly …/ Thirdly …/ Finally,* to organise your article.

Study tip

For jobs you can use *have to* to describe obligation in the past: *I **had to** talk to customers …*

9 Meeting new people

Are you ready?

- Use greetings and exclamations
- Role-play – meeting new people
- Review modals, and adverbs of probability
- Use passives

1 Discuss. *Do you like meeting new people? Why or why not?*

2 Complete the dialogues with the phrases. Then listen and check. (9.1)

What a shame!	Excuse me.	Good afternoon.
How interesting!	How's it going?	How nice!
I have to go.	nice to meet you.	Pardon?	Bye!

1 **Woman:** Good afternoon. Are you Mr Osman?

  Man: **1** _____ Yes, I am.

  Woman: I'm Bobby. I'm your driver. Welcome to Ireland.

  Man: **2** _____ Thank you.

  Woman: How are you today?

  Man: I'm very well, thank you.

2 **Teenage girl 1:** Hi, Zara! **3** _____

  Teenage girl 2: Good, thanks. You?

  Teenage girl 1: Not bad.

  Teenage girl 2: Sorry, but **4** _____

  Teenage girl 1: Cool! See you later.

  Teenage girl 2: **5** _____

3 **Man:** **6** _____ Are you Dr Goode?

  Woman: Yes, I am.

  Man: I'm Dr Tonkin.

  Woman: Are you a member of the ISTG?

  Man: **7** _____

  Woman: I said are you a member of the ISTG – are you here for the conference?

  Man: Sorry, yes. Yes, I am. I hope you can come to my presentation. It's about my latest project in international education.

  Woman: **8** _____ When is it?

  Man: Tomorrow morning at 11.00.

  Woman: **9** _____ I'm flying home this evening. I'm sorry.

  Man: How annoying! Well, **10** _____

  Woman: Nice to meet you, too.

3 Discuss.

1 In which conversation in activity 2 do the two speakers already know each other?

2 What is the informal way to ask: *How are you?*

3 Which phrase or phrases do you use:

  a when you didn't hear what a person said?

  b when you need to leave?

  c to show that something interests you?

  d to show that you would like something to be different

4 Practise the conversations in activity 2 with a partner.

> **Study tip**
>
> When you learn a new phrase or word, decide if it is formal or informal and write this next to the phrase or word in your notebook.

5 Role-play with a partner. Do Role-play 1 first, then Role-play 2.

Student A

1 Introduce yourself to Student B, a new English student at your school. Find out:

- his / her name
- how he / she is today
- what subjects he / she is studying
- what hobbies he / she has

Then end the conversation.

2 You are English. You are visiting your old friends in another country. You have just arrived at the airport. Their son / daughter (Student B) is meeting you.

Student B

1 You are an English student. You are starting at a new school. Student A is in your class.

2 You are picking up your parents' English friend from the airport. You have never met him / her before. Introduce yourself and welcome him / her to your city. Then find out:

- how he / she is today
- how his / her flight was
- what he / she would like to do in the city

Then suggest that you leave the airport and how you will travel to your house.

To respond to what someone tells you in a conversation you can use:	*How* + adjective:	*How* interesting! / nice! / annoying!
	What + noun:	*What* a pity! / a shame! / a good idea!

6 Read the email. Answer the questions.

1 What is Hilda inviting Maya to?

2 When is it?

3 What does Mr Sherman organise?

4 What subject does Mr Sherman teach?

5 What does Hilda think about the talk?

> Hi Maya
> There's a talk tonight at school about an exchange programme. On the programme you visit a student in another country, stay with their family and go to their school. Then they come and visit you. The exchange is organised by Mr Sherman. He's the geography teacher. It might be interesting. Do you want to come with me? We could meet at my house at 5.00.
> Hilda

7 Find the example of a passive sentence in the email in activity 6. Then rewrite the following sentences using the passive.

1 JK Rowling is the writer of the Harry Potter books.
The Harry Potter books were _____.

2 Many people around the world read these books.
These books _____.

3 Gustav Eiffel designed The Eiffel Tower in Paris, France.
The Eiffel Tower in Paris, France _____.

4 Nearly 7 million visitors visit it every year.
It _____.

8 Find two examples of modals that express possibility in the email in activity 6. Then choose the best way to complete the sentences.

1 It *might / perhaps* rain.

2 I *may / probably* go to bed early tonight.

3 She *probably / could* go to Africa next summer.

4 You *perhaps / may* see Aston at the party tonight.

Grammar

Passive
You use the passive when the thing is more important than the person. This is why the thing comes first in the sentence. You make the passive with the verb *to be* + the past participle. If you want to add more information about the person doing the action, use *by* + the person.

*The exchange **is organised by** Mr Sherman.*

You use past simple passive to talk about the past. You change *is / are* to *was / were*.
*The window **was broken** last night.*

More? ➜ Grammar

9.1 We are all different

1 Discuss. *Have you ever travelled to another country?*
What was different about the place you travelled to?

Learning aims

- Understand details from people talking about their experiences of school exchanges
- Listen to a discussion about a school exchange.
- Use modal passives to talk about why I would or wouldn't like to go on a school exchange

2 Listen to four students talk about their school exchanges. Match each person to the topics they are talking about.

Nadia	the house
Luis	school
Alfie	the weekend
Klara	food
	the exchange family
	daily routines

3 Listen again and answer the questions.

1 Which country did Nadia go to?

2 What time did school finish every day?

3 What time did Nadia go to bed?

Nadia

1 What country did Luis go to?

2 What does Luis usually have for breakfast?

3 What does he want his mum to do?

Luis

1 What country did Alfie go to?

2 What were his exchange family like?

3 What problem did he have?

Alfie

1 What country did Klara go to?

2 What did Klara do at weekends?

3 What does Klara usually do at the weekend at home?

Klara

4 Ruby and Lisa are going on a school exchange. Listen to them discussing the exchange. Which things does Lisa mention? 🎧9.3

| the trip | the flight | the train journey |

| the exchange school | the exchange family |

| food | culture | hobbies | language |

5 Listen again. Choose the correct answers. 🎧9.3

1 The school trip is …

   A next week   B next month   C next year

2 They are going to …

   A New Zealand   B Scotland   C Bermuda

3 Lisa is feeling … about the trip.

   A excited   B relaxed   C worried

4 Ruby and Lisa …

   A have met their exchange families.

   B met their exchange families on a video call.

   C spoken to their exchange families on the phone.

6 Match sentences 1–5 with the topics from activity 4. Listen again and check. 🎧9.3

1 It might be cancelled.

2 It might be delayed.

3 They might not be kind.

4 It might not be very nice.

5 They might be strange.

7 Read the grammar box and then decide which sentences in activity 6 are in the modal passive.

8 Put the words in the sentences in order. What is the subject in each sentence? What is the modal?

1 closed / might / the / be / the / shop

2 should / door / be / locked / the

3 oven / ought / the / cleaned / to / be

4 needs / text / translated / this / be / to

9 Discuss these questions with a partner.

● *Would you like to go on a school exchange? If yes, where would you like to go? Why?*

● *Would you be worried about going? Why or why not?*

Grammar

Modal passive
The form of the modal passive is: subject + modal verb + *be* + past participle.

You use a modal passive to express possibility.

*The flight **might be cancelled**.*

To express advice:
The lesson ought to be recorded.
The lesson should be recorded.

To express necessity:
The rabbit's cage needs to be cleaned.

More? ➜ Grammar

Vocabulary

The train is / was …
cancelled
delayed
The parents are …
kind
lovely
nice
strange
strict
I'm going to stay with the Hilton family.
The plane might be cancelled.
The plane might be delayed.

9.2 Let's celebrate!

Learning aims

- Read about different celebrations
- Understand the meaning of difficult words from context
- Understand how suffixes change verbs into nouns
- Write about my New Year celebrations

1 **Discuss:** *What special days do you and your family celebrate? What happens at your celebration?*

2 **Look at the titles of the texts. What do you know about these celebrations?**

1 Hogmanay

We're Scottish and so we celebrate Hogmanay. Hogmanay is on the 31st of December. It's a celebration of the New Year. It's very important to clean the house before the end of the old year, so my brother and I help. In the evening, our neighbours visit us. They bring a small gift like a fruit cake or biscuits and we give them something to drink. This gives us good luck for the next year. At midnight, my mum walks through the house carrying a branch which is on fire. We sing a special song and we go outside to watch the fireworks.

2 Diwali

My family is from India. We celebrate Diwali in late October or early November. Diwali lasts for five days. On the first day, we clean our houses. Then on the second day we decorate the house with flowers and small lamps called diyas. This is why Diwali is also called the festival of lights. On the third day our relatives visit and we eat lovely food. We also have fireworks. On the fourth day we visit our friends' houses and give them presents. On the fifth day there is more eating and celebrating.

3 Thanksgiving

In America we celebrate a big public holiday in November called Thanksgiving. It's a special day to say thank you for all the food we have. We go to my grandparents' house with my aunt and uncle and our cousins and have a big traditional dinner. We eat roast turkey with cranberry sauce for our main course. Then we have pumpkin pie for dessert. It's delicious! Some people go to church at Thanksgiving. There are also parades in some towns and cities with entertainment such as dancers and music.

4 Eid al-Fitr

My grandparents are from the United Arab Emirates and we are Muslim so we celebrate Eid al-Fitr. Eid al-Fitr is a three-day celebration at the end of Ramadan. It's a public holiday so we can spend lots of time with our families and friends. We get up early and go to the mosque. After that we eat together and give each other presents. We make special food like biscuits and honey cake. We often wear new clothes for the celebration and visit our friends. People hug each other to show they are friends.

Vocabulary

What do you celebrate?
We celebrate …
We go to …
church
the mosque
the synagogue
the temple
There's …
a festival
a parade
There are fireworks.
We give presents / gifts.
It's a …
celebration
public holiday
special day

3 Discuss in small groups. *Do you celebrate any of the special days from texts 1–4 in activity 2? Do you have any similar celebrations?*

4 Read the texts again. Decide if each statement is true (T) or false (F).

1 Hogmanay is in summer.   **T/F**

2 Diwali is also called the festival of lights.   **T/F**

3 Thanksgiving is an international celebration.   **T/F**

4 People often wear new clothes at Eid al-Fitr.   **T/F**

5 Find words in the texts for the following:

1 members of your family

2 a thing that explodes and makes bright lights in the sky

3 a line of people or vehicles moving through a public place to celebrate

4 a day when most people don't have to go to work or school

5 to put your arms around someone and hold them tightly

6 one of the parts of a tree that have leaves, flowers and fruit

7 to make a place look more attractive by adding things to it

8 a type of large bird that can be cooked and eaten

> ## Grammar
>
> **Suffixes**
> You can change some verbs into nouns by adding letters to the end of the word. These letters are called a suffix. There are lots of different suffixes but some common ones are:
>
> *-ation / -tion*
>
> *educate > education*
>
> *-er*
>
> *sing > singer*
>
> *-ment*
>
> *advertise > advertisement*
>
> More? ➔ Grammar

6 Read the grammar box and then find examples of each suffix in texts 1–4. What verbs do the nouns come from?

7 Copy and complete the table with the correct form of the nouns using the suffixes *–ation / -tion*, *-er* or *-ment*.

Verb	Noun
teach	
decorate	
employ	
build	
bake	
retire	
promote	

8 Complete the sentences with the correct words from activity 7.

1 We're going out to celebrate tonight because my dad got a … at work.

2 My uncle works at a secondary school. He's a maths ….

3 My grandad isn't enjoying his … He says he's bored and wants to go back to work.

9 Write a paragraph about New Year. Think about:

- Is New Year important in your family and in your country?
- Who do you celebrate it with?
- What do you do? What do you eat?
- What's your opinion of the celebrations?

9.3 What we eat

1 **Discuss.** *What food is popular in your country?*
Do you like it? Why or why not?

Learning aims

- Read an email about food in the UK
- Give a presentation about a typical British food
- Make comments on others' presentations
- Write an email about typical foods in my country
- Look at verb patterns in sentences

2 **Read the email from Tao. Where is he?**

Hi Mum and Dad,

I'm having a lovely time in London. I didn't expect to like the food, but don't worry – I'm eating very well. Sue, the mum in my exchange family, is an excellent cook. I expected to eat fish and chips every day but British people eat a lot of different types of food.

The first evening I was here, Sue cooked spaghetti. She explained to me that British people love Italian food. They often eat pasta and pizza. The next evening she made chicken korma, which is a curry. She said that British people love curries and other spicy foods. Did you know that there is a British breakfast called kedgeree? It's made from curried rice, fish and boiled eggs? Sue has promised to cook it for me next weekend. She says I can help her make it.

I asked her if the family eat roast beef every Sunday and she laughed. She told me that roast beef is a traditional meal. It started because people used to go to church every Sunday morning and they used to put the meat and vegetables in the oven and it cooked while they were out. They asked me to try it. I wasn't sure that I would like Sunday roast but it was delicious. It made me feel very happy.

See you soon!
Tao

3 **Read Tao's email again and answer the questions.**

1 What did Tao expect to eat in London?

2 Who does Tao think is an excellent cook?

3 What did Tao have for dinner on his first evening in London?

4 What meal is Tao going to help Sue cook?

5 When do people eat kedgeree?

6 Why did people used to have roast beef on a Sunday?

Study tip

When you are answering questions about a text remember to look at the question words, *What*, *Where*, *Who*, *How many*, etc. These tell you what kind of information you are looking for.

Vocabulary

I like / don't like …
beans
beef
boiled eggs
chips
curry
fish
fish and chips
meat
pasta
pizza
rice
roast dinner
salad
spicy food
vegetables
I put the meat in the oven.
She's a good cook.
She cooks dinner.
She let me help her (to) cook.
She made me try the soup.
She promised to cook it for me.
I didn't expect to like the food.

4 **Complete the sentences using the information in the first sentence.**

1 'Shall I cook?' ➜ Tao offered …

2 'Sue showed me how to make kedgeree.' ➜ Tao learned …

3 'Please do the washing up, Tao.' ➜ Sue asked …

4 'You must speak in English, Tao.' ➜ They reminded …

5 'I found the correct word in the dictionary.' ➜ The dictionary helped …

6 'You must try the soup, Tao.' ➜ Sue made …

5 **Work in pairs. Find out information about ONE of the following traditional British foods. Prepare a presentation about it.**

Cornish pasty   Eton mess   haggis

ploughman's lunch

● What does it look like? – find a photo or draw a picture

● What is it made of?

● How is it made?

● Who eats it and for what meal?

● What is its history?

● Any other interesting facts

6 **Give your presentation to your group or to the class. Listen to the other presentations and copy and complete the table for them.**

Presenters: Topic:	Excellent	Good	OK
Information			
Presentation			
English fluency			
English pronunciation			
Answers to questions			
My comments: My help:			

7 **Suzy is your friend from England. She is visiting your country. Write an email from Suzy to her parents about the food she is eating in your country.**

Grammar

Two verbs in a sentence
Sometimes we use two verbs together in a sentence.
You use a verb + *to* + infinitive with some common verbs of saying and thinking:
agree choose decide expect hope learn offer plan promise
Sue **has promised to cook** next weekend.

You use verb + object + *to* + infinitive with some verbs:
advise tell ask remind order expect
They **asked me to try** it.

You use *make* + object + infinitive (without *to*) to talk about how you feel because of someone or something.
It **made me feel** very happy.

You can use *help* + object + infinitive (without *to*) …
She says I can **help her make** it.
Or with *to*
She says I can **help her to make** it.

More? ➜ Grammar

Study tip

Speaking to others in English can be scary. But don't worry!
Follow these tips and ideas:

● Practise your presentation a lot so you know what you want to say.

● Video or audio record yourself doing the presentation. Then listen to the recording and think about what you can improve.

● Try not to read from notes – it's better for the listener if you don't.

● Look up when you are speaking and relax your face. You will speak more clearly.

● Slow down! People often speak too quickly and this is difficult for the listener. Take time to smile.

● Ask questions. This will help you to relax and keep your listeners interested in your presentation.

● Keep going. Don't worry if you say the wrong word or forget something.

9.4 Globalization

Learning aims
- Read and understand a text about globalization
- Understand some difficult words in a text from the context
- Recognise some adverbs of degree

1 Read the definition of globalization below. Discuss.
What do you know about multinational companies?
What multinational companies are there in your country?

- *I think that … are examples of multinational companies in our country.*
- *They make / sell …*
- *It's a British / American / Chinese company.*

Countries around the world are becoming more connected due to the increase in international business. Many companies now have offices or shops **all** around the world and sell or make their goods in more than one country. These companies are called multinationals and this process is called globalization.

2 Read the article below and match headings 1–3 to paragraphs A–C.

1 Why globalization is positive
2 How globalization has happened
3 Why globalization is negative

Vocabulary

It's … the price.
a quarter of
half of
a third of

All you've ever wanted to know about globalization

A Globalization is not new, but it is happening **1 much** more quickly now than in the past. This is because of **2 very** big improvements in transport, the internet and mobile technology. It can also be cheaper to produce things in another country. Many multinational companies employ workers in poorer countries at **3 just** half or a third of the salary they have to pay employees in their own countries.

B Multinational companies from rich countries often build factories or offices in poorer countries. This can bring money and jobs into that country and helps the local people. Globalization is not **4 only** about business. It also helps people to share ideas, experiences and culture. It also makes people think much more about what is happening in other parts of the world than their own, which makes them better world citizens.

C Sometimes multinational companies allow their workers in poorer countries to work in bad conditions, for example, they may work long hours without enough breaks. Sometimes it's **5 quite** hard for a small local company to compete for business against a multinational company. Some people say that multinationals are a bad thing. People **6 really** don't like seeing the same shops and businesses in every country they go to. They don't want to lose their identity and their culture.

3 **Read the grammar box. Then find the words in bold 1–6 in the text and do the following:**

1 Check the meanings.

2 Read the sentences without the adverbs of degree.

3 Notice how the adverb of degree adds emphasis to the sentence.

4 **Find these words in the text and match them with the definitions.**

citizen   identity

1 who you are and the qualities that make you different from others

2 a person who belongs to a particular place (usually a country)

5 **Read the text again. Choose the correct answers according to the text.**

1 The reason globalization is happening much more quickly now is that …

A more people are starting their own companies.

B more people speak English now.

C we have better communication.

2 People who work for a multinational country get …

A the same salary wherever they live.

B a different salary depending on where they live.

C a lower salary if they live in a rich country.

3 Globalization can …

A create more jobs.

B help people start companies.

C make everyone richer.

4 World citizens …

A travel a lot.

B know what is happening in other countries.

C have family in different countries.

5 Globalization can make people in poorer countries worry that they will …

A lose their identity.   B lose their language.

C have to build new cities.

6 Globalization might make some small companies …

A rich.   B open.   C close.

6 **Discuss.** *Do you think globalization is a positive thing? Would you like to work for a multinational company? Why / Why not?*

Grammar

Adverbs of degree
You use adverbs of degree to show how much something happens. Adverbs of degree can change verbs, adjectives and other adverbs.
*Many companies now have offices or shops **all** around the world.*

More? ➔ Grammar

Vocabulary

all
exactly
instead
just
much
not enough
only
quite
really
very
without

9.5 We are world citizens

Learning aims

- Discuss what a 'world citizen' means
- Read an article about being a world citizen
- Listen to a teenager talking about being a world citizen
- Write a magazine article about being a world citizen
- Learn the second conditional

1 **Discuss.** *What is a world citizen?*

Vocabulary

to be a world citizen
to go travelling
to have an identity
to learn another language

2 **Read the article. Decide if the sentences are true (T) or false (F).**

1	To be a world citizen you have to be interested in new ideas.	T/F
2	You have to find a new cultural identity.	T/F
3	Learning another language or languages helps you to become a better world citizen.	T/F
4	It's not important to know what is happening in other countries.	T/F
5	It's never a good thing to tell people what you think about world issues.	T/F

Do you need a passport to be a world citizen?

Don't worry! You don't need any documents to be a world citizen. You don't have to travel far either. You just have to like meeting new people, enjoy food and music from different countries and be interested in what is happening in the world.

Do I have to give up my identity to be a world citizen?

No, no one should ever give up or lose their culture or identity. We understand the world better if we know where our families and our neighbours come from and what they believe in. Ask your parents and grandparents to tell you about your family history.

How can I understand other people if we come from different cultures?

Listen and talk to other people about their country and their lives. Compare your stories. If you learn another language or go travelling, you will be able to understand those cultures better.

Why is it important to know what is happening around the world?

You must watch and read the news to find out about life in other countries. If you understand what is happening in another country and whether it is good or bad, then you will understand that culture and the world better.

Should I share what I think as a world citizen?

Yes, of course. You should say if you think something is wrong in the world. You can follow stories in the news online and tell people what you think and why.

3 **Tell your partner how much you think you are a world citizen and why.**

I think I am / am not a world citizen because …
I like / don't like …
I am / am not interested in …
I agree / disagree that you must …
I believe / don't believe that it's important to …

4 **Work in groups. Name some things that are important to world citizens.**

- *I think education is important.*
- *I agree / disagree.*

5 **In your groups, make a word cloud, like the one in the article, with your ideas from activity 4. Compare your word cloud with another group's.**

6 **Listen to Amaya talking about herself. What does she mention?** 🔊 9.4

travelling   social media   the media
languages   school

7 **Discuss. Do you think Amaya is a good world citizen? Why or why not?**

8 **Match the sentence halves. Listen again and check.** 🔊 9.4

1 If I had more time,
2 If I had better Wi-Fi at home,
3 If I lived in a big city,

a I would try and help stop climate change.
b I would read the news online.
c I would learn another language.

9 **Complete the second conditional sentences using the verbs in bold.**

1 If I _____ (have) enough money, I _____ (buy) some new trainers.

2 If I _____ (see) a famous film actor, I _____ (not speak) to them.

3 If you _____ (go) to bed now, you _____ (not feel) tired tomorrow.

4 If Karim _____ (arrive) in the next five minutes, we _____ (not miss) the start of the film.

5 If Yana _____ (tidy) her room, I'm sure she _____ (find) her black jeans.

10 **Write answers to the questions. Use the second conditional.**

1 What would you buy if you had more money?

2 What would you learn to do if you had more time?

3 Where would you go if you went travelling? How long would you go for?

11 **Write an article for your school magazine about why it's important for teenagers to become better world citizens, and how they can do this.**

Write 130–140 words.

> ### Grammar
>
> **Second conditional**
> You use the second conditional to talk about an unlikely or impossible situation.
> The second conditional has two parts to the sentence: *if* + past simple, … *would* + infinitive
> *If I had more time, I would learn another language.* = I don't have more time but I'm imagining that I do.
>
> One part of the sentence depends on the other part of the sentence happening.
> You can put either part of the sentence first. If the part of the sentence with *if* in it comes last, you don't need a comma.
> *I would learn another language if I had more time.*
>
> More? ➜ Grammar

A 'melting pot' is a phrase used to describe a place where two or more nationalities, cultures or identities live together.

New Zealand

Maori were the first people to make their homes in New Zealand. They arrived there more than 1000 years ago from islands in the Pacific Ocean. Their history, language and culture are part of New Zealand's identity. They speak their own language Te Reo Maori as well as English. Both Te Reo Maori and English are official languages in New Zealand. The names of many places in New Zealand are in the Maori language, for example Rotorua.

Many New Zealanders believe that Maori culture has a positive affect on everyone in New Zealand. They believe it helps people to understand the importance of family. It makes them listen more to older people. It also helps them to understand and accept different cultures and it makes them care more about the environment.

moko / Maori tattoo

80ᶜ

NEW ZEALAND

1 **Read the text and complete the sentences. Choose A, B or C.**

1 Maori people live in …

   A North America

   B Australia

   C New Zealand.

2 Maoris have their own …

   A language.

   B schools.

   C cities.

3 In New Zealand …

   A people do not like the Maoris.

   B Maori culture is disappearing.

   C Maoris and other New Zealanders share ideas.

Find out

1 *Where is New Zealand? Where is Rotorua in New Zealand?*

2 *What are some important Maori words? What do they mean?*

3 *The name of a famous Maori person. Why is he or she famous?*

New York, USA

New York is often called a 'melting pot'. People have come from many different places and cultures around the world to live in New York. Did you know that over 800 languages are spoken there?

Jane travelled to New York in her summer holidays. She says, "It was amazing. It was very lively with so many different people, different kinds of food, and different music. I heard lots of different languages, too. It's not like that where I live. At first, it was a bit scary, but after a while I loved it. I also saw lots of different religious buildings. There were churches, mosques, temples and synagogues. I talked to lots of people about their religion and their family history. I learned so much about different cultures. I think New York is a great place. If I didn't have to go to school, I'd move to New York tomorrow!"

2 **Read the text and answer the questions.**

1 How many languages are spoken in New York?
2 When did Jane travel to New York?
3 How did Jane feel at first in New York?
4 What did she talk to different people about?
5 What would Jane like to do?

3 **Last month you travelled to either New Zealand or New York, USA. Write an email to your friend about it.**

- Explain what the culture was like. Was it a melting pot?
- Describe a person you met.
- Say what you talked about.
- Say how you felt being there.
- Explain why you felt this way.

Write 130–140 words.

Discuss

Is it important to learn about other cultures?

Do you live in a 'melting pot'?

I think it is important / isn't important because …
What do you think?
I agree / disagree …
I think we should / ought to…
I think I live in a melting pot because there is …
I don't think I live in a melting pot because there isn't / aren't …

The same …

In 2000, more than a third of all the people who were living in New York were born in a different country.

How many people were born in a different country where you live?

but different

Review

1 Ulima is talking about herself. Listen and choose the correct answers. 🎧 **9.5**

1 Ulima is talking about her favourite …

   a food   **b** celebration   **c** part of her country

2 It happens in …

   a February   **b** March   **c** April

3 It's possible to learn about …

   a culture   **b** camels   **c** different countries

4 Ulima goes with her …

   a class   **b** friends   **c** family

5 The day is very …

   a long   **b** relaxing   **c** typical

6 The next day, Ulima …

   a goes camel riding   **b** stays at home   **c** goes to a different festival

7 If she could, she would …

   a celebrate more festivals   **b** celebrate this festival more often   **c** move to a different region in her country

2 Read and complete the postcard from Fred. Use the words from the box.

> delayed   fireworks   kind   parade   promised   public

Hi Mum and Dad,

How are you? I'm having a great time here on my school exchange. The family I'm staying with are really **1** _____. Tomorrow is a **2** _____ holiday here so no one is going to school or work. There will be a big **3** _____ in the street with dancers and music bands. The family have **4** _____ to take me. There will also be **5** _____ over the city at about 9 pm when it gets dark. I'm very excited – I'm sure it will be lovely. I'll see you on Sunday, although I think my flight might be **6** _____ because of all the celebrations.

See you soon!

Fred

3 Change these first conditional sentences into second conditional sentences.

1 If I go to college, I'll study Global Studies.

2 If my dad retires, he'll play golf every day.

3 If Mona listens in class, she'll do well in the exams.

4 If the air-conditioning at school breaks, we will go home this afternoon.

5 If the trousers are too tight, I won't buy them.

4 Choose the sentence that is true.

1 The second conditional is used to talk about things which might happen in the future.

2 The second conditional is used to talk about things which probably won't happen in the future.

5 **Talk about yourself to your partner. Answer the questions.**

- How did you celebrate your last birthday?
- What is your favourite celebration? Why? What do you do during this celebration?
- Have you ever been on a school exchange?
  If yes, where did you go? What did you enjoy? What didn't you enjoy? If no, would you like to go on a school exchange? Why or why not? If yes, where would you like to go?

- What have you learned to do this year?
- What has made you feel happy recently?
- Has anything made you cry recently?
- What would you say if you met the King or Queen of England?
- What would you do if you won lots of money?

How are you doing?

Read and copy the checklist below. Think and decide for each objective: **very well**, **quite well**, or **OK, but I need more practise**.

Use the checklist to help you improve your English.

> **How to improve**
>
> To show what you know, try to use present, past and future sentences in your writing.

I can …	Very well	Quite well	OK, but I need more practice
• greet people I know and people I don't know			
• understand people talking about their experience on school exchanges			
• use modal passives to give my opinions about school exchanges			
• read and understand texts about different celebrations			
• understand the meanings of difficult words from context			
• write about a celebration			
• recognise some noun suffixes			
• understand the writer's attitude in an email about food in the UK			
• give a group presentation about a typical British food			
• write an email about typical foods in my country			
• read and understand a text about globalization			
• recognise some adverbs of degree and how they change the meaning of a sentence			
• understand a teenager talking about herself as a world citizen			
• write a magazine article about being a world citizen			
• use the second conditional to talk about things in the future that are probably not going to be true			

Words and phrases – Unit 9

Adjectives for food

cooked _____
fresh _____
raw _____
spicy _____
sweet _____

Adverbs of degree

all _____
exactly _____
instead _____
just _____
much _____
not enough _____
only _____
quite _____
really _____
very _____
without _____

Celebrations

What do you celebrate? _____
We celebrate … _____
We go to … _____
church _____
the mosque _____
the synagogue _____
the temple _____
There's … _____
a festival _____
a parade _____
There are fireworks _____
We give presents / gifts. _____
It's a … _____
celebration _____
public holiday _____
special day _____
It's my birthday. _____
New year _____
religion _____
to celebrate _____
wedding anniversary _____

Fractions

It's … the price. _____
a quarter of _____
half of _____
a third of _____

Greetings and expressions

Bye! _____
Excuse me. _____
first name _____
Good afternoon. _____
Goodbye. _____
Good evening. _____
Good morning. _____
Hello! / Hi! _____
How are you? _____
   I'm (not) well. _____
How annoying! _____
How interesting! _____
How's it going? _____
How nice! _____
I have to go. _____
Nice to meet you _____
Pardon? _____
See you later / tomorrow. _____
Sorry. _____
surname _____
Thank you. _____
Thank you, but I can't. _____
   Let's do it another day. _____
to hug _____
to kiss _____
Welcome! _____
What a good idea! _____
What a pity! _____
What a shame! _____
Why don't we …? / _____
   Shall we … ? _____

Meals

breakfast _____
dessert _____
dinner _____
lunch _____
main course _____
meal _____
picnic _____
starter _____

On a school exchange

The train is … _____
cancelled _____
delayed _____
The parents are … _____
kind _____
lovely _____
nice _____
strange _____
strict _____
I'm going to stay with
   the Hilton family. _____
The plane might be
   delayed. _____

Things to eat with / cook with
bowl ___
chopsticks ___
cup ___
fork ___
glass ___
knife ___
mug ___
pan ___
plate ___
pot ___
saucer ___
spoon ___

Typical foods
I like … ___
beans ___
beef ___
boiled eggs ___
cheese ___
chilli ___
chips ___
curry ___
fish ___
fish and chips ___
flour ___
honey ___
meat ___
pasta ___
pepper ___
pizza ___
rice ___
roast dinner ___
salad ___
sandwich ___
seafood ___
soup ___
spicy food ___
toast ___
vegetables ___
I put the meat in the oven. ___
She's a good cook. ___
She cooks dinner. ___
She let me help her (to) cook. ___
She made me try the soup. ___
She promised to cook it for me. ___
I didn't expect to like the food. ___

Verb phrases related to globalization
to be a world citizen ___
to go travelling ___
to have an identity ___
to learn another language ___

Verbs related to food
to be full ___
to be hungry ___
to be thirsty ___
to boil ___
to chop ___
to cook ___
to drink / have a drink ___
to freeze ___
to fry ___
to get lunch / dinner ready ___
to go on a diet ___
to have a barbecue ___
to prepare food ___
to roast ___
to serve ___

10 Communication and technology

1 **Discuss.** *Which three technological devices do you use most every day?*

2 **Match the words from the box to the pictures a–l.**

> article bill book brochure certificate comic form
> letter magazine newspaper note notebook

a 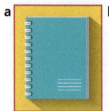 b  c  d 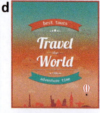 e  f

g  h  i  j  k  l

3 **Copy the table and add the items from activity 2.**
You need to use some words more than once.

read	*a book*
look at	
write	
complete / fill in	
write in	
ask for the	
get / receive	

4 **Discuss.** *Which of the items a–l do you …*

- *rarely use or need*
- *(almost) never use*
- *use mostly for studying*
- *use mostly to relax*

> Use **adverbs of degree** to talk about how much or how often you do something:
>
> I *rarely* read a book at home/to relax.
> I *mostly* take notes in my notebook at school.
> I *almost never* read a newspaper.

5 **Read the sentences about technology. Choose the correct adjective.**

1 You have to be _____ when you buy things online and make sure your money is safe.

   a careful   **b** glad   **c** well-known

2 The internet is not _____ in my country. You need to pay for it each month.

   a well-known   **b** glad   **c** free of charge

3 In my house the internet service is very _____. I can download a file in a few seconds.

   a electric   **b** comfortable **c** fast

4 I always take my phone with me when I go out. It doesn't feel _____, if I don't have my phone in my bag.

   a silly   **b** normal   **c** previous

5 You have to pay a _____ price to get the latest phone.

   a high   **b** hard   **c** free-of-charge

6 I would like an _____ car because they don't use petrol.

   a electric   **b** normal   **c** previous

7 Multinationals are usually _____ global brands.

   a hard   **b** normal   **c** well-known

8 I think it's _____ to spend a lot of money on a pair of trainers.

   a silly   **b** comfortable **c** well-known

9 The new model of this phone has a bigger screen. The _____ model was smaller.

   a well-known   **b** previous   **c** before

10 I'm _____ that I live in the modern world because I love technology.

   a comfortable   **b** hard   **c** glad

6 **Work with a partner. Do you agree with the statements in activity 5?**

- *I completely agree …*
- *I totally disagree …*
- *I'm not sure because …*

Vocabulary

to be …
careful
comfortable
electric
fast
free / free of charge
glad
hard
high
modern
normal
safe
silly
well-known
It feels / doesn't feel … if I …
silly
normal
I'm glad
The … model
previous
next
to download (a file)
(the) internet
online
screen
technology

10.1 Technology and me

1   **Discuss:** *How much do you like technology? What do you think a 'techie' is?*

Spoken language	
You sometimes use **nouns as verbs** especially when speaking:	
Can you send a *message*?	(noun)
I'll *message* you later.	(verb)
You also use **short forms** of words when speaking:	
I hate old *tech* (= technology) You're a *techie*! (= you like technology very much).	*Adding '-ie' or 'y'* often makes nouns *very informal*: He's a *foodie*! (= He loves good food.)

2   **Do the quiz. Then check your answers.**

Communication Quiz

Are you a TECHIE?

1   You need to write something. What do you do?

   A   I write with pen and paper of course!

   B   I type using a keyboard, mouse and computer. Easy!

   C   I speak into my phone and it types the words for me. It's **easier**!

2   You need to get in touch with a friend you haven't seen for a long time.

   A   I'd write a letter and post it to them. Everyone loves getting a letter, don't they?

   B   It's best to pick up the phone and speak to them, isn't it? You can't just send a message after so long, can you?

   C   It would be strange to just call them, wouldn't it? I'd message them.

3 Compare your answers and discuss. Do you agree with your 'type' A, B, or C?

4 Read about tag questions and find examples in the quiz.

5 Choose the correct tag question.

1 Mobile phones are really useful, *are / aren't* they?
2 Watching TV isn't good for you, *is / isn't* it?
3 You need new shoes, *do / don't* you?
4 This car isn't very expensive, *is / isn't* it?
5 Social media is tiring, *is / isn't it*?

6 Listen and check the sentences in activity 5. Then listen again and repeat. 🔊10.1

We use the adverb **anyway** to make an opinion or point stronger: | I don't really need a mobile phone *anyway*! You should get a new one *anyway*!'

7 Practise making and responding to tag questions. Use these ideas:

* *Technology is useful.*
* *Mobile phones are too expensive.*
* *Going to the cinema is fun.*

Technology is useful, isn't it?
Yes it is! It really helps me with school work.

Grammar

Tag questions
You use **tag questions** to check information and ask for agreement. If the sentence is positive, you use a negative tag question. If the sentence is negative, you use a positive tag question.
*You're a techie, **aren't** you?*
*You're not a techie, **are** you?*
More? → Grammar

Vocabulary

audio book
broken
expensive
headphones
landline
message / text message
social media
tech
techie
type

---

3 It's holiday time! How do you relax?

A I pick up my favourite book – a long one – and read it all day!

B I download an audio book and listen to it on my headphones.

C I don't like reading or listening to books. I prefer to spend time with my friends and look at my social media on my phone.

4 Your mobile phone is broken. What do you say?

A 'Never mind! I don't really need a mobile phone anyway. I can still make calls on the landline telephone in my house'.

B 'Mum, Dad, can I have your old phone? You should buy a new one anyway!'

C 'I'm happy, actually! My old phone was more than a year old. Now I can get a new one. All my friends have a new phone!'

Answers
Mostly 'A': You like old-fashioned communication, like books and letters. Are you over 100? Your grandparents will be pleased!
Mostly 'B': You like a mix of older types of communication and more modern ones. And you feel comfortable talking to people. Maybe your family and friends are good communicators too?
Mostly 'C': You are a techie! You love new tech, and you hate having old tech, don't you?

10.2 Life then and now

1 **Discuss.** *What technology did your parents and grandparents use to have when they were younger?*

- *How was the technology different?*
- *How was the technology the same?*

Learning aims

- Compare technology in the past and now
- Listen to someone talk about technology in the past
- Practise talking about the past and now
- Describe what is about to happen

2 Listen to a girl talking about her family and technology. Number the photos in order. (10.2)

a

b

c

d

3 Listen again and decide if the statements are true (T) or false (F). (10.2)

1 Tara's grandma, Helen, has never had a mobile phone. **T/F**

2 Helen had a phone when she was young. **T/F**

3 Tara has always had the internet. **T/F**

4 The photo shows how someone in Tara's family used to travel. **T/F**

5 There were cars in John's village. **T/F**

6 Tara's aunt has an electric bike. **T/F**

4 Complete the conversation using the correct words from the box.

> didn't have have had had used
> used to was were

- Grandma, **1** _____ there any cars when you were young?

- Yes, of course. Cars were invented a long time before I was born!

- And **2** _____ there a phone in your house?

- Yes, we **3** _____ two!

- Did you **4** _____ a car?

- No, we **5** _____. We **6** _____ travel by bus and train.

- How long **7** _____ you had your mobile phone?

- I've **8** _____ it for nearly six years.

- Why didn't you get one before?

- I didn't need one. I always **9** _____ the phone in my house instead!

5 Choose the best option to complete the sentences.

1 You're late! Dad was *about to / about* phone you.

2 This book is *about / about to* a young man who plays football.

3 I'm *going / about to* buy a new laptop.

4 *Do you / Are you* about to take a photo?

6 Discuss these questions with a partner.

- *How has technology changed in the last ten years?*

- *How has life changed because of technology?*

- *Which of these changes do you think are positive? Why? / Why not?*

Grammar

Past tense
You use different **past tenses** in different situations:
You use **past simple** for facts:
There was a phone in her house.
She *didn't have* a mobile phone.

You use **present perfect** to describe an action that started in the past and is still true.
She's had a mobile phone for about five years.

You use *used to* to describe a past habit.
He *used to go* to work by horse.

More? ➜ Grammar

Grammar

about to + infinitive
You use *to be* + *about to* + verb without *to* to say what is going to happen very soon.
He is about to go to work and that is why he's looking so smart.

She's about to buy this new electric car.

More? ➜ Grammar

Vocabulary

electric
great
picture
plug in
quiet
transport

10.3 Technology in the home

Learning aims
- Learn words to describe your home
- Read about intelligent homes
- Discuss technology in the future
- Use some phrasal verbs to give commands

1 **Discuss.** *What modern technology do you have in your home? Which rooms have technological devices?*

2 **Look at the pictures of rooms in a home and find these things. Make sentences and say where they are.**

There's a mirror above the sink in the bathroom.

> armchair carpet chest of drawers cupboard light mirror rug shelf shelves sink
> sofa tap towel

3 **Discuss.** *Have you ever been in an intelligent home? Which things can you name in this picture?*

4 Read the title of the article on the opposite page and look at the photo. What do you think it will say about intelligent homes? Make a list of words you think you will read in the text.

5 Read the article. Does the writer say intelligent homes are real or just a dream?

More Intelligent Homes

Do you ever talk to your home? Is it possible to communicate with your furniture? This is already happening in some homes, and this is what the future will be like.

Just imagine you are lying in the bath and you want to listen to some music. Say to your speakers 'Play me a relaxing song!' Is it too dark in your bedroom but you don't want to get up and turn the lights up? Just say: "Turn up the lights!"

If you notice that the temperature in your room is a little cold, don't worry! It's so easy to say: 'Turn up the heating by one degree.' But if the room is too hot, no problem. Just say what you want and it will happen. 'Open the window for five minutes and then close it again!'

After a shower, you put the dirty towels in the washing machine. When you say, 'Wash the towels at 40°', the washing machine will turn itself on. Then you walk into the kitchen and find a message on your phone. It's from your fridge and it says: 'You need more milk. I have ordered it.' And if you are out and you need to cook something that will be ready when you come home? Just send a text message to the cooker from your phone!

In fact, you can control everything in your home because of something called the IOT, or the Internet of Things. You must connect all your devices, such as your washing machine, your TV and your heating to the internet and this lets them talk to each other. And you can use the buttons in an intelligent sofa to control anything you want in your house!

6 Now read the article again and decide if the statements are true (T) or false (F).

1 The writer describes talking to a bathroom. **T/F**

2 The writer doesn't like intelligent homes. **T/F**

3 Only the bathroom is an intelligent room. **T/F**

4 The fridge in a smart home can order your shopping for you. **T/F**

5 You don't need a mobile phone to control the intelligent technology. **T/F**

6 You need to connect all the technology in your home to use the IOT. **T/F**

> **Grammar**
>
> **Phrasal verbs:** *turn + preposition*
> *turn on / off*
> the washing machine = start / stop
>
> turn *down / up*
> the lights / heating = less / more (of something)
>
> We can use phrasal verbs as commands:
> ***Turn off** the washing machine!*
>
> More? ➜ Grammar

7 Discuss the questions with a partner.

- *What will technology in the home be like in the future?*
- *What new technology will there be at school?*
- *Would you like to live in an intelligent home? Why / Why not?*

8 With your partner, play *Guess the command.*

Turn off the TV! Close / open the door! Order some coffee!

> We often use *be + like* in questions about general descriptions.
> *What will the future **be like**?*
> We don't usually use *like* in answers:
>
> | What**'s** the weather *like* today? | It**'s** ~~like~~ sunny. |
> |---|---|
>
> We can use *there + will be* to answer the question with *like* about the future:
>
> | What will technology *be like* in the future? | *There will be* more intelligent technology in our homes. |
> |---|---|

10.4 Technology in the future

1 **Discuss** *Can you imagine cities in the future? How will they be different? Will we live on a different planet?*

2 **Look at the pictures of the future. Find examples of:**

- types of power
- types of transport
- homes of the future

Learning aims

- Read and listen to predictions about the future
- Discuss cities of the future
- Use *think* + *will* to make predictions about the future
- Learn to use discourse markers

Vocabulary

Compound nouns
electric vehicle
flying car
mobile phone app
petrol car
solar power
sunlight

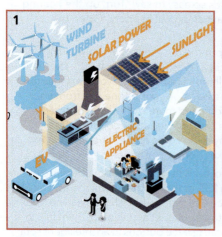

3 **Read and listen to texts A–C and match them to the pictures 1–3.** (10.3)

A

I think that in the future we will move to another planet. There will be a lot of people, so they will have to live in very small flats in tall buildings. But I think that life will be very similar to now. Children will go to school and adults will go to work. However, it will be quite dark because there won't be any sunlight. So, we will need a new type of power for lights.

Ran

B

I think that in the future our cities will look very different. We will build very tall buildings with lifts and we will have enormous parks on the outside of the cities. I also think we will move around the city in small electric flying cars. There will be cleaner air and blue skies. I don't think anyone will type or write anymore. Instead, I think we'll only talk to our computers and use our voice to control machines.

Amishi

C

I think that in the future we will live on this planet, but we will change how we use energy. We will use the wind and the sun to give power to our cars and homes. In the future we will need a very large battery at home for power. I think everybody will drive an electric vehicle. There won't be any more petrol cars. We will control cars and things in the home with mobile phone apps and our voices. And we will cycle more, so the roads will be safer.

Wang

4 **Read again. Who thinks that …**

1 … there will be a problem with weather?   Wang / Amishi / Ran
2 … we will drive electric vehicles?   Wang / Amishi / Ran
3 … we will use our voices to control things?   Wang / Amishi / Ran
4 … people will live in very tall buildings?   Wang / Amishi / Ran
5 … life won't be very different?   Wang / Amishi / Ran

5 **Discuss with your partner.** *Who do you agree with most: Wang, Amishi or Ran? Why?*

6 **Choose the correct option to complete the sentences.**

1 *I think we don't will / I don't think we* will fly in cars.
2 *I think cities won't to look / I think cities won't look* different.
3 *I will not think that / I don't think that* we will live on another planet.
4 *Do you think we will / Do you think will we* all drive electric cars?

Grammar

Predictions with *think*
You use *think (that)* + *will* for predictions, either positive or negative:
*I **think that** in the future our cities **will** look very different.*

*I **don't think we will** type with our fingers anymore.*

More? ➔ Grammar

Discourse markers show the listener or reader what ideas are coming next. For example: ***also, instead, and …, so***	You use *also* to add another idea to an idea:	*I **think** that in the future our cities will look very different.* *I **also think** we will move around the city in electric flying cars.*
	You use *instead* to talk about a different or opposite idea:	*I don't think anyone will type or write anymore.* ***Instead**, I think we'll only talk to our computers and use our voice to control machines.*
	You use *and* to add another idea, and **so** to explain the result	***And** we will cycle more, **so** the roads will be safer.*

Vocabulary

battery
building
computer
electric
energy
enormous
flat
lift*
machine
park
petrol
planet
power
sun
voice
wind
to control
to cycle
to drive
to fly
to type
to write
(*American English = elevator)

---

7 **Work with a partner. Make predictions about technology and the future. Use the topics below.**

I think … we will / won't …

I also think … we will / won't / there will be / won't be … .

I don't think we'll … .   I think we will … instead.

And we will … , so …

education   communication   jobs

food   home   transport

10.5 New worlds

1 **Discuss.** *Do you like reading comics and stories about space travel and new technology? Have you ever heard of Iron Man or other superheroes? Have you ever had dreams of inventing something new, using technologies?*

2 **Read the article about Elon Musk. Why are comic stories important for him?**

New Worlds …

In 1999, a 28 year-old businessman called Elon Musk started a company called X.com. However, this was not the first time that Elon Musk had started a business. When Elon Musk started his company X.com, he had already sold a video game to a computer company. He was 12 when he sold this video game.

Iron Man

From a young age Elon Musk dreamed of using technology for adventures. He also dreamed of going into space. As a child, he read a lot of comics, especially Iron Man. In the comics, he read about Tony Stark who built Iron Man. Elon Musk wanted to be like Tony Stark. He had seen flying cars in comics. Now he wanted to make real ones.

The Tesla Roadster

Elon Musk wanted to use technology so everyone could enjoy it. For example, he thought previous electric cars had been too expensive. He had a plan. First, he decided to make a very expensive car for rich people. He created the Tesla Roadster.

Elon Musk

Then, when Elon Musk had made a lot of money, he used it to build cheaper models. At the moment, he is trying to make space rockets for everyone. He wants to make it possible for people to travel into space. In 2018 Elon Musk sent a rocket to space with a Tesla Roadster on it! He believes that in the future people will live on another planet. Do you agree with him?

THE FUTURE IS NOW

CREW DRAGON 2019

Elon Musk's dream

3 **Read the article again. Decide if the sentences are true (T) or false (F).**

1 At the age of 27 Musk started his first business, X.com.   T/F
2 He sold something to a computer company when he was 12.   T/F
3 He thought electric cars were too expensive.   T/F
4 He made a lot of money and built cheaper cars.   T/F
5 He sent one of his cars to space.   T/F
6 He doesn't think people will ever live on another planet.   T/F

Past perfect
You use the past perfect tense to compare two actions in the past, and say which action happened *first*. The past perfect is used to talk about the 'earlier past'. Look at the timeline for Elon Musk's life.

Action 1	Action 2
He sold a video game.	He started a company.

Age 12   Age 28

*When Elon Musk started his company X.com, he **had** already **sold** a video game to a computer company.*
You use *had* + the past participle to make the past perfect. You often use the past perfect with *already*. The other verb in the sentence is usually past simple.
*This **was** not the first time that Elon Musk **had started** a business.*

More? ➔ Grammar

4 **Complete the sentences with the past perfect or past simple, using the verbs in brackets.**

1 We _____ (arrive) at the station five minutes late and the train _____ already **(leave)**.
2 I _____ **(be)** to the USA when I _____ **(be)** at school.
3 She _____ never _____ **(ride)** on an elephant before, and it _____ **(feel)** very strange!
4 Raj _____ **(dream)** of going into space when he _____ **(be)** a child.
5 When Edward _____ **(meet)** his niece Sasha again, she _____ **(grow)** twenty centimetres taller.

5 **Draw a timeline for your life.**

- Start with your birth date.
- Then add important events on the timeline with dates.
- Describe them in *past simple*: I started high school in 2018. I met my best friend in 2019. I went to France in 2020.
- Then make sentences about what happened using the *past perfect* and *past simple*: When I *met* my best friend in 2019, I *had already started* high school.

We all need language to communicate but which languages are spoken the most in the world? You might be surprised. Number one is Chinese with two billion speakers. Second is Spanish with 329 million speakers. And English is third, just behind Spanish, with 328 million speakers. Can you guess which is more popular today on the internet: English, Chinese or Spanish?

The answer is English. In 2011 there were 565 million people using English online. In 2001, there were only 187 million people using English online. But the increase in Chinese on the internet is more amazing: in 2000 there were 34 million Chinese speaking users online, and in 2011 there were 509 million! There has also been a very big increase in the number of Spanish users online.

So what are the top three languages on the internet going to be in 2050? The most popular will probably be Chinese and then Spanish. English will be the third most popular online language. These languages will probably be most the most important languages in the next 100 years. So, you should start studying them!

1 **Read the text and decide if the sentences are true (T) or false (F). Correct the false sentences.**

1 The English language is the most spoken language in the world.

2 There are more Spanish speakers in the world than English speakers.

3 There are more English users online than any other language.

4 The biggest increase online is with Spanish speakers.

5 The most popular language in the world in 2050 will be English.

2 **Write the questions for these answers.**

1 2 billion

2 329 million

3 565 million

4 509 million

Find out

1 *How many people speak English, Chinese, and Spanish in your country?*

2 *Where or how can someone in your country learn these languages?*

Study tip

Nationalities
You use the ending *-ese* for some countries:
China> Chin*ese*
Japan> Japan*ese*
Portugal> Portugu*ese*

My name is Clara and I go to an international school in the USA. In my high school we are learning English, Chinese and Spanish. My teachers say that in the future I will need all these languages to find a good job. I think the most difficult language is Chinese because there are so many characters to learn. In English there are only 26 characters! Also, the pronunciation of Chinese is quite difficult. Many words are spelled the same way but have very different meanings, and you have to learn these. I think English grammar is easier than Chinese or Spanish, but I think Spanish pronunciation is the easiest.

3 **Read the text and answer the questions about Clara.**

1 Which languages do Clara's teachers think will be most important in the future?

  a Chinese

  b English and Spanish

  c all three

2 Which is the hardest language for Clara?

  a Chinese b English c Spanish

3 Which is the easiest grammar for Clara?

  a Chinese b English c Spanish

4 Which is the hardest pronunciation for Clara?

  a Chinese b English c Spanish

4 **Write an email to a friend.**

- Give them advice about learning English, Chinese or Spanish.

- Tell them why you think they should learn this language.

- Tell them what you think will be difficult or easy for them.

Write 130–140 words.

Discuss

Is it important to learn more than one language for communication? Why / Why not?
How many languages have you learned?
How many languages do you think you will learn in the future?
I think it is / isn't important because …
What do you think?
I think people should …
I think / don't think we should learn more than one language because because in the future we will / won't …

The same …

One of the most difficult language to learn for native English speakers is Chinese.

What is the most difficult language to learn for speakers of your first language?

but different

Review

1 Ugo is talking about himself. Listen and choose the correct answers. 🔊10.4

1 Ugo has different types of …

   a phones   **b** technology   **c** computers

2 He's going to buy a new phone …

   a next year   **b** very soon   **c** in a year

3 There are really … apps on the phone he wants to get.

   a good   **b** expensive   **c** fast

4 Ugo's mum … new technology.

   a likes   **b** doesn't understand   **c** isn't interested in

5 Her phone doesn't …

   a take photos   **b** make calls   **c** have games on it

2 Read and complete the letter from Ginnie. Use the words from the box.

> be   instead   like   so   think   will

Sometimes I think about technology in the future. What will the future be
1 _____? I like to think about that. I think that in the future we
2 _____ fly cars 3 _____ of driving them. And I think that
they will 4 _____ electric 5 _____ there will be cleaner air.
I don't 6 _____ we'll live on another planet.

3 Choose the best words to complete the text.

> There is some cool **1** *technology / technologies* in our lives today. My friend Sally has an amazing bathroom. It's an **2** *ugly / intelligent* bathroom. It's so cool. She can turn **3** *in / on* the taps using her **4** *hands / voice*. I stayed in her house last week and I was so surprised when she told the lights to turn on and off again! I **5** *will / had* never seen anything like that before. I **6** *have / had* had a smart phone for years, but this was completely different. Now I want an intelligent home! It's strange to think that people **7** *use / used* to have houses with no electricity, and now our houses are controlled by our phones!

4 Choose the correct rule.

The past perfect describes:

a a single action in the past

b an action or event which happens before another.

c an action or event which follow another action.

5   **Talk about yourself to your partner. Answer the questions.**

- What are you about to do? And what is about to happen in your favourite TV show?
- When you woke up this morning, what had already happened?
- What's your favourite way to communicate with friends, parents, or grandparents? Why?

- What objects or types of technology have you turned on, turned off, turned up or turned down today?
- Do you think life will be very different next year? Why or why not?
- What will life be like in 10 years?
- If you could invent / change one thing in the future, what would it be?

How are you doing?

Read and copy the checklist below. Think and decide for each objective: **very well, quite well,** or **OK, but I need more practise**.

Use the checklist to help you improve your English.

> **How to improve**
>
> To show what you know, try to use different past tenses together in your speaking and writing.

I can ...	Very well	Quite well	OK, but I need more practice
• use words to describe documents and texts.			
• use adverbs of degree			
• use a variety of adjectives to describe people, places and things			
• understand details from people talking about their experiences of technology			
• talk about how I use technology			
• use tag questions to check facts and opinions, and to see if someone agrees with me			
• understand a text about intelligent homes			
• use future tenses to discuss technology in the future			
• use *be like* to make predictions for the future			
• use phrasal verbs to make commands			
• understand and use words to describe natural energy and types of transport			
• read, listen to and make predictions about the future			
• discuss cities of the future			
• learn and use *think + will*			
• use discourse markers to build an argument			
• read a text about a famous businessman and his inventions			
• discuss technology in the future			
• talk about past events using the past perfect and past simple			
• Make and discuss my personal timeline			

Words and phrases – Unit 10

Common adjectives

careful _____
comfortable _____
electric _____
expensive _____
fast _____
free of charge _____
glad _____
hard _____
high _____
normal _____
previous _____
safe _____
silly _____
strange _____
well-known _____

Compound nouns related to the future

electric vehicle _____
flying car _____
mobile phone app _____
petrol car _____
solar power _____
sunlight _____

Discourse markers

also _____
and _____
instead _____
so _____

Documents and texts

article _____
bill _____
book _____
brochure _____
certificate _____
comic _____
form _____
letter _____
magazine _____
message / text message _____
newspaper _____
note _____
notebook _____

In the bathroom

bath _____
comb _____
hairbrush _____
mirror _____
shampoo _____
shower _____

soap _____
tap _____
toilet _____
toothbrush _____
towel _____

In the home

armchair _____
carpet _____
chest of drawers _____
cupboard _____
light _____
rug _____
shelf _____
shelves _____
sink _____
sofa _____

Numerical vocabulary

a lot (of) _____
all / every one _____
almost _____
approximately _____
around _____
both _____
double _____
each _____
enough _____
everything _____
half _____
how much / how many _____
little _____
many _____
more _____
more or less _____
most _____
nearly _____
nothing _____
number _____
once, twice, three times, etc _____
plenty _____
several _____
some _____
the only one _____
total _____
various _____

Technology

broken _____
digital camera _____
DVD _____
landline _____
mobile phone / phone _____
model

photograph   _____
program   _____
software   _____
tech   _____
techie   _____
type   _____
upgrade   _____
voice   _____

Time expressions

afterwards / later / then   _____
again   _____
already   _____
at last   _____
before   _____
date   _____
day / week / month   _____
during / while   _____
finally   _____
firstly   _____
future   _____
immediately   _____
it's my / your turn   _____
last   _____
late   _____
meanwhile   _____
moment   _____
monthly   _____
next   _____
past   _____
previous   _____
season   _____
since   _____
sometimes   _____
soon   _____
still   _____
suddenly   _____
the day before yesterday   _____
the following (week)   _____
till / until   _____
today   _____
week / last week /
  next week   _____
weekend   _____
when   _____
year / annual / yearly   _____
yesterday   _____
yet   _____

The future

battery   _____
building   _____
computer   _____
electric   _____
energy   _____
enormous   _____
flat   _____

lift / elevator   _____
machine   _____
park   _____
petrol   _____
planet   _____
power   _____
to control   _____
to cycle   _____
to drive   _____
to fly   _____
to type   _____
to write   _____
sun   _____
voice   _____
wind   _____

Reading

Read the information about three people and five advertisements for different restaurants. Which restaurant should each person choose? For each person A–C, choose the correct restaurant 1–5.

A

If Laura could choose her perfect meal, she would have a burger and chips. She knows it's not very healthy, but she loves it anyway. She doesn't really like cooking so she would order a takeaway. However, she lives a long way from town but doesn't mind paying for a taxi.

B

Peter doesn't like any food unless it's really spicy, and a bit different. So if he could choose, he would always decide to have something he doesn't usually eat. However, he's studying at university so it can't be too expensive.

C

If Sara could choose any kind of food to eat for a celebration, she would choose roast dinner and she would cook it herself and eat it at home. However, she is always busy, so she doesn't have much time.

1

Hannah's Home Cooking

Do you love the taste of traditional cooked food but are always in a hurry? Try our delicious, prepared meals. Just place in the oven and wait!

2

Ronnie's Roasts

We serve the best roast lunches and dinners in the city! Call now to reserve a table or you might be disappointed!

3

Freddie's Fast Food

Fast food, made fast, delivered fast! Call us now! Only available for city centre addresses.

4

Simon's Surprises

Delicious curries, available for delivery. Get bored easily of the same thing? Recipes change daily! Can be delivered or collected. 50% cheaper for all students.

5

Farshad's Food Hall

All types of food served and delivered to any address for a small charge. We have a big menu from fish and chips to salads to burgers and pasta. Healthy options are also available.

Study tip

Remember that if a question seems too easy, the answer is probably wrong! So, you need to find information which tells you your answer is definitely correct.

Listening

You will hear an interview with Josh about his school exchange.

Listen and choose the correct answers (A, B, C or D). You now have some time to read the questions.

1 **Josh didn't go to France because …**

  A it was too far

  B some people were unwell

  C it was too expensive

  D of the food

2 **Josh went on a different trip to …**

  A London

  B Spain

  C Sri Lanka

  D the United Kingdom

3 **Josh learned how to …**

  A read music

  B cook new foods

  C play new music

  D make new friends

4 **After a few days Josh …**

  A ate burgers

  B liked the food more

  C didn't feel well

  D wanted to go home

5 **Next year Josh will …**

  A go back to the same country

  B visit a different country

  C learn to cook different food

  D have students in his house

Study tip

In exams, you will often listen twice. It is important you relax and really listen the first time. Make some notes. Then read through the sentences and options again. Do your notes help you to choose the correct answers?

Speaking

Work with a partner.

Student A

Ask Student B these questions.

- What food would you choose if you could have anything? Why?
- What countries would you visit if you had enough money? Why?
- How would you travel there if you could choose? Why?
- What job would you choose if you could do any job? Why?
- If you could change anything about the world, what would you change? Why?

Student B

Ask Student A these questions.

- How is technology different from when you were young?
- Give me examples of technology we don't use anymore.
- Tell me about technology your parents or relatives didn't have when they were younger?
- What technology did you use before you went to bed last night?
- What will mobile phones be like in the future?

> **Study tip**
>
> To describe a situation which is not real yet, or is a dream, use: *If I could choose to …, I would … because I think it would be* + adjective.

> **Study tip**
>
> If someone asks you about how things were different in the past, remember to use *used to*: *I used to … My mum used to … There didn't use to be any ….*

Writing

Technology and languages

- Describe the technology you like using. When / Why do you use it?
- What technology don't you use? Why not? / How does it make you feel?
- Which languages would you choose to learn in the future? Why?
- Which languages wouldn't you choose to learn in the future? Why not?

Write 100–110 words in English.

Grammar

Contents

Reported speech 237

- – statements (e.g. *She said (that) she had it.*)
- – commands (e.g. *She told me to save money.*)
- – questions (e.g. *She asked her parents if she could go out.*)

Nouns

singular and plural

A bird > birds
*I have a **bird**.*

possessives (...'s and ...s')

You use possessives to say who something belongs to.
You use **'s** for one person: *It is John's coat.* = the coat that belongs to John
You use **s'** when something belongs to more than one person and the plural noun ends in **s**:
Those are my cousins' rabbits. = the rabbits that belongs to my cousins.

countable and uncountable nouns

Many nouns in English have a singular form > *carrot* and a plural form: *carrots*.

These nouns are called countable nouns because you can count them:
one carrot, two carrots, three carrots, many carrots

You can use *a* or *an* with countable nouns: **an apple, a banana**

compound nouns

A compound noun is a noun with two words:
ice cream = ice + cream
post office = a place where you post a letter and buy stamps.
airport = a place you go to travel by plane
bookcase = a set of shelves for books
bedroom = a room for your bed; where you sleep

compound nouns can be one word (**grandmother**) or two words (**ice cream**).

noun phrases

You use noun phrases to make sentences. You usually start a noun phrase with a determiner, such as *a / an* or *the*: **my mum; the woman; an apple**.

Noun phrase		Noun phrase	Noun phrase
subject		indirect object	direct object
My mum	bought	the woman	an apple.

suffixes (e.g. -er, -tion, -ment)

You can change some verbs into nouns by adding letters to the end of the word. These letters are called a suffix. There are lots of different suffixes, but some common ones are:

-ation / -tion for an action or resulting state: educate > education; invite > invitation

-er or **-or** for a job; sing > singer; act > actor

-ment for a state, an act or a condition:
advertise > advertisement

-ese for some nationalities: China > Chinese; Japan > Japanese

Adjectives

order of adjectives

You use adjectives in a special order:

	adjectives					noun
	quality	size	age	colour	special information/ shape	
a		huge	old	black	haunted	house
an	interesting		new			idea
a	beautiful	tiny		blue	Italian	vase
the	poisonous			green		frog
the	soft			pink	rectangular	clouds

-ing and -ed adjectives

You use **–ing** adjectives to describe what something is like.
*We go on lots of interest**ing** school trips.*

You use **–ed** adjectives to describe how you feel.
*I'm very interest**ed** in other cultures.*

comparatives

You use comparative adjectives to talk about the difference between two or more things.

Regular forms:
big > bigg**er**: *A rabbit is bigger than an ant.*
hun**gr**y > hungr**ier**: *A rabbit is hungrier than an ant.*
tall > taller: *She is taller than him /He is not as tall as her.*

For longer words of more than two syllables you use *more / less* + adjective + *than*: intelligent:
*My mouse is **more intelligent than** my rabbit.* ~~intelligenter~~
*My rabbit is **less intelligent than** my mouse.*

You use (not) as ... as to compare:
*I am **as tall as** my sister.* (we are the same height)
*I am **not as tall as** my mum.*

You often use this pattern: **too** + adjective + **to / (not)** + adjective + **enough to**:
*My baby brother is **too young to** talk.*
*My grandmother is **too old to** walk a long way.*
*My grandmother is **not strong enough to** walk a long way.*

superlatives

You use a superlative to say that one thing or person has more of a particular quality than all the others in a group.

You use the **adjective + -est** for short adjectives.
cold > the coldest: *the coldest part of the world*
tall > *the tallest building in the world*

For longer adjectives (three syllables or more) you add *the most* before the adjective:
important > *the most important*
difficult > *It was **the most** difficult exam.*

regular forms (e.g. -est, -iest, (the) most / least ...)

One syllable: **high** > high**est**; **late**> la**test** ; **dry**> dr**iest**

Two syllable: **happy** > happ**iest**;

Three syllable: **incredible** > **the most** incredible; **unbelievable** > **the most** unbelievable: *We had **the most** incredible holiday!*

You use *least* to say which of three or more things is the most negative:
interesting > **the least** interesting > *London was **the least** interesting place.*

irregular forms (e.g. (the) best / worst)

Some adjectives are irregular:

good	better	worse	*My exams results were **worse** than my brother's.*
far	further	furthest	*I walked **the furthest** - 112 kilometres!*
bad	worse	worst	*It was **the worst** day of the week - it rained all day.*

possessives (e.g. *my, your, his, her,* etc.)

my	
your	
his	
her	
its	**name**
our	
your	
their	

You use possessives to say A belongs to B.
*This is **my** rabbit.* (A is the rabbit; B is me).
*It is **their** rabbit.* (A is the rabbit; B is them)
*What is **its** name? **Its** name is Chip.* (A is the name; B is the rabbit. The name belongs to the rabbit.)

compound adjectives

Some adjectives have more than one word in English. These are called compound adjectives. We usually use a hyphen (-) to connect the two words.
*There are many **after-school** activities.*
*It's a **four-wheeled** car.*
*Let's take the **long-distance** train.*
*I'm having a **two-week** holiday.*

Adverbs

adverbs of degree (very, quite, too)

You use adverbs of degree in front of adjectives to show the intensity of the adjective.

(not strong meaning) **quite** > **very / really** > **too** (very strong meaning)
*It's **quite** big.*
*It's **very quiet** in town today.*

You can also use **really** instead of **very**:
*It's **really quiet** in town today.*

*The film was **really** good.*

*It's **too** hot for me today!* (this has a negative meaning = more than enough = I don't like it.)

adverbs of time (e.g. *then, next week, already, just, yet*)

You use **then** to mean 'at that time'. It can mean in the past:
*I met my best friend at school. I was still at primary school **then**.*
Or it can refer to the future:
- Let's meet at the cinema at 3:15 pm.
*- Okay, see you **then**.*

You use **next week** to refer to the future
*See you **next week**!*

You often use **already**, **just** and **yet** with present perfect:
You use **already** to mean earlier than expected, or done before:
- Shall we get the bill?
*- It's OK. I've **already** paid.*

You use **just** to say something happened very recently:
*I've **just** woken up! = I was sleeping seconds ago.*

You use **yet** to say something is nearly happening, you want it to happen, or is nearly finished:
*I haven't finished my homework **yet**.*
*Have you seen the film **yet**?*
*No, I haven't. / **Not yet**, but I want to.*

adverbs of place (e.g. *here, there*)

You use adverbs of place to say where:
*When did you get **here**?*
*Would you like to live **there**?*
*He's **upstairs**.*
*Come **up**!*
These adverbs are often at the end of the sentence.

adverbs of manner

You use adverbs of manner to express how you do something.

Most adverbs of manner are formed by adding **-ly** to an adjective.
bad – badly

You use adverbs of manner to say how someone does something, or how something happens. Adverbs give information about a verb.
*I mixed two gases together **slowly**.*

The adverb comes after the verb:
*Do you usually sleep **well** or **badly**?*
*What helps you to think **positively**?*

adverbs of probability

You use adverbs of probability to say how sure you are about something.

You use **definitely** to say you are sure that something is true.
*John was **definitely** here in the house. His clothes are in the bedroom.*

You use **probably** to say you think something is true but you are not sure.
*This is **probably** because he needed somewhere to stay.*

You use **possibly** to say you are less sure.
Can you come on Monday?
Possibly.

You can also use **perhaps** or **maybe** instead of **possibly**. They mean the same thing.
Perhaps / Maybe are usually at the start of the sentence.
Perhaps they were John's clothes.

Maybe they were John's clothes.

100% ←—————————————————→ 30%

definitely   probably   possibly
                                      perhaps
                                      maybe

adverbs of frequency

You use adve rbs of frequency to say how often something happens:

100% ←—————————————————→ 0%

always   often   usually   sometimes   rarely   never

Adverbs of frequency usually come before the main verb:
*I **rarely watch** TV.*   *You can **sometimes see** the sun.*

But they come after the verbs: *am, is, are, was, were* when they are used as main verbs:
*She **is usually** very late.*   *He **is rarely** friendly.*

Some adverbs (*sometimes, normally, usually*) can come at the start of the sentence:
***Sometimes** I go swimming at the weekend.*

adverbs of sequence (e.g. *first, last*)

You use adverbs of sequence to say who or what happened in which order:
*There was a running race. Kim finished **first**. John was **next**. And Simon finished **last**. = 1 Kim; 2 John 3 Simon*

adverbs of direction (e.g. *left, right*)

You use these to describe how to get somewhere:
*Go **left** and then **right**. You will see the cinema **in front of** you.*

comparative adverbs

If you want to compare how two or more things or people do something, you can use comparative adverbs.

Buses travel **more slowly** than planes.
Jack draws **more carefully** (**than** Peter).
Peter draws **more quickly** (**than** Jack).
He drives **too slowly** sometimes – it's dangerous!
She doesn't drive **carefully enough** – she sometimes has accidents.
She sings **better** (than me).
He drives **worse** at night because he can't see well in the dark.

superlative adverbs

If you want to say that one thing or a person does something in a particular way, different from all the others in the group, you can use a superlative adverb.

We run fast, but Sally runs **(the) fastest**.
We both drive carefully, but John drives **(the) most carefully**.
Our friend Paul is a bad driver. He drives **(the) least carefully** of all of us.
We all sing well, but Andy sings **(the) best**.
They play the video game badly, but I play it **(the) worst**.

Articles

When talking about what job someone does, you use *a* or *an* before the job.
*She's **a** doctor.*

You use *an* before singular countable nouns that start with a vowel.
*He's **an** actor.*

Quantifiers: *some, many, a lot of, much, enough, too much, (a) few*

You use *a* or *an* to describe 'one' of something e.g., *an apple*. You can use *some* when there is more than one of something (*some* apples). With plural nouns you can use some when you don't want to or can't count: *some* apples.

You can also use *many* to describe nouns: *There were **many** people in the park.*

You can't count some nouns: ~~one bread, two breads~~. These are called uncountable nouns. You can say: *some bread*. But you can use uncountable nouns with *of*: *a piece **of** bread.*
You can't use 's': *some ~~informations~~.*   ✗
But you can say: *some information*   ✓
*This is an important piece **of** information*   ✓

You can use *a lot of* or *lots of* with countable **and** uncountable nouns:
a lot of / lots of apples/ information, bread, etc.

When you ask about quantities, use *How much* …? or *How many* …?
You use *How much* with uncountable nouns: *How much beef would you like?*
You use *How many* with countable plural nouns: *How many potatoes do you want?*
How many would you like?
Five, please.

You use *Is this enough (water)?* to ask if something uncountable is the right amount.
You can answer: *Yes, that's **enough*** to say something *uncountable* is the right amount
You can answer: *No, that's **too much*** to say that something *uncountable* is more than you want.

You use *too* to say that something is more than enough / something negative:
*It's **too** hot.* = negative; you don't feel good when it is this hot
*There are **too many** people at the party* = there isn't enough space – it doesn't feel comfortable.

You use *few* for countable nouns:
Few dogs bite. Most are friendly. = not many
A few dogs bit me last week. = There were many dogs. Some bit me.

You use **both** to say you want A and B. *Which fish would you like? **This** one or **that** one?*
*I'd like **both** (of them) please.*

You use **all (of them)** to say you want everything there is:
Which of these apples would you like?
***All of them**, please!*

Conjunctions

coordinating conjunctions (e.g. *and, but, because, so, or, either*)

You use coordinating conjunctions to join two sentences together.
You use *and* to add more information: *The room has lots of flowers **and** it's very beautiful*
You use *but* to add contrasting information: *The living room is big, **but** the dining room is small.*
You use *because* to give an explanation for something or to say why.
*I have a desk **because** I work from home.*

You use *so* to add a reason for something.
*I work from home **so** I have a desk at home.*
You use *or* to give an option or choice:
*You can have a car **or** a bike.*
You can use *either* to give an option, but you need or for the other option:
*You can have **either** a car **or** a bike.*
You use *so* to give a reason:
*I didn't have much money **so** I bought a bike.* = because I didn't have much money.
You use *so that* to explain how something is then possible:
*I gave her money **so that** she could buy some food.*
You can't say: *I work from home **so that** I have a desk at home.*

subordinating conjunctions (e.g. *when, where, because, if, although, as soon as, unless*)

You use subordinating conjunctions to link a main clause with a subordinating clause (a clause that adds information to the main clause or explains the main clause). Some subordinating conjunctions refer to time.
*Some of my friends want to be pilots or mechanics **when** they are older.*
*I went to a normal secondary school **before** I came to this school.*
***As soon as** I finish my exams, I will go to university.*

*The apartment is quite big, **although** it's in the centre of the city.*
In sentences with *although*, there is often a contrast or something surprising. You need a comma between the two clauses.

*We'll miss the festival **unless** we change our dates* = If we don't change our dates, we will miss the festival = we must change our dates or we will miss the festival
In sentences with *unless*, you are talking about things which won't happen until you do something.
Although and *unless* can also go at the beginning of the sentence.
***Although** it's in the centre of the city, the apartment quite big.*
***Unless** we change our dates, we'll miss the festival.*

Prepositions

prepositions of place

You use prepositions of place to say where something is.
*It is **next to / beside** the museum.*
*It is **behind** the museum.*
*It is **between** the clinic and the castle.*

in, on, at

The prepositions *in*, *on* and *at* are used very frequently in English to talk about places.
Sometimes it can be difficult to know which one you should choose in a particular phrase or sentence. The table below shows some of the very common uses. It gives examples to help you learn them.

	in	on	at
PLACE	geographical regions: in Spain in the mountains	surfaces: on the wall / roof on the table / shelf on the first floor on a piece of paper	specific places: At the bus stop at home / work at Amy's house at the back of the book
	cities/ large areas: in York		addresses: She lives at 5, Regent Street.
	roads/streets: There are lots of shoe shops in that street.	Roads/ streets: The bank is on Kings Road.	public places: at the station / theatre at the doctor's
	rooms/buildings: I heard a noise in the kitchen. There is a wedding in the church.	Transport: I was on the number bus	shops: at the supermarket
	containers: in a box in the fridge		Events: at Steve's party at last year's conference
	liquids: I'd like sugar in my coffee.		

prepositions of time

The prepositions *in*, *on* and *at* are used very frequently in English to talk about times.

Sometimes it can be difficult to know which one you should choose in a particular phrase or sentence. The table below shows some of the very common uses. It gives examples to help you learn them.

	in	on	at
TIME	months / years: days: clock times: in February on Monday at 10 o'clock in 1996 at midnight in the last century	days: on Monday parts of the day: on Tuesday evening	clock times: at 10 o'clock at midnight
			meals: at breakfast
	seasons: in winter in (the) summer	dates: on the ninth of May on Friday 29th	festivals: at Christmas at Easter
	parts of days: in the morning		
	to say when something will happen in the future: I'll talk to you in ten minutes.	special days: on Christmas Eve	

for

You can use the preposition *for* to talk about how long you do an activity.
How long did you sleep *for*?
I slept for an hour.

You can also use *for* to say how far you travel.
How long did you walk for?
We walked for 20 miles.

But you can also say:
We walked 20 miles.

You can use *for* to describe giving someone something:
This present is for you!

with

You can use the preposition *with* to talk about the other people also doing an activity.
Who did you go to Spain with?
I went to Spain with my brother.
I'm staying in London with my sister.

You can also use *with* to describe something that accompanies something else:
I always have my phone with me.
I got this pen free with the newspaper = When you buy the newspaper, you get a pen.

direction

You use prepositions of direction to give directions.
Walk from the shops to the train station. Then walk towards the park.

method (e.g. *by, with*)

You often use *by* + *-ing*, or *with* to explain how something happens:
You start the phone by pressing this button.
You open this door with this key.

like, between, among

You use the preposition *like* to compare things or people:
John is like his father = similar to
Like London, New York has tall buildings.= both have tall buildings

You use the preposition *as* to compare things or people:
He is as tall as a house!
He is as quiet as a mouse!

You use the preposition *between* to say where something is in comparison to two other things or times:
The number 2 is between 1 and 3.
The letter B is between A and C.
'The window was broken between 7 a.m. and 7.15 a.m.'

You use the preposition *among* to say where something is in comparison to three or more other things or people:
The town of Bluestone is among several lakes.
Don't worry – you are among friends! We can help you.

You use the preposition *due to* to say why or how something happened:
There is a lot of rain today due to a storm at sea. = because of a storm
The train is delayed due to a problem at the station. = because of a problem

prepositional phrases

You use these to talk about where something is. You can sometimes leave these out of a sentence and it will still make sense. They add more information.
There's a bridge at the end of the road.
There's a car park on the left next to the traffic light.
This postcard is from my brother.
Go with the teacher please.

adjectives + dependent prepositions.

Many adjectives go with a certain preposition.
I am worried about the game tonight.
We're excited about the game tonight.
I'm interested in the environment.
I'm keen on running.

prepositions before or after nouns and adjectives

You use *between* to compare two things:
There is a difference between travelling and going on holiday.

You use prepositions after some adjectives:
I am frightened of spiders. I can't sleep if they are in my room.

Pronouns

subject / object (e.g. *he, she, they*)

Pronouns are words that you use to talk about someone or something when you do not need to use a noun. You use subject pronouns as the subject of the verb. You use object pronouns as the object of the verb.

Subject pronouns

Singular	Plural
I	we
you	you
he	they
she	they
it	they

Subject pronoun	Example	Object pronoun	Example
I	*I am a boy.*	me	*She gave **me** £5.*
you	*You are a girl.*	you	*Can I help **you**?*
he	*He is tall.*	him	*She saw **him** in town.*
she	*She likes rabbits.*	her	*Can you give the rabbit to **her**?*
it	*It is good.*	it	*Can you give me **it**?*
we	*We are friends.*	us	*Can you help **us**?*
you	*You are sisters.*	you	*Can I help **you**?*
they	*They are late.*	them	*Can you help **them**?*

You can also use object pronouns after a preposition: *She was waiting **for us**. I talked **to him** yesterday.*

This table lists the different possibilities for singular and plural pronouns. There are examples below.

		Subject pronoun	Object pronoun	Possessive Determiner	Possessive Pronoun	Reflexives
singular	1st person	I	me	my	mine	myself
	2nd person	you	you	your	yours	yourself
	3rd person	he	him	his	his	himself
		she	her	her	hers	herself
		it	it	its	-----	itself
plural	1st person	we	us	our	ours	ourselves
	2nd person	you	you	your	yours	yourselves
	3rd person	they	them	their	theirs	themselves

possessive (e.g. *his, hers, theirs*)

Determiner	...rabbit .	The rabbit is ...	Pronoun
my			mine
your			yours
his			his
her			hers
its			-----
our			ours
your			yours
their			theirs

(Possessive)

reflexive (e.g. *myself, ourselves, etc.*)

Subject pronoun	verb	Reflexive
I	clean	myself
you	clean	yourself
he		himself
she	cleans	herself
it		itself
we	clean	ourselves
you	clean	yourselves
they	clean	themselves

You can use a reflexive pronoun to show that you did something to, for or by yourself.(not involving another person)
*I hurt **myself**.*
*Have you hurt **yourself**?*
*He taught **himself** to ride a bike.*

demonstrative (e.g. *this, that, these, those*)

You use the demonstrative pronouns *this* (singular) and *these* (plural) to talk about people or things near you, and to introduce or identify people and things.
***This** is the River Yarra.*

You use the demonstrative pronouns *that* (singular) and *those* (plural) to talk about people or things not so near you.
***This** table is OK (e.g., next to you). Or maybe **that** table is better? (= another table further away).*
*Do you want **these** black shoes? (= the shoes near you) Or do you want **those** red shoes? (= the shoes further away).*

You can use **ones** so you don't need to repeat the noun (*here, bananas*).

You can also use *this*, *that* and *those* and these as pronouns (= as the object).
*Do you like **this / that**?*
*Do you prefer **these / those**?*

quantitative (e.g. *one*, *some*)

We use *one* for singular nouns:
How many cups of coffee do you want?
One please. = one cup of coffee

*Look! There are **some** lions! They're running!* (= it is impossible to count)
*I'd like **some** soup.* (uncountable)

indefinite (e.g. *another*, *several*)

You use *another* and *several* for quantity:
*Can I have **another** cup of coffee please?* (= I had one and now I want one more.)
*I had **several** cups of coffee yesterday.* (= I had more than two.)

You also use *another* as a pronoun:
*I finished my drink. I think I'd like **another**.*

relative (e.g. *which*, *who*)

You use relative pronouns to link two sentences. For objects you use *which*:
*It's the cat. It lives next door. = It's a cat **which** lives next door.*

For people use *who*:
*It's my uncle. He lives next door. = It's my uncle **who** lives next door.*

impersonal (e.g. *it*, *there*)

You use *it* and *there* to describe situations:
***There** is a lot of rain today.*
***It** is raining today.*
***There** is a train leaving in five minutes.*
***It** doesn't matter.*
***It's** amazing.*

general use of *you*

Sometimes you can use *you* to talk in a general way about something, especially when you are speaking.
*- So do **you** do this job inside?* = (do people do this job inside?)
*- Yes, **you** do.* = (yes, they do)

You can also use present passive, but this more formal. You often find this in writing instead of speaking.
This job is usually done outside.

You also use *you* with obligation:
***You** don't have to wear gloves. But **you** can if you want to.*

Verbs and tenses

to be: *am, is, are*

The verb forms *am, is, are* are followed by:
a noun group: *Mr Brown **is a teacher**. It **isn't my book**. **Are** you **a student**?*
an adjective: *She's **tall**. I'm **tired**. **Are** you **happy**? They're **hungry**.*
an expression of place or time: *Mary's **at home**. It's **six o'clock**. It's **on the table**.*
an expression of age: *I'm **sixteen**. She's **fourteen years old**.*

present simple forms

Positives	
Full form	**Short form**
***I am** late.*	***I'm** late.*
***You are** next.*	***You're** next.*
***She is** in.*	***She's** in.*
***He is** at home.*	***He's** at home.*
***It is** here.*	***It's** here.*
***We are** happy.*	***We're** happy.*
***They are** ready.*	***They're** ready.*

Negatives		
Full form	**Short form (1)**	**Short form (2)**
*I **am not** late.*	*I'm **not** late.*	
*You **are not** next.*	*You're **not** next.*	*You **aren't** next.*
*She **is not** in.*	*She's **not** in.*	*She **isn't** in.*
*He **is not** at home.*	*He's **not** at home.*	*He **isn't** at home.*
*It **is not** here.*	*It's **not** here.*	*It **isn't** here.*
*We **are not** happy.*	*We're **not** happy.*	*We **aren't** happy.*
*They **are not** ready.*	*They're **not** ready.*	*They **aren't** ready.*

Questions	Short answers
***Am I** late?*	*Yes, I **am**. / No, **I'm** not.*
***Are you** next?*	*Yes, you **are**. / No, **you're** not. / No, you **aren't**.*
***Is she** in?*	*Yes, she **is**. / No, **she's** not. / No, she **isn't**.*
***Is he** at home?*	*Yes, he **is**. / No, **he's** not. / No, he **isn't**.*
***Is it** here?*	*Yes, it **is**. / No, **it's** not. / No, it **isn't**.*
***Are we** happy?	*Yes, we **are**. / No, **we're** not. / No, we **aren't**.*
***Are they** ready?*	*Yes, they **are**. / No, **they're** not. / No, they **aren't**.*

to have: *has*, *have*

You use *have* when you talk about someone owning something or you are talking about their characteristics.

present simple forms

Positives
I have a brother.
You have a rabbit
She has a bird.
He has brown hair.
It has a big garden.
We have blue eyes.
They have a car.

You don't often use contractions with *have* so there aren't many short forms:
I've a brother. ✗

present simple

You use present simple:
to talk about things that are always true: *February is the shortest month.*
to talk about habits: *I get up late at the weekend.*
to talk about general facts about our lives: *We live in a small house.*

The form of the verb changes with *he / she / it*.

I work from 9 to 5.
You work very hard.
She works for her father.
He works in the supermarket.
We work in town.
They work at the hospital.

With verbs that end in *-o / -s / -ch / -sh* the present simple form is *-es*:
He goes out every weekend.   *She watches* a lot of TV.

With verbs that end in *consonant + y* the present simple form is: *-ies*:
He studies languages at university.

BUT I **play**, he **plays**   I **buy**, she **buys**

auxiliary verb *do*

You use *do* for questions and negatives in the present simple:
A: Do you like this music? B: Yes, I do. / No, I don't.

You use *does* and *doesn't* (*does not*) for questions and negatives with *he / she / it*:
A: Is Helen at home? B: Helen? She doesn't live here.

Questions	Short answers
Do I have a brother?	*Yes, I do. / No, I don't.*
Do you have a rabbit?	*Yes, you do. / No, you don't.*
Does he have brown hair?	*Yes, he does. / No, he doesn't.*
Does she have a bird?	*Yes, she does. / No, she doesn't.*
Does it have a big garden?	*Yes, it does. / No, it doesn't.*
Do we have blue eyes?	*Yes, we do. / No, we don't.*
Do they have a car?	*Yes, they do. / No, they don't.*

Negatives	
Full form	**Short form**
I do not have a brother.	*I don't have* a brother.
You do not have a rabbit.	*You don't have* a rabbit.
She does not have brown hair.	*She doesn't have* brown hair.
He does not have a bird.	*He doesn't have* a bird.
It does not have a big garden.	*It doesn't have* a big garden.
We do not have blue eyes.	*We don't have* blue eyes.
They do not have a car.	*They don't have* a car.

present continuous

1   The form of the present continuous is:
am / is / are + '-ing'
For the negative you add *not* after **am / is / are**:
I am not working at the moment.
I'm not playing today.
You can use the short forms **aren't** and **isn't**:
We aren't going by bus.

2   You use the present continuous:

a   **to talk about an activity or something happening now:**
It isn't raining now.
They're talking; they're not eating.
It's raining, but it's not snowing.
The kids are playing tennis; they're not working.

b   **to talk about a temporary situation:**
I'm living with my friends at the moment.
We're staying at a wonderful hotel.
I'm not feeling well today.
My sister's working as a waitress for a month.

c   **to talk about a future plan:**
Mike is coming home on Thursday.
They're having a party next week.

d   **to talk about change, development and progress:**
Life is getting easier thanks to technology.
Do you think your English is improving?

e   **with always to criticize or complain about what someone does:**
You're always interrupting me!
My father is always losing his car keys.

present continuous to talk about the future

You can use present continuous to talk about plans and arrangements in the future.
Form: to be + ing + time
Is she taking her driving test *today*?
Yes, she is.
We're opening a small café *next month*.
He's leaving tomorrow afternoon.

past tenses

You have a lot of choices with past tenses. Here is a quick way of thinking about past tenses:

Use past simple for short, finished actions:
*He **opened** the door and **looked** in the room. There was no one there.*

Use present perfect for actions which started in the past and still have an effect now.
*I **have been** to Italy.* = I went in the past (and now I still remember it).
*I **haven't seen** the film but I want to.* = Something didn't happen (see the film) but now I want to see it.
*We've **been** friends for five years* = we started being friends and now we still are friends.

You use ***used to*** to describe something that was true in the past and isn't true now.
*When I was young **I used to have** pets.* = now I don't have pets.

past simple

1   You use the past simple to talk about things that happened in the past:
I stayed in that hotel last week.
He worked all night and finally finished the project when the secretaries arrived in the morning.

2   **You also use the past simple to talk about the general past, and about regular actions in the past:**
We lived in Rome for a year when I was a child.
Our friends often visited us there.

3   **For most verbs, the past simple form ends in -ed.**
Some verbs have an irregular past form:
begin> began; break> broke; buy> bought; come> came; do> did; drink> drank; drive> drove; eat> ate; find> found; get> got; give> gave; go> went; have> had; make>made pay> paid; say>said; see> saw; take>took; tell> told; write> wrote

4   **For all regular and irregular verbs, the form is the same for all persons:**
I / you / he / she / It / we / you / they said

5   **You use *did* ... + Infinitive to form questions in the past.**
***Did** you **get** home all right?*
***Did** he **go** out last night?*
***Did** you **tell** them about the party?*
*Who **did** you **see**?*
*Where **did** you **buy** that hat?*
*When **did** she **arrive**?*

6   **You use *did not* (or *didn't*) + infinitive to form negatives in the past:**
*I **didn't understand**, so I asked a question.*
*He **didn't give** me his address.*
*They **didn't buy** anything.*

present perfect

The form of the present perfect is: ***have / has*** + past participle.

You use the present perfect to ask questions about the past up to the present.

You often add ***ever*** to these questions.
*Have you **ever** played sport for your school?*

You can use short form answers.
Yes, I have. No, I haven't.

To make negative statements with the present perfect you can use ***never***.
*I've never **seen** my neighbour.*

present perfect with *for* and *since*

You use the present perfect with ***for*** and ***since*** for something which started in the past and is still going on now.

You use for to talk about the length of time:
*I've lived here **for five years**.*

You use since with a specific time or date in the past.
*I've lived here **since I was eleven years old**.*

For the question form we use '***how long***':
***How long has** your grandma lived here?*
*My grandma has lived here **since 1994 / Since 1994**.*

present perfect with *already, just, still* and *yet.*

You use the present perfect with ***already*** to refer to something that happened earlier than expected. You often use already to show this:
-Go and do your homework, Lisa.
*-Don't worry, Mum, **I've already done** it.*

You use the present perfect with ***just*** to refer to an action in the very recent past.
*I've **just finished** my homework.*

You use the present perfect with ***still*** in negative sentences to talk about something that has not happened, and you are waiting to happen.
*I'm not happy! I **still haven't received** my new laptop. Today was the delivery day!*

You use the present perfect with ***yet*** for something that still hasn't happened but you expect to happen soon.
*I **haven't finished** my homework **yet**.*
*-**Have** you **finished** your homework **yet**?*
*-Not **yet**! Nearly!*

past continuous

1   The form of the past continuous is:
was / were + verb ***-ing***

2   You use the past continuous for an action which was interrupted by another action:
*I **was reading** the newspaper when the doorbell rang.*
*They **were flying** from London to New York when the accident happened.*
Question: *Where **were they flying** when the accident happened?*

WARNING: If two things happen one after the other you use two verbs in the past simple tense:
*As soon as Jack **saw** me, he **waved**.*
*I **woke up** when my alarm clock **rang**.*

3 You use the past continuous for an action which was still in progress at a particular time:
*At 2.15 we **were** still **waiting** for the bus.*
*It was just before midnight. We **were talking** quietly.*

4 You often use the past continuous to set the scene for a story or for a series of events:
*It was 1985.We **were living** in a small house in Liverpool.*
*On the day I had my accident, I **was preparing** for my examinations.*

5 You use the past continuous to show that something was changing, developing or progressing:
*The children **were growing up** quickly.*
*We **were learning** a lot.*

past perfect

You use the past perfect tense to compare two actions in the past, and say which action happened first.
*When the police arrived, the burglar **had gone**.*
*The burglar **had gone** when the police arrived.*
The meaning is 'already gone', so we often use *already*:
*The burglar **had** already **gone** when the police arrived.*
***Had** the burglar (already) **gone** when the police arrived?*
*Yes, she **had**. / No, she **hadn't**. She was still there.*

You often use *it* with *never*:
*I'd **never seen** the sea before- it **was** amazing!* = it was the first time; I was amazed.
You do not need *before*:
*I'd **never seen** the sea! It was amazing.*

Careful! When you speak you use present perfect: *I **have never seen** the sea before – it **is** amazing.*

present simple to talk about the future

You use present simple to describe facts in the future:
You need a time word: e.g. ***tomorrow**, **when**, **6 p.m.**:*
*I **leave** at 10 am tomorrow.*
***When** do you **arrive**?*
*I **arrive** at 6pm in New York.*

going to to talk about plans

You use (be) ***going to** + verb* to talk about plans, often in the near future.
I am / I'm not
You are / aren't
She / he is / isn't   + ***going to*** + verb
We are / aren't
They are / aren't

*Are you **going to** the park this afternoon?*
*No, Henry and I are **going to go** to the cafe this afternoon.*

future with *will / shall*
will

You use: subject + *will* + verb

When you are predicting what will happen in the future, you use *will*.
*I think it **will be** fun.*

You often use a contraction:
*It**'ll be** dangerous! Be careful!*
*We**'ll** probably **go** swimming a lot.*

When you ask about a prediction you use *do* + subject + *think* + *will*:
*Do you **think we'll go** swimming a lot?*
*Does he **think we'll be** on time? Yes, he **does**. / No, he **doesn't**.*

When you are asking a question about the future, you can use *will*.
***Will** you **visit** me?*
***Will** it **be** cold?*

predictions with *think + will*

You use *think + will* to talk about a possible decision.
*I **think I'll study** business.*

After *I **think*** you usually use a contraction: *I **think I'll** …*
*I **think I'll study** English* = I'm not sure but it is very likely.
*Do you **think** you **will** study English? Yes, I do. / No I don't.*

shall

When you make an offer or a suggestion to someone in British English, you use *shall*.
We can also use *will* for offers: *I'll book some tickets for you!* [offer]
***Shall I book** some train tickets for you?* [offer]
***Shall we go** shopping in the city?* [suggestion] This is similar to *let's*:
***Let's go** shopping in the city!* [suggestion]

future plans

You have a lot of choices when you talk about the future:
You use *think + will* to talk about a possible decision.
*I **think I'll be** a doctor.*

After *I **think*** you usually use a contraction: *I **think I'll** …*
*I **think I'll have** a big family one day* = I'm not sure but it is very likely.
*Do you **think** you **will** study English? Yes, I do/ No I don't.*

You use want with the infinitive form of the verb to talk about a personal choice or preference.
*Which coffee do you **want**?*
*I **(don't)** / **want** a coffee with milk.*

You use *would like* with the infinitive form of the verb to talk about future ideas.
*I'**d like to go** to France.*
*Where **would you like to go**?*
*What job **would you like** to do?*

You use *might* with the infinitive form of the verb without *to* to talk about things that are possible but you are not sure about:
*I **might have** the pasta. **Might** you **have** a pizza?*
*What **might** you **have**?*
*I think the pasta **might be** good.*

You use *going to* when we have a very strong intention:
*I'm **going to have** a salad.*

You use the present simple to talk about fixed times in the future.

*I **have** a reservation for the new restaurant.*
Great! What time?
It's** at **9 p.m.

Verb forms

imperatives

You can use the imperative to give advice. Use the infinitive of the verb without **to**.
***Think** about what you post on social media websites.*

You use **Do not** or **Don't** in the negative.
***Do** use another name. / **Don't** use your real surname.*

You can also use **never / always** + the imperative. This makes the meaning stronger.
***Never upload** photos that show where you live.*
***Always tell** an adult if someone you don't know asks to meet you.*
***Try** different sports.*
***Drink** lots of water!*

You use **Do not** or **Don't** in the negative.
***Don't sit** for a long time.*

infinitives / infinitives of purpose

You use **to** + infinitive to say why you do something. This follows another verb.
- I'm going to the restaurant
- Why?
*- **To have** dinner.*

*I'm going to the restaurant **to have** dinner with Jack.*
*He sent her a card **to say** Happy Birthday.*
Why did he send her a card?
***To say** Happy Birthday.*

Why didn't you call me?
*I didn't **want to** wake you*

You do not use infinitives with **to** with some verbs:
*He **let** the girl watch TV.*
*They **should** know the time.*
***Let's** go!*
*I **make** the children wash up.*

gerunds

You use verbs + **ing** (gerunds) as nouns to talk in general about activities you like or don't like.
***Shopping** online is fun.*
*I like **shopping** online.*
*I don't like **trying on** clothes in shop.*

The spelling sometimes changes when you use the -**ing** form of a noun:
get> ge**tt**ing; begin> begi**nn**ing; swim> swi**mm**ing
You double the final consonant in these examples.
When there is an 'e' you do not pronounce it and you do not use it in the gerund:
have> hav**ing**; love> lov**ing**

You use gerunds after some verbs:

1   to give advice: ***Keep exercising** regularly- it is very good for you.*

2   for directions: ***Keep walking** straight for five minutes. Then take the next right.*

3   for processes: ***After swimming**, I have a shower.*

two verbs in a sentence

Sometimes we use two verbs together in a sentence.

You use a verb + **to** + infinitive with some common verbs of saying and thinking.

agree choose decide expect hope learn offer plan promise
*Sue **has promised to cook** it for me next weekend.*

You use verb + object + **to** + infinitive with some verbs.
advise tell ask remind order expect
*They **asked me to try** it.*

You use **make** + object + infinitive (without **to**) to talk about how you feel because of someone or something.
*It **made me feel** very happy.*

You can use **help** + object + infinitive (without **to**) …
*She says I **can help her make it**.*
Or with **to**:
*She says I **can help her to make it**.*

passive (present and past simple)

You use the passive when the thing (object) is more important than the person (subject). You use the passive:

1   to talk about a process.
    *Often 250 mg of caffeine **is put** in an energy drink.*

2   to talk about facts where the thing is more important than the person doing the action.
    *Energy drinks **are** often **drunk** by students to help them study.*
    *Sometimes caffeine   **is**   **added** to soft drinks.*
    *Form: object +   **to be**   + past participle.*

If we want to say more about the person doing the action, we often use **by** + subject at the end.
To make the present passive you use an object:
    *energy drinks   **are** often   **drunk by students***
To make the question we use:
***is / are** +   object +   past participle   (**by** + object)*
***Are**   energy drinks   (often)   **drunk by students**?*

In this sentence, we want to know if these drinks are popular with students, so we use **by** + subject (students) at the end of the sentence.
You can make a sentence without a subject:
***Is** oil **produced** in your country? We don't need by people / someone as it is obvious.*
*Yes, it **is**. / No, it **isn't**.*

You use past simple passive to talk about the past. You change **is / are** to the past: **was / were**:
***Was** oil **produced** in your country a hundred years ago?*

Sometimes we also need a time word / phrase: *last year / ten years ago*:
***Were** energy drinks **drunk** (by many people) in your country **twenty years ago**?*
***Yes**, they **were**. / **No**, they **weren't**.*

phrasal verbs (e.g. *look after, find out*, etc.)

Some verbs in English consist of a verb + a preposition (*in / out / on / up* etc.).
These are called phrasal verbs. A phrasal verb does not have the same meaning as the first part of the verb. For example, *put* has one meaning, and *put out* has a different meaning.
Colette **puts on** gloves and boots to protect herself.
Sam's job is to **put out** fires.

He should **give up** smoking = stop smoking
I want to **find out about** the new wind farm. = I want to discover
Carry on writing. You have ten more minutes! = don't stop
The café has **run out of** coffee = there is no more coffee/ it's finished
Please **fill in** this form = complete the form
Leave me **out of** the argument! = don't include me/ don't make me say anything!
My parents **look after** me = care for me.

Phrasal verbs: *turn* + preposition for everyday objects
We use these to describe how we use objects.
turn on / off the washing machine = start / stop
turn down / up the lights / heating = less / more (of something)

You need to learn these phrasal verbs as fixed phrases.

verbs + dependent prepositions

You use many verbs with a certain preposition.
I **care about** the environment and climate change.
Do you belong to any groups? = are you a member of any groups
I **belong to** a local painting group.
She **applied for** a new job. = she completed forms to try and get a new job.
I **paid for** the car = I bought the car.
They **listen to** music every night.
He **believes in** having pets = he thinks it's a good idea.
My parents **care for** me = give me food, somewhere to live etc.
My sister **relies on** me for everything = I have to do everything for her.

You have to learn these verbs together with the preposition.

make for feelings

You use *make* to talk about how people make you feel.
You use the object pronoun after *make* or *makes*: *me, you, him, her, it, us, them*

Subject pronoun	make / makes	Object pronoun	Adjective / Verb
I	make	him	happy.
You	make	him	smile.
He / She / It	makes	him	sad.
We	make	him	cry.
They	make	him	angry.

Negative: *I don't make you happy. She doesn't make us sad.*

Question: *Do I make you happy?* Short answer: *Yes, you do.*

verb + object + infinitive + (in) direct object (e.g. *make* someone *do* something)

1 The form is

subject +	*make* or *makes* +	object + infinitive without *to*
My	mum	**makes**	me wash up.
My	parents	**make**	my sister do homework.

Question:

Do your parents	**make**	your sister	do homework?

Yes, they do/ don't.

2 You use **make** someone **do** something to describe a job your parents or boss says you must do. You have no choice.

about to + infinitive (e.g. *I was about to call*)

You use **to be** + **about to** + verb without '*to*' to say what is going to happen very soon.
He is **about to** go to work and that is why he's looking so smart.
She's **about to** buy this new electric car.
Are you **about to** leave? Yes, I am. I'm **about to** go to the office.

have / get something done

You use **get / have** something done to talk about something someone else does for us or another person.
You use **have** or **get** + object + past participle.
How often do you **get your hair cut**?
I **get my hair cut** every month.
My parents often **have their windows cleaned**.
I went to the camera shop **to get my camera fixed**.

used to (past habit)

You use **used to** talk about things that happened a lot (habits) in the past.
How **did** people **use to** go across the bridge?

Careful! You don't use a '*d*' in the question and the negative form:
Did you **use**d to have a pet when you were young?
No, I **didn't use**d to have a pet when I was young.

People **used to** travel across it on horses. They **didn't use** to travel in cars.
I **used to** have toys. Now I don't because I am 18!

   Careful! You do not pronounce the '*d*' in **used to**.

tag questions

You use tag questions check information and ask for agreement. If the sentence is positive, you use a negative tag question.

Positive	Negative
- **You're** John,	**aren't** you?

- Yes, I am.

If the sentence is negative, you use a positive tag question.

Negative	Positive
- **You're not** American,	**are** you?

- No, I'm not. I'm French.

Modals

can / can't (ability)

You use *can / can't* to say that someone knows how to do something or has the ability to do something.
Can / can't is a modal verb so it comes before the main verb in the sentence.
I can swim.
I can't sing.
Can you swim? Yes, I can / No, I can't.

could / couldn't (past ability)

You use *could / couldn't* to say that someone knew how to do something or had the ability to do something in the past.
Could is a modal verb so it comes before the main verb in the sentence.
I couldn't read her writing very well.
We couldn't wake Luisa up.
I could run fast when I was young.

could (polite requests)

You use *could* for polite requests. We often use *please* at the start or end of the sentence.
Could you lie down over there, please?
Could you help me, please?
Could my grandmother sit there, please?

The answer to the last question is not ~~Yes she could~~.
The correct reply is *Of course!* = yes. Or "*Sorry,(the seat is taken)* = no.

You use *could* to say you are not completely sure if something is possible:
They said that these bones could be from a dinosaur.

might / may (possibility)

You use *might* or *may* to talk about something which is possible, but you are not 100% sure of.
I thought it might be the bone of a horse.
It might rain. Let's take an umbrella.

Might is less formal and more common than *may*.
This may be because people caught lots of mammoths and ate them.
I may take the bus. Or I may walk. I'm not sure.

Careful! *I may be late* is correct. *I maybe late* is not. You can say: *Maybe I'll be late.*

would like (desire, offer)

Use *would + like* to ask and answer questions about what you want.
This is more polite than using *want*. You often use it when talking to people you don't know in shops and restaurants.
Would you like the chicken salad?
I'd like the green salad, please.

You also use it when talking about dreams:
What job would you like to do?
I'd like to be an actor = maybe this is not a real plan but it is something I want.

You also use *would you like* to make offers.
Would you like a table?
Yes, please / Yes, I would.

You use *can* to make and reply to requests:
Can we have a table near the window, please?
Yes, you can.

BUT! People working in shops and cafes use *can* for offers
Can I help you?
Yes, I'd like a table for two, please.

shall (suggestion, offer)

You use *shall* for suggestions or offers:
Shall we go shopping?
Shall I help you?

should / shouldn't / ought to (advice)

Use *should* or *ought to* when you are giving someone advice about what to do. *Should* is used more often than *ought to*. *Must* is stronger than *should / ought to*.
You should go for a walk in the evening.
You ought to do yoga for one hour in the evening.
Remember you use to with ought.

Use *shouldn't* when you are giving advice about what not to do.
You shouldn't eat too much before bedtime.
Should I call him?
Yes, you should.

You don't use *ought* in questions:
~~Ought I to call~~ them?> Should I call them? Yes, you should. / No, you shouldn't.

Mustn't is stronger than *shouldn't*.
No, you mustn't call them!

have to / must / don't have to (obligation)

You use **have to** and **must** when you talk about something that must happen because someone else says it is necessary or important.
You can use **have to** + verb or **have got to** + verb
*In our school we **have to** wear a school uniform.*
*In our school we **have got to** wear a school uniform.*

When you use **have got to**, **got** has the main stress:
*you have **got** to*
When you use **have to**, **have** is the main stress: *you **have** to walk*

You use **don't have to** when something is a choice, or is not necessary.
*We **don't have to** stay at school for lunch.* = you choose if you want to stay at school for lunch.
OR
*We **haven't got to** stay at school.*
*He **doesn't have to** stay at school.*
These have the same meaning:
*Does he **have** to stay at school? No, he doesn't.*
*Has he **got** to stay at school? No, he hasn't.*

You use **must to** explain a rule or obligation.
*You + **must** + verb:*

You do not use 'to': *You must to wash your hands.*
*You **must** wash your hands.*
*She **must** wash her hands.*

The question is different. We usually use **have to**.
This is possible: **Must I wash** my hands?
But this is more common: **Do I have to wash** my hands?

mustn't (prohibition)

You use **mustn't** when you talk about what is not allowed.
*You + **must** + not + verb:*
*You **mustn't take** photos.*
*Stop! You **mustn't walk** on the grass!*
*Students **mustn't talk** in exams!*

We don't use usually use **mustn't** in questions: *Mustn't I sit here?*
Can't I sit here? / Can I sit here? > No, you mustn't.

need / needn't (necessity)

You use **need** + to + verb
You use **need to** when you want to say something is necessary:
*You **need to study** hard for the exam. It's difficult.*
Question: **Do I need to study** hard for the exam? >Yes, you do. / No, you don't.

You use **needn't** when something is not necessary.
*You **needn't buy** any food. My dad is cooking tonight.* = it is unnecessary to buy food

don't have to and **needn't** have the same meaning.
*We **don't have to run**. We have lot of time.*
*We **needn't run**. We have lots of time.*

will (offer)

You use **will** for an instant offer:
These bags are heavy!
***I'll help** you!*
Thank you!

I'm thirsty!
***I'll make** you a cup of tea.*

modal passive (e.g. The game might be postponed.)

You use a modal passive to express possibility, ability, advice, obligation, prohibition, necessity or permission.

The form of the modal passive is: subject + modal verb + **be** + past participle.
*The flight **might be cancelled***
*You **could be invited**.* = it's possible you will get an invitation.

Conditionals
zero conditional

You can use **if** or **when** for zero conditionals because you are describing a real situation.
Form:

*When / **if** + present tense + comma (,) +   present tense*
***When** / **if** it   **rains**   , I   **take** my umbrella.*
The **when** / **if** clause can come at the start or at the end:
*I **take** my umbrella **if** it rains.*
***When** it rains   do you **take** your umbrella?*
***Do** you **take** your umbrella   **if** / **when** it rains?*

You use zero conditionals:

1   to talk about the things that are generally true.
    If it rains, you get wet.

2   to describe present habits or scientific facts
    If you heat water to 100 degrees Celsius, it boils.

first conditional

You use the first conditional to talk about things in the future that are possible. The first conditional form is:
***if**   + present simple   ,   ... **will** + infinitive*
***If I**   get more money   ,   I will   buy a bike.*
*What **will** you **buy** if you get more money?*
If it   rains   ,   I will buy an umbrella.
It is possible (but not certain) it will rain and I can buy an umbrella.
*What **will** you **do** **if it rains** today?*
***I'll buy** an umbrella, **if it rains**.*

second conditional

You use the second conditional to talk about things in the future that probably are not going to be true. The second conditional form is:
***if**   + past simple   ,   ... would + infinitive*
***If I**   had more time   ,   I would learn another language.*
*What **would** you **do** if you had more time?*
*What **would** you **buy** if you were rich?*
You usually use were not was to show this is not real; it is imagined.
I'd buy a big house if I were rich.

Reported speech

statements (e.g. *She said (that) she had it.*)

To report what someone says or states, you normally change the tense of what the speaker says.
You change the main verb back one tense in the past: *is > was*; *will> would*
Here you use *said* + **past simple**
I'm very happy to talk to everyone. > *Mrs Mansour **said** that she **was** very happy to talk to everyone.*
*Building **will** take four months.* > *Mrs Mansour **said** that the building **would** take four months.*
If something is still the truth, you do not need to change the tense:
Everyone is worried about climate change.> Linda said that we are all worried about climate change.

commands (e.g. *She told me to save money.*)

You use reported commands to quickly say what someone said, for example, in a newspaper.
'Jump, Dave!' said Mandy.
*Mandy **told Dave to jump.***
'Don't tell John!' said Clare to Sally.
*Clare **told Sally not to tell John.***

questions (e.g. *She asked her parents if she could go out.*)

You use reported questions to quickly explain what someone asked:
'Can I go out?' Jane asked her parents.

You use *ask* + *if* + past of the verb (here it is *can> could*) + verb
*Jane **asked if she could go out.***

Exam-style questions

Listening

Questions 1–8 🔴E1

You will hear some short recordings. You will hear each recording twice. For questions **1–8**, tick (✓) the correct box (**A–D**).

You are in a restaurant with your friend.

1 The waitress comes to your table. She tells you something.

What can't you have for lunch?

A   B   C   D

☐   ☐   ☐   ☐

[1]

2 Your friend orders a drink.

What does your friend order to drink?

A   B   C   D

☐   ☐   ☐   ☐

[1]

3 You order and ten minutes later the waitress brings your starters.

What does your friend need?

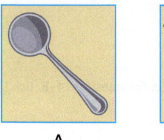   

A □   B □   C □   D □

[1]

4 Your waitress asks if you would like something.

What does the waiter ask you if you would like?

   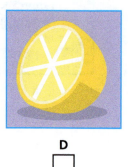

A □   B □   C □   D □

[1]

5 Your friend says something.

Who is your friend talking about?

A □   B □   C □   D □

[1]

The questions that appear in this book were written by the author.
In examination, the way marks are awarded may be different.

6 Your friend continues.

Where is your friend going this evening?

A ☐ B ☐ C ☐ D ☐

[1]

7 Your friend continues.

What time are they meeting?

A ☐ B ☐ C ☐ D ☐

[1]

8 Your friend finishes what she is saying.

What is she going to wear?

A ☐ B ☐ C ☐ D ☐

[1]

[Total: 8]

The questions that appear in this book were written by the author.
In examination, the way marks are awarded may be different.

You will hear an announcement at a sports competition. You will hear the announcement twice. There will be a pause during the announcement. For questions **9–14**, tick (✓) the correct box (**A–D**). You now have some time to read the questions.

9 The competition is …

A ☐   B ☐   C ☐   D ☐

[1]

10 The Indian team are …

A ☐   B ☐   C ☐   D ☐

[1]

11 The Indian team's captain has …

A ☐   B ☐   C ☐   D ☐

[1]

[PAUSE]

The questions that appear in this book were written by the author.
In examination, the way marks are awarded may be different.

12 The player has hurt her …

A ☐   B ☐   C ☐   D ☐

[1]

13 Fans can have a free …

A ☐   B ☐   C ☐   D ☐

[1]

14 The gift shop is next to the …

A ☐   B ☐   C ☐   D ☐

[1]

[Total: 6]

The questions that appear in this book were written by the author.
In examination, the way marks are awarded may be different.

You will hear two teenagers having a conversation about what to buy a friend as a birthday present. You will hear the conversation twice.

For questions **15–19**, choose the information (**A to F**) that matches each present.

For each present write the correct letter (**A to F**) on the answer line. Use each letter only once. There is one extra letter which you do not need to use.

You now have some time to read the information below.

Information

A	It is too much money.

B	It isn't the right size.

C	Edie doesn't wear gold jewellery.

D	It is not modern.

E	It feels nice.

F	It is broken.

Presents

15 belt .... [1]

16 necklace .... [1]

17 bracelet .... [1]

18 scarf .... [1]

19 jumper .... [1]

[Total: 5]

The questions that appear in this book were written by the author.
In examination, the way marks are awarded may be different.

You will hear two interviews, one with Marta and one with Luca. They are talking about school. There will be a pause between the two interviews.

Part 1: Questions 20–24

You will now hear the interview with Marta twice. For questions **20–24**, tick (✓) the correct box (**A–C**).

You now have some time to read the questions.

20 What does Marta say about school?

   A The subjects are boring. ☐

   B It's easy to study in class. ☐

   C It's very loud. ☐ [1]

21 Marta's favourite subject is …

   A history ☐

   B maths ☐

   C physics ☐ [1]

22 Marta thinks homework is …

   A useless ☐

   B boring ☐

   C useful ☐ [1]

23 Marta thinks to do an after-school club or activity you have to be …

   A good at the sport or activity ☐

   B very confident ☐

   C a good student ☐ [1]

24 When Marta finishes school she plans to …

   A go to university ☐

   B get a job ☐

   C go travelling ☐ [1]

[PAUSE]

The questions that appear in this book were written by the author.
In examination, the way marks are awarded may be different.

You will now hear the interview with Luca twice. For questions **25–28**, tick (✓) the correct box (**A–C**).

You now have some time to read the questions.

25 What does Luca say is the best thing about school?

    A The people   ☐

    B The lessons   ☐

    C The food   ☐   [1]

26 Luca's favourite sport is …

    A badminton   ☐

    B cricket   ☐

    C swimming   ☐   [1]

27 Luca thinks at the weekends teenagers should …

    A help at home   ☐

    B have jobs   ☐

    C have fun   ☐   [1]

28 Luca will decide what job he wants to do when …

    A he knows his exam results   ☐

    B he finishes university   ☐

    C he has talked to his parents   ☐   [1]

[Total: 9]

You will hear an interview with Polly about her company. You will hear the interview twice.
There will be a pause during the interview.

For questions **29–34**, tick (✓) the correct box (**A–D**).

You now have some time to read the questions.

29 Why did Polly start her company?

   A She wanted to be rich. ☐

   B She couldn't buy any new clothes. ☐

   C Her friend gave her the idea. ☐

   D She wanted to help her mum. ☐   [1]

30 What did Polly do first?

   A sold her old clothes ☐

   B made a website ☐

   C made posters ☐

   D sent a message on social media ☐   [1]

31 What doesn't Polly like about having her own company?

   A When customers are unhappy. ☐

   B She's too busy to see her friends. ☐

   C When she doesn't like the clothes she is selling. ☐

   D She doesn't have time to study. ☐   [1]

[PAUSE]

The questions that appear in this book were written by the author.
In examination, the way marks are awarded may be different.

32 What has Polly learned from the experience?

    A It's important to have satisfied customers. ☐

    B Advertisements have to be attractive. ☐

    C People like cheap clothes. ☐

    D It's difficult to own a company. ☐ [1]

33 Who did Polly go on holiday with?

    A Her grandparents ☐

    B Her friends ☐

    C Her family ☐

    D By herself ☐ [1]

34 What is Polly's advice to other teenagers who want to start a company?

    A Wait until you have finished school. ☐

    B Make sure people like your business idea. ☐

    C Ask your teachers to help you. ☐

    D Ask your family and friends to help you. ☐ [1]

[Total: 6]

Questions 35–37 🎧 E6

You will hear a radio interview with Izzy Fletcher, who is a young nature photographer. You will hear the interview twice. There will be two pauses during the interview.

For each question (35–37), choose the **two** true statements (A–E) and tick (✓) the correct boxes.

You now have some time to read the questions.

35 A Izzy lives in Hawaii.   ☐

  B Izzy's winning photo is of a forest in Hawaii.   ☐

  C Izzy took the photo on her mobile phone.   ☐

  D Izzy has family in Australia.   ☐

  E Izzy's prize is a photography course.   ☐   [2]

[PAUSE]

36 A Izzy's mum works in a hospital.   ☐

  B Izzy's sister is older than her.   ☐

  C Izzy will continue taking photographs when she is older. ☐

  D Izzy wants to be a photographer when she is older.   ☐

  E Izzy doesn't want to live abroad.   ☐   [2]

[PAUSE]

37 A Izzy thinks a great nature photo has to show something we don't often see. ☐

  B It's Izzy's summer holidays.   ☐

  C Izzy would like to have a party.   ☐

  D Izzy doesn't want her winning photo to be in a book.   ☐

  E Izzy is going to give the book to her grandmother.   ☐   [2]

[Total: 6]

The questions that appear in this book were written by the author.
In examination, the way marks are awarded may be different.

Reading

1 Read the texts. For each question, tick (✓) the correct box (A–D).

a

> Hi Lucia
> I'll be home at about 5.30, so I'll cook dinner then. I'm cutting someone's hair at 4.00 and then I'm going to the pharmacy to get some more medicine for Jorge. Please do the laundry for me. See you later.
> Mum x

What is Lucia's mum's job?

A She's a chef. ☐

B She's a hairdresser. ☐

C She's a doctor. ☐

D She's a cleaner. ☐ [1]

b

To: Milo

Hi Milo,
Thanks for a great weekend in the mountains. It was so good to improve my skiing. Next time I'd like to try snowboarding too.
Grayson

What is Grayson telling Milo?

A when he will visit him ☐

B where he has been ☐

C what his favourite hobbies are ☐

D what sport he would like to learn ☐ [1]

c

Wet paint

The sports hall is being painted so students are not allowed to walk in the corridor outside the sports hall today. Students should walk through the main hall instead to get to their geography classrooms. At lunchtime, students who want a hot meal must go across the sports field to get to the canteen.

Where can't students go?

A To the sports hall ☐

B To the main hall ☐

C To their geography classrooms ☐

D To the canteen ☐ [1]

[Total: 3]

The questions that appear in this book were written by the author.
In examination, the way marks are awarded may be different.

2 Read the email. For each question, tick (✓) the correct box (A–C).

> Hi! ✉ 🗁 🏷 🗑
>
> I want to tell you about my new Saturday job. It's at my local supermarket. I start at 8.00 in the morning and finish at 5.00 in the afternoon. My dad drives me there and I walk home with my friend Suze who also has a job at the supermarket. We have lunch between 12.30 and 1.30. There is a café at the supermarket but we usually go to the park.
>
> I like having a job because Suze and I often go into town on Sundays and now I have money to buy the clothes that I want. I can also join the gym now. My parents used to give me money if I cooked, but it wasn't very much.
>
> See you soon!
> Mica

a Mica is writing to tell you about her …

   A work ☐   **B** best friend ☐   **C** school ☐

[1]

b Mica works …

   A at a cafe ☐   **B** in a shop ☐   **C** in an office ☐

[1]

c Mica goes to work by …

   A car ☐   **B** train ☐   **C** bus ☐

[1]

d Mica and Suze have food …

   A in a café ☐   **B** at home ☐   **C** outside ☐

[1]

e On Sundays, Mica and Suze often …

   A go shopping ☐   **B** do their homework ☐   **C** meet friends ☐

[1]

f Mica wants to …

   A go to more concerts ☐   **B** do more exercise ☐   **C** change her job ☐

[1]

g Mica's parents used to pay her to …

   A do the gardening ☐   **B** do the laundry ☐   **C** make dinner ☐

[1]

[Total: 7]

The questions that appear in this book were written by the author.
In examination, the way marks are awarded may be different.

3 Read the text and choose the correct word to fill the gaps (**a**) to (**g**). For each question, tick (✓) the correct box (**A–D**).

Las Fallas

Las Fallas is a Spanish festival. It takes place from the 1st to the 19th of March **a** .... year, in the city of Valencia in the east of Spain. It's a very interesting and special spring festival because the local people design and build huge statues of famous people, places and news events. **b** .... statues are called ninots. The ninots are put all around Valencia in the parks, streets and squares. People walk around and take photos of them. Then on the night **c** .... the 19th March, firefighters set fire to the ninots. You **d** .... be careful because it's dangerous to stand **d** .... near. However, each year, the people **f** .... one ninot not to burn. This ninot is **g** .... in the museum in Valencia.

a

A many		**B** one		
C all		**D** every		[1]

b

A This		**B** That		
C These		**D** Those [1]		

c

A on		**B** of		
C at		**D** for		[1]

d

A shouldn't		**B** ought		
C must		**D** can		[1]

e

A too		**B** enough		
C much		**D** a lot		[1]

f

A decide		**B** ask		
C tell		**D** choose		[1]

g

A approached		**B** preferred		
C put		**D** torn		[1]

[Total: 7]

The questions that appear in this book were written by the author.
In examination, the way marks are awarded may be different.

4 Read the email and answer the questions in English.

Hi!
I'm writing to tell you that I can't come to your party this weekend, because I'm in hospital. I was skating last Friday and I fell down. I hit my head on the ice. It hurt but I felt fine. I went home, had dinner and watched some TV with my sisters, and then I went to bed. But the next day, my head hurt more and I felt very tired. My mum gave me some medicine and I spent the day on my bed listening to music and sleeping. On Sunday, I couldn't see very well and I felt sick. My mum called an ambulance. I've been here for three days now.

I feel much better, but the doctor said that I have to stay here for another three days. I'm bored now. I want to go back to school and see my friends. Maybe you could visit me? If you do visit, please could you bring me some good books or comics? I did make a friend here – a boy called Tom. He was in the bed next to mine. He broke his leg and hurt his head skateboarding. He was very funny. But he's gone home now.

I hope you have a great party. Please take lots of photos and send them to me. I have a present for you. Why don't you come to my house next week and I'll give it to you?

See you soon!
Rami

a Where is Rami?

.... [1]

b **(i)** What was Rami doing last Friday?

.... [1]

(ii) What happened?

.... [1]

c What did Rami do on Saturday?

.... [1]

d How did Rami get to hospital?

.... [1]

e How long has Rami been in hospital?

.... [1]

f What would Rami like his friend to bring him?

.... [1]

g Who did Rami meet in hospital?

.... [1]

h **(i)** Did Rami like Tom?

.... [1]

(ii) Why or why not?

.... [1]

i What does Rami ask his friend to do at the party?

.... [1]

j What does Rami suggest his friend does next week?

.... [1]

The questions that appear in this book were written by the author.   [Total: 12]
In examination, the way marks are awarded may be different.

5 Read the information about five students (**a–e**) and the eight advertisements for houses to live in at university (**1–8**).

Which house should each person choose?

For each person (**a–e**), write the correct number (**1–8**) on the line.

a  Claudio wants to make lots of new friends. He likes going out and would like to cook and eat meals with other people in the house.

....

b  Tara likes to cook for other people. She would like to live in a tidy house with a big kitchen. She likes gardening and would like to be able to grow vegetables.

....

c  Declan plays the guitar, the piano and the clarinet. He practises every evening for two hours. He doesn't like cooking.

....

d  Priya wants to be in the centre of the city. She is studying art and she likes going to museums. She also likes going to cafes and restaurants.

....

e  Yanlin would like to live near the university, but she doesn't have a lot to spend on accommodation. She needs a job so that she has money to go out with her friends.

....

The questions that appear in this book were written by the author.
In examination, the way marks are awarded may be different.

1

155 Preston Place
Large, cheap room available for the right person in our family home, which is very close to the university. We have two small children and we would love it if you would look after them some evenings. We can pay twenty euros per evening for this. Girls only.

2

24 Frederik Road
One room still available to live in this house with three other female students. We are all serious science students and we like to study at home. We are looking for a quiet fourth person. Sorry – no boys!

3

Rose Cottage
Retired music teacher has two rooms available in cosy cottage in the countryside. I have a lovely garden. The house is not near any restaurants, but I am happy to cook dinner every evening for us all and enjoy chatting over a meal. Music students or musicians preferred.

4

Flat 1A Hope Court
Small but light room available in flat with two other female students in busy, lively area of the city. You can walk everywhere, so you will save money on transport. There are lots of places to meet your friends and to eat out. No garden. Women only.

5

82 Freshfield Road
Room available in new house with one other male student. Three kilometres from university but there is a bus stop at the end of the road and a parking space if you have a car. I spend a lot of time in the library and at work so you will have the house to yourself most of the time.

6

51 Park Place
Female student wanted to live in beautiful old house with garden near the park with four other girls. We usually cook together and we all do the cleaning together on Saturday morning. Must like gardening.

7

17 Wentworth Drive
Room available for quiet student. Lots of families live on this road so we are not allowed parties or lots of friends coming to the house. Only 1 and a half kilometres to the university.

8

7 Ash Road
Nice room available in house with eight other students. We are looking for someone who is friendly and doesn't get annoyed easily. We eat together most evenings and love going dancing at the weekends. 45 minutes from the city centre.

[5]

The questions that appear in this book were written by the author.
In examination, the way marks are awarded may be different.

6 Read the text and answer the questions (**a–i**) in English.

> ### The Belfont Band
> ### by Jacob Van Gelder
>
> I went to my first Belfont Band concert with my grandparents and my older sister when I was just five years old. Both our parents were in the band. My dad played the violin and my mum played the clarinet. I loved it. Back then the band was quite small – there were only 25 members. Now the band has grown and there are more than 100 musicians in it.
>
> Some people join the band after school, when they are 18, but most people join when they leave university at about 21 or 22. I joined when I was 15. I was the youngest player the band had ever had. I started learning the piano and the violin when I was six years old and I took lots of music exams. I preferred the piano to the violin, but the band didn't need a piano player, so I play violin in it. I love being in the band because I enjoy playing music with other people. I think the sounds of the different instruments together is amazing. I don't like travelling to concerts though. We do a lot of concerts in other cities, especially in the winter. We go by train and we have to carry our instruments and suitcases with us. The journeys are long and I get tired.
>
> I'm planning to go to university next year, so I won't be able to play with the Belfont Band for a while. I'm hoping to join a university band and maybe I can play piano for them. I'm also having flute and guitar lessons, and I'd quite like to get some drums for my birthday, so maybe they will let me play one of those. I'm not going to study music at university though; I want to study architecture.

a Why didn't Jacob go to his first Belfont Band concert with his parents?

.... [1]

b How many musicians were in the band when Jacob was five?

.... [1]

c What age do people usually join the band?

.... [1]

d Which instrument did Jacob want to play in the band?

.... [1]

e What two things does Jacob like about playing in a band?

1 ....

2 .... [2]

f When does the band do most of its concerts?

.... [1]

g How does the band travel to concerts?

.... [1]

h Which two new instruments is Jacob learning to play?

1 ....

2 .... [2]

i What course does Jacob want to do at university?

.... [1]

[Total 11]

The questions that appear in this book were written by the author.
In examination, the way marks are awarded may be different.

Speaking Card

1

Role-play
It's your birthday next week. You are planning your birthday party.
Student: yourself
Teacher: your friend
The teacher will start the role play.
Answer all the questions.

2

Conversations	
Conversation 1:	The teacher will start the conversation.
	Answer all the questions.
Conversation 2:	The teacher will start the conversation.
	Answer all the questions.

Writing

1 Your name is Jane Holtom. You are starting at a new school.

Complete the form for the school.

Your name	Jane Holtom
Your favourite school subject	.... [1]
Languages you speak	.... [1]
Now give more information about your favourite school subject. Write about: • how often you study this subject • who teaches you this subject • why you like this subject.	....

[Total: 5]

The questions that appear in this book were written by the author.
In examination, the way marks are awarded may be different.

2 Your country

- Describe your country. (What is it called? What part of the world is it in? What languages do people speak? What is the weather usually like?)
- What is your favourite city or town in your country? Why?
- What is traditional to eat or drink in your country? Do you like eating or drinking this? When do you eat or drink it?
- Why should people visit your country?

Write 80–90 words **in English**.

[12]

3 Answer Question 3(a) or Question 3(b).

Write 130–140 words in **English**.

> **a** A new home
>
> Last month, you and your family moved to a new house. Write an email to your friend about this.
>
> - Describe your new house.
> - Say what you would like to change in or buy for your new bedroom.
> - Talk about your neighbours and the neighbourhood. Say what there is to do in your neighbourhood.
> - Compare your new house with your old house. Say which you prefer and why.
> - Invite your friend to come and visit you in your new home.

[28]

OR

> **b** A sport competition
>
> Last weekend, you won a sporting competition. Write an article for your school website about this.
>
> - Say what, when and where the competition was.
> - Say how long you have been doing this sport for and how often you do it.
> - Explain how you felt during the competition, and when you won.
> - Describe how you prepared for the competition and how you stay fit and healthy.
> - Explain why it's important for teenagers to do sport.

[28]

The questions that appear in this book were written by the author.
In examination, the way marks are awarded may be different.